Cairo

THE CITY OF THE CALIPHS

A Popular Study of Cairo and Its Environs and the Nile and Its Antiquities

By

EUSTACE A. REYNOLDS-BALL

B. A. (Oxd.), F. R. G. S.
Author of "Paris in Its Splendor"

ISBN: 978-1-63182-819-5

All Rights reserved. No part of this book maybe reproduced without written permission from the publishers, except by a reviewer who may quote brief passages in a review to be printed in a newspaper or magazine.

Printed: March 2023

Published and Distributed By:
Lushena Books
607 Country Club Drive, Unit E
Bensenville, IL 60106
www.lushenabks.com

ISBN: 978-1-63182-819-5

"*He who hath not seen Cairo hath not seen the world: its soil is gold; its Nile is a wonder; its women are like the black-eyed virgins of Paradise; its houses are palaces; and its air is soft — its odours surpassing that of aloes-wood, and cheering the heart: and how can Cairo be otherwise when it is the Mother of the World?*" — "The Thousand and One Nights."

CONTENTS.

CHAPTER		PAGE
INTRODUCTION		1
I.	EGYPT UNDER THE PHARAOHS	5
II.	THE EMPIRE OF THE PTOLEMIES	22
III.	THE RULE OF THE CALIPHS	42
IV.	THE MAKING OF EGYPT	55
V.	ALEXANDRIA AND THE NILE DELTA	90
VI.	THE STORY OF THE SUEZ CANAL	105
VII.	CAIRO AS A RESORT FOR INVALIDS	114
VIII.	CAIRO IN ITS SOCIAL ASPECT	122
IX.	THE BAZAARS AND STREET LIFE	132
X.	THE MOSQUES	139
XI.	THE TOMBS OF THE CALIPHS	149
XII.	THE NATIONAL MUSEUM	157
XIII.	THE ACROPOLIS OF CAIRO	169
XIV.	OLD CAIRO AND THE COPTIC CHURCHES	181
XV.	SOME SIDE-SHOWS OF CAIRO	191
XVI.	THE PYRAMIDS OF GHIZEH	202
XVII.	THE CITY OF THE SACRED BULLS	215
XVIII.	THE CITY OF THE SUN	227
XIX.	MINOR EXCURSIONS	235
XX.	THE NILE AS A HEALTH-RESORT	249
XXI.	THE NILE FROM CAIRO TO THEBES	261
XXII.	"THE CITY OF A HUNDRED GATES"	277
XXIII.	ASSOUAN AND PHILÆ	294
XXIV.	FROM THE FIRST TO THE SECOND CATARACT	304
XXV.	RECENT EGYPTOLOGICAL DISCOVERIES	312
	APPENDIX	337

LIST OF ILLUSTRATIONS

	PAGE
GENERAL VIEW OF CAIRO (photogravure)	*Frontispiece*
THE SUEZ CANAL	110
THE ROUTE TO THE PYRAMIDS	116
INTERIOR OF THE MOSQUE OF KAIT BEY	140
THE TOMBS OF THE CALIPHS	149
THE MOSQUE OF KAIT BEY	152
THE TOMBS OF THE MAMELUKES	154
PYRAMID, SPHINX, AND TEMPLE OF GHIZEH	202
ASCENDING THE GREAT PYRAMID	206
THE SPHINX	212
STATUE OF RAMESES II.	217
OBELISK OF HELIOPOLIS	227
VIEW OF EDFU	276
STATUE AT THE ENTRANCE OF THE TEMPLE OF RAMESES III.	286
LUXOR	292
GENERAL VIEW OF DAR-EL-BAHARI	314
LOWER LEVEL SLUICES, ASSOUAN BARRAGE	339

THE CITY OF THE CALIPHS.

INTRODUCTION.

IF a plebiscite were taken among travellers in general as to the dozen most interesting and striking cities of the globe, it is probable that Cairo would be included in the list. It is inferior in world-wide interest, of course, to Jerusalem or Rome, or even Athens, but it would probably take a higher rank than many historic capitals. No doubt Cairo, compared with the great capitals of Europe, is modern, or, at any rate, mediæval, and, indeed, historically of little importance; but it cannot be denied that to the average traveller Cairo is not easily dissociated from Egypt, — the cradle of the oldest civilisation and culture in the world. The proximity of the Pyramids and the Sphinx have no doubt something to do with this vague and erroneous view, and with the fictitious antiquity ignorantly attributed to the City of the Caliphs. The most elementary history, handbook or guide-book will, of course, correct this general impression; but it is not, perhaps, an exaggeration to say that some casual visitors to Egypt begin their sightseeing with a vague, if unformulated, impression that Cairo was once the capital of the Pharaohs, and the Pyramids its cemetery.

The historic and artistic interest of Cairo is, in short, purely mediæval and Saracenic; and, perhaps, no Eastern city, except Damascus, in the beaten track of tourist travel, embodies so many of the typical characteristics of an Oriental city.

Mehemet Ali and Ismail may be considered by the artist and antiquarian to have done their best to vulgarise, that is, Europeanise, the City of the Mamelukes; but the rebuilding and enlarging under Mehemet, and the hausmannising tendencies of Ismail, have done little more than touch the surface. The native quarter of Cairo still remains a magnificent field of study for the intelligent visitor, especially if he ignores the hackneyed and limited programme of the guides and interpreters; and the artist who knows his Cairo will find the Moslem city full of the richest material for his sketch-book. "Every step," observes Mr. Stanley Lane-Poole, " tells a story of the famous past. The stout remnant of a fortified wall, a dilapidated mosque, a carved door, a Kufic text, — each has its history, which carries us back to the days when Saladin went forth from the gates of Cairo to meet Richard in the plain of Acre, or when Beybars rode at the head of his Mamelukes in the charge which trampled upon the Crusaders of Saint Louis. A cloistered court recalls the ungodly memory of the prophet of the Druses; a spacious quadrangle, closely filled by picturesque, albeit scowling, groups of students, reminds us of the conquering Caliphs of 'Aly's heretical line, who, disdaining the mere dominion of Roman 'Africa,' carried their triumphant arms into Egypt and Syria, Sicily and Sardinia, whilst their fleets disputed the command of the Mediterranean with the galleys of Moorish Spain."

Cairo is full of these picturesque associations connected with the magnificent age of the Mameluke Sultans, but most visitors know little about them. Probably this is mainly attributable to the fact that most of the books on Egypt rather ignore its capital; and the age of the Saracens is a period as much overlooked by modern historians as that of the Ptolemies.

There are, of course, the standard guide-books, — a most skilful condensation of a mass of erudition, — but the compilers find the Upper Nile, with its antiquities, of such surpassing interest, that little room can be found for Cairo itself. Besides, guide-books are read of necessity, and not for pleasure or continuously; and in the wealth of dry detail it is difficult sometimes to "see the wood for the trees."

There is, however, another aspect besides the sentimental or devotional one, which should not be disregarded; and in the chapter dealing with the regeneration of Egypt under British influence, I have attempted to show how modern Egypt strikes the political observer and the man of practical affairs.

Egypt, with its wealth of antiquities and artistic relics, is, no doubt, of the highest importance to the tourist and sight-seer. Regarded, however, as a community or modern state, the Egypt of to-day holds a very low rank among semicivilised countries. There is a certain amount of reason in the complaint of some modern historians that Western minds seem to lose all sense of proportion and historic perspective when describing this Land of Paradox, which is, after all, but a tenth-rate territory, with an acreage less than that of Belgium, and a population hardly more numerous than that of Ireland. These indisputable facts will, perhaps, come as a surprise to the tourist, who takes several weeks to sail along the thousand miles of its mighty river, — its one and only highway, — from Cairo to the Soudan frontier. One is apt to forget that, above the Delta, Egypt simply means a narrow fringe of desert stretching for a few miles on each side of the Nile. This, no doubt, is true; and visitors are perhaps too apt to "see the country looming in a mist of mirage," and are unable to resist the weird charm of this unique land.

At the same time, one cannot deny the enormous international importance of Egypt in spite of its small acreage and population. This importance, no doubt, is to some extent fictitious, and is due partly to its peculiar geographical position, which makes it the great highway between the Eastern and Western hemispheres, and partly to its climate, which has converted it into the great winter residence and playground of civilised nations. Besides, magnitude is not, of course, an absolutely reliable test of a country's greatness. Little states, as we all know, have filled a most important part in the world's history, — Athens, Sparta, Venice, Florence, Genoa, for instance. Then, the Holy Land itself is about the size of Wales, and the area of Attica was no wider than that of Cornwall.

In preparing this book, I have consulted many of the standard English and French works which have been recently published; and I am especially indebted to the valuable information to be found in the works of Professor Flinders Petrie, Professor Mahaffy, the late Miss A. B. Edwards, Sir Alfred Milner, and Mr. Stanley Lane-Poole. For the preliminary chapter on Alexandria and the Nile Delta, I have utilised portions of an article on Alexandria which I contributed to "The Picturesque Mediterranean," published by Cassell & Co., Ltd., London, and my grateful acknowledgments are due to this firm for permission to reproduce these portions.

E. A. R. B.

CHAPTER I.

EGYPT UNDER THE PHARAOHS.

THE history of the City of Cairo, as distinct from that of Egypt, is simple and easily mastered, being confined within reasonable limits. It does not go back further than mediæval times. Unlike the history of Egypt, which is concerned mainly with the rise and fall of alien states, Cairo, whether Arabic or Turkish, is a wholly Mohammedan creation. It is, indeed, more Mohammedan in some respects than any city in the world, just as Rome is more Roman than any other city. Constantinople, of course, is a decidedly hybrid city in comparison, and its very name recalls an alien civilisation; while its chief temple, Justinian's great church of St. Sophia, is a Christian building, dedicated to a Christian saint, although the Turks naturally try to disguise its heretical origin by calling it Agia Sophia (Holy Wisdom).

The history of Cairo, then, falls naturally into two periods: that of Arab rule when it was virtually the seat of the Caliphate; and the period of Turkish dominion, from its capture by the Ottoman Turks in 1517 down to the present time. In short, we need consider it under two aspects merely, — first as the capital of the Caliphs, and next as the chief city of a Turkish pachalic.

The history of Egypt, on the other hand, is that of the oldest civilised country in the world, — though as a community it is perhaps one of the newest. It is hardly an exaggeration to say that all literature, ancient and modern, from the works of Homer and Aristotle down to the masterpieces of Dante and Shakespeare, is indirectly due to the ancient Egyptian civilisation. Philologists of the highest authority are agreed that the Phœnician origin of the alphabet cannot be substantiated. Even Tacitus seems to have suspected that this nation had won a spurious renown as the inventors of letters, — *tanquam repererint quæ acceperant.* The Egyptian cursive characters to be found in the Prissé papyrus of the eleventh dynasty — " the oldest book in the world " — are pronounced by the best philological scholars to be the prototype of the letters afterwards copied by the Greeks from the Phœnicians, and thence transmitted to the Latins.

Though Egypt, as the cradle of the alphabet, may be considered the foster-mother of all literature, yet it must be allowed that the one thing needful to history, namely, literary material in documentary form, is wanting in the case of Egypt. We have nothing but the fossilised history of the monuments. Only the baldest annals (*pace* Brugsch Bey) can be compiled from stone inscriptions. Then, as Mr. David Hogarth, in his " Wanderings of a Scholar in the Levant," pertinently observes, contemporary documents carved on stone, whether in Greece or in the Nile Valley, have often been accepted far too literally. The enthusiasm of archæologists has inclined them to regard insufficiently the fact that to lie monumentally to posterity is a failing to which the Pharaohs, prompted by their colossal vanity, were particularly subject.

From the Hyksos invasion down to the conquest of the country by the Ottomans, — a period of nearly five thousand years, — Egyptian history is simply that of foreign conquests, and is inseparably bound up with that of alien nations, its conquerors, — Semitic (Hyksos kings), Ethiopian, Assyrian, Persian, Greek, Roman, Saracen, and Turkish. A cardinal fact in the history of this remarkable country is its perpetual subjection to foreign influences. Yet, in spite of this, the Egyptians have, during these thousands of years of foreign dominion, preserved their national characteristics, and the same unvarying physical types. This racial continuity, in spite of all these adverse circumstances and interminable succession of alien immigrations, which might be supposed to modify materially the uniformity of the Egyptian type, is one of the greatest puzzles in ethnography.

What is known as the prehistoric period of Egypt can be dismissed in a paragraph. This history is based, of course, on mythical legend, and is purely conjectural. It is supposed that the country was divided into a number of small, independent states, each with its own tutelary chief; or, according to some writers, these sovereigns were deities and kings in one, and they have been termed god-kings. To emphasise the distinction, Menes and the kings of the first dynasty are designated as the first earthly kings of Egypt.

As to the origin of the Egyptians, scholars are divided into two schools; for though there are innumerable theories, if we eliminate the more fanciful ones it will be found that all historians of note have adopted one or other of the two following theories. Those who adopt the Biblical narrative have come to the conclusion that the ancestors of the Egyptians came originally from Asia, and that, in short, the tide of civilisation flowed up the Nile. Philologists, too, who have discovered many points of resemblance in the roots of the ancient Egyptian and Semitic languages, have adopted this theory. Ethnographists and anthropologists, however, hold an opposite view, and consider that a study of the customs of the ancient Egyptians, and an examination of their implements and utensils, which are very similar to those of the tribes living on the banks of the Niger and Zambesi, rather point to an Ethiopian or South African origin; and that civilisation began in the Upper Nile Valley and spread northwards and downwards. It is probable, however, that each of these historical schools may be partly right; and possibly the true explanation is that, whether an Asiatic or African origin be granted, the immigrants found an aboriginal race settled on the banks of the Nile, whose racial characteristics and distinctive physical types were probably as little modified by these alien invaders as they have been by their Mohammedan conquerors in the seventeenth century.

Most modern historians, then, fortified by the opinion of ethnographical authorities, after the scientific examination of the ancient monumental sculptures and drawings, are satisfied that the ancient Egyptians differed in all essential racial characteristics from the African negroes, and belonged to a branch of the great Caucasian family.

It would be futile to attempt here anything but the barest summary of the chief facts of Egyptian history. A very slight thread of narrative may, however, connect the most important historical landmarks under which the leading facts of Egyptian history may be grouped. Without attempting, then, anything of the nature of a scientific chronological *précis*, a practical and rough-and-ready division, ignoring, of course, the dynasties and Ancient, Middle, and New Empires, and other conventional divisions of historians, would be something as follows:—

1. The age of the Pharaohs, which would include the first twenty-six dynasties, down to the first Persian invasion under Cambyses.

2. The Empire of the Ptolemies, which includes the prosperous reigns of the dynasty founded by Alexander the Great.

3. The Saracenic era, during which Egypt became once more a centre of arts and sciences, in spite of the interne-

cine feuds of the rival Caliphs. This period closes with the conquest by the Ottoman Turks.

4. The Political Renaissance of Egypt under Mehemet Ali.

5. Modern Egypt, when the country of the Pharaohs entered upon its latest phase, after the fall of the Khedive Ismail, as a kind of protegé of the Great Powers, under the stewardship, first of Great Britain and France, and finally of Great Britain alone.

The division of Egyptian history into Ancient, Middle, and New Empires is as artificial and arbitrary as the popular divisions into dynasties. The Ancient Empire begins with Menes, the first really historical king of Egypt. Little is known of this monarch's achievements, but he at any rate affords us a sure starting-place for our survey of the early monarchy.

The sources from which we derive our knowledge of these primeval kings are from the monumental inscriptions, lists (more or less imperfect or undecipherable) in the Turin papyrus, and the history of the Ptolemaic priest, Manetho. Mena, or Menes, is supposed to have been descended from a line of local chiefs at This, near Abydos, the traditional burying-place of Osiris. Coming south, he made Memphis the capital of his new united kingdom. This was the chief centre of the worship of the god Ptah, creator of gods and men; and it was here that the cult of the Apis bull (the Serapis of the Greeks) was first instituted. The kings of the first three dynasties, with the exception of Menes, have left few records, though certain inscriptions on the cliffs at Sinai have been attributed to one of the kings of the third dynasty, and the Pyramid of Medum, in the opinion of Doctor Petrie, was built by Seneferu. These three dynasties cover the period B. C. 4400 to 3766, according to Brugsch. But Egyptian chronology is one of the most disputed departments of

Egyptology, and the dates given are, of course, only approximate.

With the fourth dynasty we come to the familiar names of the great pyramid-builders, Cheops, Chephren, and Mycerinos. It is not till the age of the Theban Pharaohs that we find sovereigns who have left such lasting records of a highly developed civilisation. Cheops and Chephren, in the Egyptian traditions, probably coloured a good deal by the biassed accounts of Herodotus and other Greek historians, have been held up to the execration of posterity as heartless tyrants and profligate despisers of the gods. Mycerinos's memory is, however, revered by Herodotus as a just and merciful king. "To him his father's deeds were displeasing, and he both opened the temples and gave liberty to the people, who were ground down to the last extremity of evil, to return to their own business and sacrifices; also he gave decision of their causes juster than those of all the other kings." The actual bones of this king can be seen in the British Museum, so that this panegyric has a peculiar interest for English people.

To the fifth dynasty, known as the Elephantine from the place of origin, belongs Unas, whose pyramid-tomb was discovered by Professor Maspero in 1881. The sovereigns of the sixth dynasty distinguished themselves by various foreign conquests. To this family belongs the famous Queen Nitokris, the original of the fabled Rhodopis of the Greeks.

It is permissible to skip a period of some six hundred years, during which four dynasties reigned, whose history is almost entirely lost. So far as we can judge, it was a period of struggle between weak titular sovereigns and powerful feudal chiefs who left the kings a merely nominal sovereignty, having apparently acquired the control of the civil and military authority.

Egypt during this period was invaded by Libyan and

Ethiopian tribes. With the eleventh dynasty, founded by powerful princes from Thebes, begins the Middle Empire, with Thebes as its capital. It will be noticed that the seat of government is often shifted during the thirty dynasties which comprise Egyptian history from Menes to Nectanebo I.

Under the Ancient Empire, Memphis, as we have seen, was the seat of government, and may be regarded as the first historic capital of Egypt. This, near Abydos, no doubt can boast of an earlier history; but this was merely the cradle of the first Egyptian kings, of whom we have no records more authentic than those semi-mythical traditions which centre round the prehistoric god-kings, and it cannot, of course, be considered as a seat of government. The political centre was shifted, under different kings, for dynastic, strategic, or political motives, to various places in Egypt, from the Upper Nile Valley to the Delta.

As the power of the kings increased, the capital was fixed at Abydos, Elephantine, and other southern cities. Under the Middle Empire, the period of Egypt's greatest splendour, the great city of Thebes was the capital. Then, during a period of internal disturbance or foreign invasions, it was transferred again to the north, to Memphis, Tel-El-Amarna, and other cities of Lower Egypt. From the thirteenth to the seventeenth dynasties, Egyptian history is intricate and difficult to follow. The Shepherd Kings had conquered Lower Egypt, and held sway in the Delta, while the old Theban royal race still maintained the chief authority in Upper Egypt. So, during these five dynasties, there were two capitals, Tanis (Zoan) and Thebes. During the later Asiatic wars the political centre was shifted towards the Asiatic frontier, and Rameses the Great and his successors held their court principally in the northern city of Tanis. Under the New Empire, — the period of decadence and foreign oppression, — the centre was continually transferred, and it was shifted with each political change, — now to Thebes, now to Memphis, and finally to Bubastis and Sais.

The twelfth dynasty is an important period in Egyptian history. The reigns of Usertsen I. and III. and Amen-Em-Het III. are renowned for the famous permanent engineering achievements which did more, perhaps, for the prosperity of the country than many of the architectural enterprises and foreign conquests of the eighteenth and nineteenth dynasties. Amen-Em-Het III. conferred the greatest benefit on Egypt by his vast engineering works for regulating the inundations of the Nile. His most famous work, by which Egypt has benefited even down to the present day, was the construction of the great artificial lake, called by the Greeks Moeris, now called by the Arabs El-Fayyum. This monarch also gave later sovereigns the idea of a Nilometer, as on the cliffs at Semni he made regular measurements of the rise in the Nile inundation.

We now enter a dark period of about five hundred years, when Egypt passed under the foreign domination — incidentally referred to above, from which she freed herself only after a long and severe struggle.

The thirteenth dynasty appears at first to have carried on the government with the success inherited from its predecessors; but there are indications that the reigns of its later kings were disturbed by internal troubles, and it is probable that actual revolution transferred power to the fourteenth dynasty, whose seat was Sais in the Delta. The new dynasty probably never succeeded in making its sway paramount; and Lower Egypt, in particular, seems to have been torn by civil wars, and to have fallen an easy prey to the invader. Forced on by a wave of migration of the peoples of Western Asia, in connection, perhaps, with the conquests of the Elamites, or set in motion by some internal cause, the nomad tribes of Syria made a sudden irruption into the northeastern border of Egypt, and, conquering the country as they advanced, apparently without difficulty, finally established themselves in power at Memphis. Their course of conquest was undoubtedly made smooth for them by the large foreign element in the population of the Lower country, where, on this account, they may have been welcomed as a kindred people, or at least not opposed as a foreign enemy. The dynasties which the newcomers founded we know as those of the Hyksos, or Shepherd Kings, — a title, however, which is nowhere given to them in genuine Egyptian texts. It has been conjectured that the name Hyksos (which first occurs in the fragment of Manetho) is derived from "Hek-Shasu," King of the Shasu, an Egyptian name for the thieving nomad race.

After the rough work of conquest had been accomplished, the Hyksos gradually conformed to Egyptian customs, adopted Egyptian forms of worship, and governed the country just as it had been governed by the native kings. The fifteenth and sixteenth dynasties are Hyksos dynasties, probably at first holding sway over Lower Egypt alone, but gradually bringing the Upper country into subjection, or at least under tribute. The period of the seventeenth dynasty, whether we are to call it Hyksos or native Theban, or to count it as being occupied by kings of both races, was a period of revolt. The Theban under-king, Sekenen Ra, refused tribute, and the war of liberation began, which, after a struggle of nearly a century, was brought to a happy conclusion by the final expulsion of the Hyksos by Aahmes, or Amasis I., the founder of the eighteenth dynasty.

The period of the foreign domination has a particular interest on account of its connection with Bible history. It appears from chronological calculations, which are fairly conclusive, that it was towards the end of the Hyksos rule that the Patriarch Joseph was sold into Egypt. A king named Nubti (B. C. 1750) is supposed to have occupied the throne at the time; and the famous Hyksos king, Apepa II., is said to have been the Pharaoh who raised Joseph to high rank, and welcomed the Patriarch Jacob and his family into Egypt.[1]

Aahmes I. (Amasis), the conqueror of the Hyksos usurpers, was the son of Ka-mes, the last of the royal race of Thebes of the seventeenth dynasty; and his mother was Queen Aah-hetep, whose jewels in the National Museum at Cairo are only exceeded in beauty and interest by those of the Princess Hathor. This monarch is the first of the eighteenth dynasty, in which the history of Egypt enters upon a new phase, and what may be called the "Expansion of Egypt" begins. Hitherto the Egyptian sovereigns had been satisfied with waging war only with their immediate neighbours. Now begins an active foreign policy, and we note an expansion of the national spirit. An Egyptian Empire was founded, which, by the end of the reign of Thotmes I., extended from the Euphrates in the north to Berber in the Soudan. This policy of foreign conquest was, no doubt, forced upon Aahmes and his successors by circumstances. It was essential to find employment for their large armies, whose energies had been hitherto confined to overthrowing the Hyksos dynasty. But this foreign policy, which brought Egypt into collision with the great Asiatic empires, eventually proved a source of danger, when Egypt was no longer ruled by the warrior-kings of the eighteenth, nineteenth, and twentieth dynasties.

Thotmes II. and his sister, the famous Hatasu (Hatshepset), whose achievements are more fully referred to in the chapter on Thebes, followed up the Asiatic victories of Thotmes I. with successful expeditions into Arabia. It

[1] E. A. Wallis-Budge.

was, however, reserved for her son Thotmes III. to bring the neighbouring nations into complete subjection; and Egypt, under this famous monarch, perhaps the greatest prototype of Alexander the Great in history, reached the period of its greatest material prosperity.

It was his proud boast that he planted the frontiers of Egypt where he pleased; and this was, indeed, no hyperbolical figure. "Southwards, as far, apparently, as the great Equatorial Lakes, which have been rediscovered in our time; northwards to the Islands of the Ægean and the upper waters of the Euphrates; over Syria and Sinai, Mesopotamia and Arabia in the East; over Libya and the North African coast as far as Cherchell in Algeria on the West, he carried fire and sword, and the terrors of the Egyptian name."[1]

Queen Hatasu was one of the most famous royal builders of Egypt. "Numerous and stately as were the obelisks erected in Egypt from the period of the twelfth dynasty down to the time of Roman rule," remarks Miss Edwards, "those set up by Hatasu in advance of the fourth pylon of the Great Temple of Karnak are the loftiest, the most admirably engraved, and the best proportioned. One has fallen; the other stands alone, one hundred and nine feet high in the shaft, cut from a single flawless block of red granite."

Thotmes III. was famed as much for his achievements of peace as for his foreign conquests, and some of the finest monuments at Thebes and Luxor testify to his merits as an architect. In fact, his cartouche occurs more frequently even than that of Rameses II. on antiquities of every kind, from temples and tombs down to scarabs. The fame of Thotmes's successors, Amen-hetep II., and Amen-hetep III., though vigorous and warlike kings, has been eclipsed by that of their great ancestor, though their campaigns in Syria and Nubia were equally successful.

[1] "Pharaohs, Fellahs, and Explorers."

The reign of Amen-hetep IV. is noteworthy for an important religious reform or revolution. This king, probably influenced by his mother, a princess of Semitic origin, "endeavoured to substitute a sort of Asiatic monotheism, under the form of the worship of the solar disk, for the official worship of Egypt. The cult and the very name of Amen were proscribed, the name being erased from the monuments wherever it occurred, and the king changed his own name from Amen-hetep to Khun-Aten, the 'Glory of the Solar Disk.' In the struggle which ensued between the Pharaohs and the powerful hierarchy of Thebes, Khun-Aten found himself obliged to leave the capital of his fathers, and build a new one farther north called Khut-Aten, the site of which is now occupied by the villages of Tel-El-Amarna and Haggi Qandil. Here he surrounded himself with the adherents of the new creed, most of whom seem to have been Canaanites or other natives of Asia, and erected in it a temple to the solar disk as well as a palace for himself, adorned with paintings, gold, bronze, and inlaid work in precious stones."[1]

The worship of Amen was, however, too firmly established to be permanently overthrown, and the great god was paramount among the Egyptian gods. Consequently the new cult took no hold upon the people. After Amen-hetep's death the new worship died out, and the god Amen was restored as the national deity by Amen-hetep IV. (Horus). In fact, the very stones and decorations of the Temple of the Solar Disk were used in embellishing the temple of the victorious Amen at Karnak.

With the nineteenth dynasty (B. C. 1400-1200), the age of the earlier Pharaohs,— for in popular estimation the generic names of Rameses and Pharaoh are convertible terms, though etymologists would, of course, draw a distinction,— we enter upon the most popular period of

[1] "Murray's Handbook for Egypt."

ancient Egyptian history,— popular, that is, in the sense of familiar. Rameses I. is the least important sovereign of the Pharaonic monarchs, and is known chiefly for the war he waged with the traditional enemies of the Theban monarchs, the Khita of Northern Syria. His victories were, however, but moderate, and the campaign was continued with greater success by his son, Seti I. This sovereign successfully undertook the task of subjugating the Phœnicians and the Libyans. He cut, too, the first canal between the Red Sea and the Nile. It is true that this honour has been claimed for Queen Hatasu, but the authority is doubtful, being mainly based on the sculptures in which this Queen's famous expedition to the Land of Punt is pictorially described, some of these paintings apparently indicating that there was some kind of waterway between the Nile Valley and the Red Sea.

Rameses I. was succeeded by the famous Rameses II., the Sesostris of the Greeks, and known to us as the Pharaoh of the Oppression. Rameses II. is, no doubt, the one dominant personality in the whole field of Egyptian history. His name is more widely known than that of any other Egyptian monarch. Many reasons for this universal posthumous fame can be assigned. No doubt his unusually long reign, seven years longer than the present reign of Queen Victoria (1897), has something to do with this. Then, too, the prominence given to this monarch's reign by Herodotus and other Greek historians, and the wealth of traditionary lore which has centred round the legendary Sesostris, and his intimate associations with the Old Testament history, have contributed not a little to exalt the fame of Rameses above that of all other monarchs.

It must not, however, be forgotten that his renown is to a considerable extent factitious. For instance, owing to his overweening vanity (in which, however, he did not differ from most other sovereigns of Egypt) in usurping the architectural monuments of his predecessors by carving upon them his own cartouche, he got credit for these magnificent works, as well as for those which were undeniably his own, of which the most famous are the Ramesseum, at Thebes, and the rock-hewn Temple of Abru-Simbel, in Nubia.

Then Rameses's greatest achievement in arms, the famous campaign against the Khita, which is commemorated at such inordinate length on the mural sculptures of so many temples, has been naturally somewhat magnified by Pentaur, the poet laureate of the Theban court. In a poem virtually written to order, it is necessary, of course, to discount a certain leaning towards fulsome hyperbole in this stone-graven epic. It is absurd to accept as an historical fact the extravagant statement which makes Rameses rout, single-handed, the whole Khita host.

Without wishing to deny the title of Great to this monarch, we need not follow the example of the Greek historians and accept without reserve achievements which would be more suited to the mythical god-kings of the prehistoric period.

In the reign of Rameses the Great's successor, Mer-en-Ptah II. (Seti III.), took place, according to most modern historians, the Exodus of the Israelites. Some chronologists have, however, given a later date to this national emigration. "With the expiration of the nineteenth dynasty," writes Dr. Wallis-Budge, "the so-called Middle Empire of Egypt came to an end, and we stand upon the threshold of the New Empire, a chequered period of occasional triumphs, of internal troubles, and of defeats and subjection to a foreign yoke."

The period from the twentieth to the end of the twenty-fifth dynasty can be rapidly summed up. Rameses III., the founder of the twentieth dynasty, was the only strong sovereign of the half-dozen who bore this dynastic name, and was the last of the warrior-kings of Egypt. After his death, the country enters upon a period of degeneration and decadence, which lasted for over five hundred years. The later kings of this dynasty fell gradually under the dominion of the priests, which was finally consummated by the usurpation of a race of priest-kings from Tanis, who formed the twenty-first dynasty. The Trojan war was probably waged about this time. The rule of the high-priest of Amen was eventually overthrown by the Libyan prince, Shashank (Shishak of the Old Testament), who founded the twenty-second dynasty and made Bubastes the seat of government.

Egypt was now entering upon the stage of disruption, and the authority of one sovereign was virtually replaced by that of a host of petty kings, and the two following dynasties (twenty-third and twenty-fourth) are made up of a list of the more powerful of these sovereigns, who had gained a nominal supremacy. During these troublous times of internecine strife, Egypt was being harassed by two powerful neighbours, Assyria and Ethiopia. The latter country, which, during the nineteenth and twentieth dynasties, had been a mere province of the empire of the Pharaohs, was now independent, and from about 715 B. C. they got the better of their former masters and founded what is known as the twenty-fifth dynasty. This dynasty was, however, short-lived, and in 672 B. C. the Assyrians under Esarhaddon invaded Egypt, captured Thebes and Memphis, and, occupying the whole Delta, became masters of the country.

The history of Egypt at this period is difficult to follow, but it appears that one of the more powerful of the native princes — Psammetichus, King of Sais, who was nominally a viceroy of Assyria in Egypt — took advantage of the disruption of the Assyrian Empire caused by the revolt of Babylonia, to rebel against his suzerain and expel the Assyrian army of occupation. Then, by a judicious marriage with a Theban princess, the heiress of the older dynasties, Psammetichus was able to win over Upper Egypt as well as the Delta, and to found what is known as the twenty-sixth dynasty. A transitory period of tranquillity now begins, and a sort of revival of the arts and sciences takes place, — one of the many periods of renaissance which Egypt has known, — which proved that many centuries of civil war and foreign oppression had not entirely crushed the artistic spirit which had been bequeathed to the Egyptians by their ancestors. Necho, the son of Psammetichus, next reigned. He seems to have paid as much attention to the domestic welfare and the material prosperity of his country as to foreign conquest, and among his achievements was an attempt to cut a canal between the Nile and the Red Sea. His efforts in encouraging the development of trade did a good deal towards reviving the commercial spirit of the people. It was in Necho's reign, too, that certain Phœnician mariners in this sovereign's service made a voyage round Africa, — an enterprise which took nearly three years to accomplish. This is the first complete circumnavigation of the African continent recorded in history.

For the next one hundred years Egyptian history is merged in that of Syria, Babylonia, and Persia. The historical sequence of events is rendered more difficult to follow by the fact that, after the victory of Cambyses in 527 B. C., till the subjugation of the Persians by Alexander the Great at the battle of the Issus in 332 B. C., — one of the most "decisive battles of the world," — Egypt was practically a satrapy of the Persian Empire though historians reckon three short-lived Pharaonic dynasties during this period, called the twenty-eighth, twenty-ninth, and thirtieth, which synchronised with the twenty-seventh, or Persian dynasty. This is accounted for by the fact that whenever a native prince got possession of the Delta, or of a considerable portion of Egypt, he became nominally sovereign of Egypt, though it was to all intents and purposes a province of Persia.

The twenty-seventh dynasty was, in short, a period of Persian despotism, tempered by revolts more or less successful on the part of the native viceroys or satraps appointed by Darius, Xerxes, Artaxerxes, and other Persian monarchs. For instance, for a few years, under Amyrteus (twentieth-eighth dynasty), Mendes (twenty-ninth dynasty), and the last native sovereign, Nectanebo II. (thirtieth dynasty), Egypt was almost independent of Persia. In B. C. 332, when the Persian power had succumbed to the Macedonians under Alexander the Great, this anomalous period of Egyptian quasi-independence came to an end. On the death of this monarch, Egypt fell to the share of his general, Ptolemy, who founded the important dynasty of the Ptolemies, and was hailed as the Saviour (Soter) of the country.

This concludes a necessarily brief summary of the age of the Pharaohs. In order to confine in a few pages a sketch of the history of a period covering over four thousand years and comprising thirty different dynasties, one can do little more than give a bare list of names of the principal sovereigns and of their more important wars. In fact, like all ancient history, the history of the pre-Ptolemaic period is in a great degree a history of empires and dynasties, foreign wars and internal revolutions, and is in a much less degree the history of the political and social progress of the people. For, as Professor Freeman truly observes, it is to the history of the Western world in Europe and America that we must naturally look for the highest development of art, literature, and political freedom.

CHAPTER II.

THE EMPIRE OF THE PTOLEMIES.[1]

THE dynasty of the Ptolemies is thus appropriately designated, as it emphasises the fact that these Macedonian sovereigns were not merely kings of Egypt, but rulers of a great composite empire.

"None of Alexander's achievements was more facile, and yet none more striking, than his Egyptian campaign. His advent must have been awaited with all the agitations of fear and hope by the natives of all classes; for the Persian sway had been cruel and bloody, and if it did not lay extravagant burdens upon the poor, it certainly gave the higher classes an abundance of sentimental grievances, for it had violated the national feelings, and especially the national religion, with wanton brutality. The treatment of the revolted province by Ochus was not less violent and ruthless than had been the original conquest by Cambyses, which Herodotus tells us with graphic simplicity. No conquerors seem to have been more uncongenial to the Egyptians than the Persians. But all invaders of Egypt, even the Ptolemies, were confronted by a like hopelessness of gaining the sympathies of their subjects. If it was comparatively easy to make them slaves, they were perpetually revolting slaves. This was due, not to the impatience of the average native, but rather to the hold which the national religion had gained upon his life. This religion

---

[1] I am indebted for much of the information in this chapter to Professor Mahaffy's admirable monograph on the age of the Ptolemies.

was administered by an ambitious, organised, haughty priesthood, whose records and traditions told them of the vast wealth and power they had once possessed, — a condition of things long passed away, and never likely to return, but still filling the imaginations of the priests, and urging them to set their people against every foreign ruler. The only chance of success for an invader lay in conciliating this vast and stubborn corporation. Every chief who headed a revolt against the Persians had made this the centre of his policy; the support of the priests must be gained by restoring them to their old supremacy, — a supremacy which they doubtless exaggerated in their uncriticised records of the past.

"The nobles or military caste, who had been compelled to submit to the generalship of mercenary leaders, Greek or Carian, were also disposed to welcome Alexander. The priestly caste, who had not forgotten the brutal outrages to the gods by Cambyses, were also induced to hail with satisfaction the conqueror of their hereditary enemies, the Persians. Alexander was careful to display the same conciliatory policy to the priests of Heliopolis and Memphis which he had adopted at Jerusalem. These circumstances partly explained the attitude of the Egyptians in hailing Alexander as their deliverer rather than their conqueror."

In order to understand the comparatively peaceful accession of the Ptolemaic dynasty, we must bear in mind the cardinal principle which governed Alexander's occupation of Egypt, and his administration of the conquered province.

"Alexander had asserted the dignity and credibility of the Egyptian religion, and his determination to support it and receive support from it. He had refused to alter the local administrations, and even appointed some native officials to superintend it. On the other hand, he had placed the control of the garrison and the central authority in the hands of the Macedonians and Greeks, and had founded a new capital, which could not but be a Hellenistic city, and a rallying point for all the Greek traders throughout the country. The port of Canopus was formally closed, and its business transferred to the new city."

On Alexander's death, in 323 B. C., after a very short illness, Ptolemy, one of his lieutenants, took over the regency of Egypt, and in 305 B. C. he was strong enough to declare himself king, and to assume the title of Soter (Saviour).

The history of the sixteen Ptolemies who form the Ptolemaic dynasty is made up of the reigns of a few powerful monarchs who held the throne sufficiently long to insure a stable government, and of a large number of short-lived and weak sovereigns, most of whom suffered a violent death. In short, the large proportion of those who died by violence is as noticeable as in the remarkable list of the prehistoric kings of Ireland. The Ptolemaic dynasty made a propitious commencement with the first three Ptolemies, who were able and powerful monarchs. During this period the prestige of Egypt among foreign nations was very high.

In 283 B. C. Ptolemy Soter died, in the eighty-fifth year of his age, leaving a record of prosperity which few men in the world have surpassed. Equally efficient whether as servant or as master, he made up for the absence of genius in war or diplomacy by his persistent good sense, the modcration of his demands, and the courtesy of his manners to friend and foe alike. While the old crown of Macedon was still the unsettled prize for which rival kings staked their fortunes, he and his fellow-in-arms, Seleukos, founded dynasties which resisted the disintegrations of the Hellenistic world for centuries.

Perhaps of all Ptolemy's achievements, whether foreign or domestic, his famous museum and library deserves to rank the highest. Very little is known about this remarkable seat of learning, and Strabo's description is painfully meagre. This great institution was rather a university than a museum, and was certainly the greatest glory of Ptolemaic Alexandria. The idea of making his capital, not merely a great commercial centre, but a centre of arts, sciences, and literature, seems to have gradually matured in the mind of Ptolemy Soter. The college or university, or whatever we call the museum, was under the most direct patronage of the king, and was, in fact, a part of the royal palace. It included, in addition to lecture-halls, class-rooms, dining-hall, etc., courts, cloisters, and gardens, and was under the rule of a principal nominated by the king, who also performed the offices of a kind of high-priest. This Alexandrian foundation was apparently as much a teaching and residential university as the famous European universities of Paris, Padua, or Oxford. In fact, it served equally with the renowned academies of Athens as a model for modern universities.

"It is indeed strange that so famous an institution should not have left us some account of its foundation, its constitution, and its early fortunes. No other school of such moment among the Greeks is so obscure to us now; and yet it was founded in broad daylight of history by a famous king, in one of the most frequented cities of the world. The whole modern literature on the subject is a literature of conjecture. If it were possible to examine the site, which now lies twenty feet deep under the modern city, many questions which we ask in vain might be answered. The real outcome of the great school is fortunately preserved. In literary criticism, in exact science, in geography, and kindred studies, the museum made advances in knowledge which were among the most important in the progress of human civilisation. If the produce in poetry and philosophy was poor, we must attribute such failure to the decadence of that century, in comparison with the classical days of Ionia and Athens. But in preserving the great masters of the golden age the library, which was part of the same foundation, did more than we can estimate."

On the death of his father, Ptolemy Soter, Philadelphus, in accordance with the traditional policy of that age, puts to death his stepbrother, Argens, his most formidable rival. According to the historians of that period, Philadelphus is said to have complained in after-life that one of the hardships in a despot's life was the necessity of putting people to death who had done no harm, merely for the sake of expediency!

Having now cleared the way to the throne, Philadelphus makes arrangements for his coronation. We borrow the following vivid picture of these magnificent ceremonies of Philadelphus from the pages of "Greek Life and Thought:"

"The first thing that strikes us is the ostentation of the whole affair, and how prominently costly materials were displayed. A greater part of the royal treasure at all courts in those days consisted not of coin, but of precious gold and silver vessels, and it seems as if these were carried in the procession by regiments of richly dressed people. And although so much plate was in the streets, there was a great sideboard in the banqueting-hall covered with vessels of gold, studded with gems. People had not, indeed, sunk so low in artistic feeling as to carry pots full of gold and silver coin, which was done in the triumph of Paulus Æmilius at Rome, but still a great part of the display was essentially the ostentation of wealth. How different must have been a Panathenaic festival in the days of Pericles! I note further that sculpture and painting of the best kind (the paintings of the Sicyonian artists are specially named) were used for the mere purpose of decoration. Then, in describing the appearance of the great chamber specially built for the banquet, Callixenus tells us that on the pilasters round the wall were a hundred marble reliefs by the first artists, in the space between them were paintings, and about them precious hangings with embroideries, representing mystical subjects, or portraits of kings. We feel ourselves in a sort of glorified *Holborn Restaurant*, where the resources of art are lavished on the walls of an eating-room. In addition to scarlet and purple, gold and silver, and skins of various wild beasts upon the walls, the pillars of the room represented palm-trees, and Bacchic thyrsi alternated, a design which distinctly points to Egyptian rather than Greek taste.

"Among other wonders, the Royal Zoölogical Gardens seemed to have been put under requisition, and we have a list of the various strange animals which joined in the parade. This is very interesting as showing us what can be done in the way of transporting wild beasts, and how far that traffic had reached. There were twenty-four huge lions,— the epithet points, no doubt, to the African, or maned lions,— twenty-six snow-white Indian oxen, eight Æthiopic oxen, fourteen leopards, sixteen panthers, four lynxes, three young panthers, a great white bear, a cameleopard, and an Æthiopic rhinoceros. The tiger and the hippopotamus seem to have missed the opportunity of showing themselves, for they were not mentioned.

"But the great Bacchic show was only one of a large number of mummeries, or allegories, which pervaded the streets; for example, Alexander, attended by Nike and Athene, the first Ptolemy escorted and crowned by the Greek cities of Asia Minor, and with Corinth standing beside him. Both gods and kings were there in statues of gold and ivory, and for the most part escorted by living attendants,— a curious incongruity all through the show.

"The procession lasted a whole day, being opened by

a figure of the Morning Star and closed by Hesperus. Eighty thousand troops, cavalry and infantry, in splendid uniforms, marched past. The whole cost of the feast was over half a million of our money. But the mere gold crowns, offered by friendly towns and people, to the first Ptolemy and his queen, had amounted to that sum."

The literary materials we possess for the reign of this Ptolemy are deplorably meagre, the few extant documents being, for the most part, fulsome panegyrics of Greek chroniclers, or bare records of isolated facts, which are not of great historical value. The most interesting event in this reign is the coronation ceremony, which was conceived and carried out on a scale of unparalleled splendour and magnificence. Contemporary writers seem to have been as much dazzled by these fêtes as the Alexandrian populace. Possibly there was some deep political motive behind these magnificent spectacles, which amused the people and induced them to forget the atrocious domestic murders with which Philadelphus inaugurated his reign.

"We have from Phylarchus a curious passage which asserts that, though the most august of all the sovereigns of the world, and highly educated, if ever there was one, he was so deceived and corrupted by unreasonable luxury as to expect he could live forever, and say that he alone had discovered immortality; and yet, being tortured many days by gout, when at last he got better and saw from his windows the natives on the river bank making their breakfast of common fare, and lying stretched anyhow on the sand, he sighed: 'Alas that I was not born one of them!'"

Philadelphus is perhaps best known for his work in connection with the Alexandrian Museum, which had been founded by his father. He is generally allowed to have the credit of ordering the Greek translation of the Old Testament, known as the Septuagint; but his actual responsibility for this is still a matter of controversy with ecclesiastical historians. It is not, however, disputed that Philadelphus commissioned Manetho to write his famous History of Egypt. Of Ptolemy's architectural achievements, the most important is the Pharos at Alexandria. This famous tower, from which the French and other Latin nations derive their name for lighthouse (Phare), once ranked among the seven wonders of the world. It was made of white marble, and was several stories high, and inside ran a circular causeway on a gentle incline, which could be ascended by chariots. It is not known how long this lighthouse remained erect, but it was supposed to have been destroyed by an earthquake in 1203 A. D.

A clever epigram of Posidippus, on a second century papyrus found a few years ago, is worth quoting:

"Ελληνων σωτηρα Φαρου σκοπον, ω ανα Πρωτεν,
Σωστρατος εστησεν Δεξιφανους Κνιδιος
ου γαρ εν Αιγυπτωι σκοποι ου ριον οι' επι νησων
αλλα χαμαι χηλη ναυλοχος εκτεταται."

It is said that on a very calm day it is possible to discern the ruins beneath the sea off the head of the promontory.

In this reign a great impetus was given to the building of temples and other commemorative structures. In addition to the world-renowned Temple of Isis, a gem of Ptolemaic architecture, Ptolemy built several temples on the Delta, — notably one at Naukratis, and one of great size on the site of the ancient Sebennytus. He also built an important port on the Red Sea, named after his daughter Berenice, which is thus described in an article in the Proceedings of the Royal Geographical Society, 1887:

"The violent north winds that prevail in the Red Sea made the navigation so difficult and slow for the poor ships of the ancients that Ptolemy Philadelphus established the port of Berenike. This is two hundred miles south of the ancient ports at or near Kosseir, and consequently saved that distance and its attendant delays and dangers to the mariners from South Arabia and India. I suppose the best camels and the worst ships would choose Berenike, while the best ships and the worst camels would carry the Kosseir traffic. For it is interesting to note that Philadelphus, at the same time that he built Berenike, also rebuilt the old Kosseir port, and Myos Hormos was still kept in repair. In former days it is probable that many a sea-sick traveller, buffeted by contrary winds, landed joyfully at Berenike, and took the twelve-days' camel journey sooner than continue in his cramped ship, — just as now they disembark at Brindisi rather than Venice, on their way from India."

An engineering work of the highest importance, and one which, as we shall see later, in the chapter on Modern Egypt, proved of permanent value in the development of the agricultural resources of the country, was the draining of Lake Moeris, and the reclamation and irrigation of a vast tract of country now known as Fayyum.

In a sketch of this important reign, some mention should be made of Ptolemy's famous consort, his second wife, Arsinoe. This, to add to the difficulties of ancient chroniclers and modern historians, was also the name of Philadelphus's *first* wife; but the fame of the latter is altogether eclipsed by that of the former. Even in the age of Berenices and Cleopatras, and other great princesses, Arsinoe stands out prominently. Though most Egyptian queens were in a manner deified, none, with the exception of the last Cleopatra, exercised greater political influence. She took her place beside the king, not only on coins, but among those statues at the entrance of the Odeum at Athens, where the series of the Egyptian kings was set up. She was the only queen among them. At Olympia, where there were three statues of the king, she had her place. Pausanias also saw, at Helicon, a statue of her in bronze, riding upon an ostrich. It is very likely that this statue, or a replica, was present to the mind of Callimachus, when he spoke, in the "Coma Berenices," of the winged horse, brother of the Æthiopian Memnon, who is the messenger of Queen Arsinoe. Arsinoe died some three or four years before her royal husband, and Pliny tells us that the disconsolate king, after her death, lent an ear to the wild scheme of an architect to build her a temple with a lodestone roof, which might sustain in mid-air an iron statuette of the deified lady, who was identified with Isis (especially at Philæ) and with Aphrodite. She had an *Arsinoeion* over her tomb at Alexandria, another apparently in the Fayyum, and probably many elsewhere. Her temple on the promontory between Alexandria and the Canopic mouth, dedicated to her by Kallikrates, where she was known as Aphrodite Zephyritis, is mentioned by Strabo, and celebrated in many epigrams. He also mentions two towns in Ætolia and Crete, two in Cilicia, two in Cyprus, one in Cyrene, besides those in Egypt, called after her. She seems only to have wanted a Plutarch and a Roman lover to make her into another Cleopatra.

Of all the Ptolemies, Euergetes I. is the only great conqueror, and his reign should be the most interesting to the student were it not for the scantiness of material. Very little is known of this shadowy and enigmatic sovereign, and of the actual part he took in the great campaigns against the Seleucides and Cilicia — one exceeded in importance only by the chief ones of Alexander — nothing is told us by the Greek chroniclers. The events of the great campaign known as the Third Syrian War have, indeed, only within recent years been known to modern historians through the accounts in the famous Petrie papyrus. Other important evidence for the history of this Ptolemy is the famous stone inscription known as the Decree of Canopus, recovered by Lepsius, in 1865, from the sands of Tanis. It was passed by the Synod of Priests in the ninth year of this reign. It is hoped that similar decrees may be found at Philæ, for in 1895 the Egyptian government intrusted the researches here to Colonel Lyons, R. E.

The difficulty of unravelling the intricate labyrinthine maze of Egyptian history during the three hundred years of Ptolemaic rule is intensified, owing to the bewildering recurrence of certain royal names. It is difficult to differentiate the innumerable princesses bearing the names of Berenice, Arsinoe, or Cleopatra, and, indeed, some of the Greek historians have mixed these names up in a most bewildering fashion. Another difficulty which confronts the student of this period is the custom of the sovereigns marrying their sisters. Then again, many of the kings and queens reign conjointly. For instance we have Philometer (Ptolemy VIII.) and Euergetes II. (Ptolemy IX.) together on the throne of Egypt.

In a sketch of the age of the Ptolemies, a notice of the first three sovereigns must necessarily occupy a space which seems somewhat disproportionate for a period which fills barely a hundred years,—about one-third of the whole dynasty. But considering the importance of these reigns, this prominence does not, I think, show a want of appreciation of historic proportion, which has, of course, little to do with chronological proportion.

"Tried by a comparative standard," writes Mr. David Hogarth, "the only monarchs of the Nile Valley that approach to absolute greatness are Ptolemy Philadelphus I., Saladin, certain of the Mamelukes, and Mehemet Ali; for these held as their own what the vainglorious raiders of the twelfth and nineteenth dynasties but touched and left, and I know no prettier irony than that, among all those inscriptions of Pharaohs who 'smite the Asiatics' on temple walls and temple pylons, there should occur no record of the prowess of the one king of Egypt who really smote Asiatics hip and thigh, — Alexander, son of Philip."

With the reign of Ptolemy IV. (Philopater), a tyrannical and self-indulgent king, begins the decline of the Egyptian kingdom under a series of dynastic monarchs. Philopater continued the traditional foreign policy of his ancestors; and though successful in his campaign against Syria, now ruled by Antiochus the Great, Egypt derived but little benefit, as the war was terminated by a peace in which the terms were distinctly unfavourable to Egypt, and were due to the weakness and incapacity of Philopater.

The early events of the reign are thus summarised by Polybius:

"Immediately after his father's death, Ptolemy Philopater put his brother Magas and his partisans to death, and took possession of the throne of Egypt. He thought that he had now freed himself by this act from domestic danger, and that by the deaths of Antigonus and Seleucus, and their being succeeded by mere children like Antiochus and Philip, fortune released him from danger abroad. He therefore felt secure of his position, and began conducting his reign as though it were a perpetual feast. He would attend to no business, and would hardly grant an interview to the officials about the court, or at the head of the administrative departments of Egypt. Even his agents abroad found him entirely careless and indifferent, though his predecessors, far from taking less interest in foreign affairs, had generally given them precedence over those of Egypt itself. For being masters of Cœle-Syria and Cyprus, they maintained a threatening attitude towards the kings of Syria, both by land and sea; and were also in a commanding position in regard to the princes of Asia, as well as the islands, through their possession of the most splendid cities, strongholds, and harbours all along the seacoast, from Pamphylia to the Hellespont and the district round Lysimachia. Moreover, they were favourably placed for an attack upon Thrace and Macedonia from their possession of Ænus Maroneia and more distant cities still. And having thus stretched forth their hands to remote regions, and long ago strengthened their position by a ring of princedoms, these kings had never been anxious about their rule in Egypt, and had naturally, therefore, given great attention to foreign politics.

"But when Philopater, absorbed in unworthy intrigues and senseless and continual drunkenness, treated these several branches of government with equal indifference, it was naturally not long before more than one was found to lay plots against his life as well as his power: of whom the first was Cleomenes, the Spartan."

The decisive battle of Raphia, which terminated the Fourth Syrian War, is described with great circumstantial detail by Polybius. We can only find room for the following graphic specimen from this despatch of the most famous Greek prototype of modern war correspondents:

"Ptolemy, accompanied by his sister, having arrived at the left wing of his army, and Antiochus with the royal guard at the right, they gave the signal for the battle, and opened the fight by a charge of elephants.

"Only some few of Ptolemy's elephants came to close quarters with the foe. Seated on these, the soldiers in the howdahs maintained a brilliant fight, lunging at and striking each other with crossed pikes; but the elephants themselves fought still more brilliantly, using all their strength in the encounter, and pushing against each other, forehead to forehead.

"The way in which elephants fight is this: they get their tusks entangled and jammed, and then push against one another with all their might, trying to make each other yield ground, until one of them, proving superior in strength, has pushed aside the other's trunk; and when once he can get a side blow at his enemy, he pierces him with his tusks, as a bull would with his horns. Now, most of Ptolemy's animals, as is the way with Libyan elephants, were afraid to face the fight, for they cannot stand the smell or the trumpeting of the Indian elephants, but are frightened at their size and strength, I suppose, and run away from them at once without waiting to come near them.

"This is exactly what happened on this occasion, and upon their being thrown into confusion and being driven back upon their own lines, Ptolemy's guard gave way before the rush of the animals; while Antiochus, wheeling his men so as to avoid the elephants, charged the division of cavalry under Polycrates. At the same time the Greek mercenaries, stationed near the phalanx and behind the elephants, charged Ptolemy's peltasts and made them give ground, the elephants having already thrown their ranks into confusion.

"Thus Ptolemy's whole left wing began to give way before the enemy. Echecrates, the commander of the right wing, waited at first to see the result of the struggle between the other wings of the two armies; but when he saw the dust coming his way, and that the elephants opposite his division were afraid even to approach the hostile elephants at all, he ordered Phoxidas to charge the part of the enemy opposite him with his Greek mercenaries, while he made a flank movement with the cavalry and the division behind the elephants, and so getting out of the line of the hostile elephants' attack, charged the enemy's cavalry on the rear or the flank, and quickly drove them from the ground. Phoxidas and his men were similarly successful; for they charged the Arabians and Medes, and forced them into precipitate flight. Thus Antiochus's right wing gained a victory, while his left was defeated. The phalanxes, left without the support of either wing, remained intact in the centre of the plain, in a state of alternate hope and fear for the result. Meanwhile, Antiochus was assisting in gaining the victory on his right wing; while Ptolemy, who had retired behind his phalanx, now came forward in the centre, and showing himself in the view of both armies, struck terror into the hearts of the enemy, but inspired great spirit and enthusiasm in his own men; and Andromachus and Sosibius at once ordered them to lower their sarissæ and charge. The picked Syrian troops stood their ground only for a short time, and the division of Nicarchus quickly broke and fled.

"Antiochus, presuming, in his youthful inexperience, from the success of his own division that he would be equally victorious all along the line, was pressing on the pursuit; but upon one of the older officers at length giving him warning, and pointing out that the cloud of dust raised by the phalanx was moving towards their own camp, he understood too late what was happening, and endeavoured to gallop back with the squadron of royal cavalry to the field. But finding his whole line in full retreat, he was forced to retire to Raphia, comforting himself with the belief that, as far as he was personally concerned, he had won a victory, but had been defeated in the whole battle by the want of spirit and courage shown by the rest.

"Ptolemy, having secured the final victory by his phalanx, and killed large numbers of the enemy in the pursuit by means of his cavalry and mercenaries on his right wing, retired to his own camp and there spent the night. But next day, after picking up and burying his own dead, and stripping the bodies of the enemy, he advanced towards Raphia. Antiochus had wished, immediately after the retreat of his army, to make a camp outside the city, and there rally such of his men as had fled in compact bodies; but finding that the greater number had retreated into the town, he was compelled to enter it himself also. Next morning, however, before daybreak, he led out the relics of his army, and made the best of his way to Gaza. There he pitched a camp, and having sent an embassy to obtain leave to pick up his dead, he obtained a truce for performing their obsequies. His loss amounted to nearly ten thousand infantry and three hundred cavalry killed, and four thousand taken prisoners. Three elephants were killed on the field, — two died afterwards of their wounds. On Ptolemy's side the losses were fifteen hundred infantry and seven hundred cavalry; sixteen of his elephants were killed and most of the others captured."

Such was the result of the battle of Raphia between King Ptolemy and Antiochus for the possession of Cœle-Syria.

Though as a warrior and statesman the fourth Ptolemy shows a decided inferiority to his father, he seems to have been deserving of some praise as a patron of literature, and showed his admiration of Homer by building a magnificent temple in his honour. Then, as a builder, he emulated Rameses or Thotmes, and remains of his work are to be seen at Edfu and Philæ, as well as at Thebes, where he raised that exquisite shrine known as Deir-el-Medinet, of which some account is given in a later chapter, on Thebes and its temples.

We may profitably skip the short and unimportant reigns of several Ptolemies to the ninth Ptolemy, called usually Euergetes II. Antiochus IV. of Syria had conquered a great part of Lower Egypt and attempted to restore Philometer, a son of Ptolemy V. The Alexandrians, however, who, as Professor Mahaffy points out, "voiced" the will of Egypt more completely than Paris does of France at the present day, supported the claims of Euergetes. All through this reign, or rather joint reigns, of Euergetes and Philometer, we find the Roman Senate acting as arbiter, and both sovereigns went to Rome to prosecute their claims in person. A curious side-light is thrown on these intrigues by Plutarch, who mentions that Euergetes offered the chance of becoming Queen of Egypt to Cornelia, the high-souled mother of the Gracchi. No doubt " a Cornelia on the throne at Alexandria would have been a real novelty among the Cleopatras. But the great Roman lady probably held him in such esteem as an English noblewoman now would hold an Indian rajah proposing marriage."

In 146 B. C., Philometer led an army to help his son-in-law, Alexander, recover Syria from Demetrius, and died from wounds received in battle. There is a striking contrast between the characters of the two brother-kings, who for nearly a quarter of a century jointly controlled the destinies of Egypt. Philometer (Ptolemy VII.) was one of the most able of the later sovereigns of the house of Ptolemy. A good and apparently unbiassed sketch of his life is given in the following passage from Polybius:

"Ptolemy, King of Syria, died from a wound received in the war; a man who, according to some, deserved great praise and abiding remembrance; according to others the reverse. If any king before him ever was, he was mild and benevolent, a very strong proof of which is that he never put any of his own 'friends' to death on any charge whatever, and I believe also not a single man at Alexandria owed his death to him. Again, though he was notoriously ejected from his throne by his brother in the first place, when he got a clear opportunity against him in Alexandria, he granted him a complete amnesty; and afterwards, when his brother once more made a plot against him to seize Cyprus, though he got him body and soul into his hands at Lapthus, he was so far from punishing him as an enemy, that he even made him grants in addition to those which formerly belonged to him in virtue of the treaty made between them, and, moreover, promised him his daughter. However, in the course of a series of successes and prosperity, his mind became corrupted; he fell a prey to the dissoluteness and effeminacy characteristic of the Egyptians, and these vices brought him into serious disasters."

Space fails us for a sketch of the reigns of the four Ptolemies who succeed Philopater. Under Epiphanes (Ptolemy V.), the domestic affairs of Egypt fell into a state of deplorable confusion; "one rebellion succeeded another, and anarchy prevailed everywhere." In order to maintain his authority, Epiphanes was fain to ask the protection of the Roman Senate. From this time down to the conquest of Egypt by Octavius, the country of the Pharaohs was, to all intents and purposes, a Roman province under a viceroy, who was allowed the titular rank of king.

On the death of Ptolemy VI., in 181 B. C., a period of alternate despotism, anarchy, and joint-sovereignty begins, which is difficult to follow. In B. C. 146, Euergetes II. (Ptolemy IX.) besieges Alexandria and occupies the throne, though he is nominally merely the regent of the kingdom, and guardian of the infant sovereign, Ptolemy, surnamed Neos. Euergetes, however, when he had got the Alexandrians on his side, did not scruple to put the infant king to death, and occupy himself the blood-stained throne of Egypt. After having reigned some fifteen years at Alexandria, Euergetes has to flee to Cyprus, having alienated his subjects through his cruelties and debauchery. Some years later he appears to have returned from exile and regained possession of his throne.

It is difficult to unravel the confused and conflicting statements of the great historians as regards the later events of his throne, but the date of his death, 117 B. C., is not disputed.

With his death the history of Ptolemaic Egypt, so far as it is worth recording, may be brought to a close. "There is nothing of public interest to follow till we come to the

THE EMPIRE OF THE PTOLEMIES. 39

last scene," to the reign of the notorious Cleopatra VI., the Cleopatra of Shakespeare.

This famous, or rather infamous, queen, daughter of Auletes (Ptolemy XIII.), who came so near to revolutionise the history of the Roman Empire, was born about 69 B. C.

Auletes, who died 51 B. C., has earned the bad eminence of being the most worthless, incapable, and cruel of all the Ptolemies. If we take Cicero's estimate as correct, he was pliant and persuasive when in need, making boundless promises of money to men of influence at Rome, but tyrannical and ruthless when in power, taking little account of human life when it thwarted his interests, or even balked his pleasures. With the priests, however, he seems to have been on friendly terms.

With the succession of Cleopatra we enter upon one of the most familiar epochs of Egyptian, or rather Roman, history, and the intrigues of the Egyptian queen with Cæsar, and subsequently with Antony, are familiar to every one. The real cause of the war which broke out between Rome and Egypt in 31 A. D. seems a little obscure. In fact, the conduct of Antony in celebrating a grand Roman triumph at Alexandria, after a doubtful victory (34 B. C.) over the Parthians, seems to have alienated and disgusted the Roman Senate. But it was the formal distribution of provinces which gave most offence at Rome, and proved the chief *casus belli* put forward by Octavius. This was naturally regarded as a theatrical piece of insolence and contempt of his country: "For, assembling the people in the exercise-ground, and causing two golden thrones to be placed on a platform of silver, the one for him and the other for Cleopatra, and at their feet lower thrones for their children, he proclaimed Cleopatra Queen of Egypt, Cyprus, Libya, and Cœle-Syria, and with her, conjointly, Cæsarion, the reputed son of the former Cæsar. His own sons by Cleopatra were to have the style of 'king of kings;' to Alexander he gave Armenia and Media with Parthia, so soon as it should be overcome; to Ptolemy, Phœnicia, Syria, and Cilicia. Alexander was brought out before the people in Median costume, with the tiara and upright peak; and Ptolemy, in boots and mantle and Macedonian cap done about with the diadem, — for this was the habit of the successors of Alexander, as the other was of the Medes and Armenians. And as soon as they had saluted their parents, the one was received by a guard of Macedonians, the other by one of the Armenians. Cleopatra was then, as at other times when she appeared in public, dressed in the habits of the goddess Isis, and gave audience to the people under the name of the new Isis."

The usual view of historians is that Cleopatra's flight to Egypt, after the disastrous battle of Actium, was prompted by cowardice; but in view of the strong character of this queen, it is more likely that she came to the conclusion early in the fight that Antony's cause was lost, and that her naval contingent would only swell the spoils of Octavins. She probably knew, too, that her life would be forfeited if she were taken prisoner with her fleet. But there was still a chance, if Antony were killed or taken prisoner, that she might negotiate with the conqueror as Queen of Egypt with her fleet and treasure intact. Besides, as Professor Mahaffy points out, who could tell what effect her personal charms, although now somewhat mature, might have upon Octavius? She had already subjugated two far greater Romans,— Cæsar and Antony,— why not a third? For the closing scenes of Cleopatra's life we can go to Shakespeare, whose history here is less at fault than is the case in his English historical plays, as the whole narrative is scrupulously reproduced from Plutarch. The last scene of the tragedy is vividly pictured by Dion:

"After her repast, Cleopatra sent Cæsar a letter which she had written and sealed, and putting everybody out of the monument but her two women, she shut the doors. Cæsar, opening her letter, and finding pathetic prayers and entreaties that she might be buried in the same tomb with Antony, soon guessed what was doing. At first he was going himself in all haste, but, changing his mind, he sent others to see. The thing has been quickly done. The messengers came at full speed and found the guards apprehensive of nothing; but on opening the doors they saw her stone-dead, lying upon a bed of gold, set out in all her royal ornaments. Iras, one of her women, lay dying at her feet; and Charmion, just ready to fall, scarce able to talk and hold up her head, was adjusting her mistress's diadem. And when one that came in said angrily, 'Was this well done of your lady, Charmion?' 'Perfectly well,' she answered, 'and as became the daughter of many kings;' and as she said this, she fell down dead beside the bedside."

When modern people wonder at the daring of the last of the Cleopatras, who has been embalmed in the prose of Plutarch and the verse of Shakespeare, they seldom know or reflect that she was the last of a long series of princesses, probably beautiful and accomplished, certainly daring and unscrupulous, living every day of their lives in the passion of love, hate, jealousy, and ambition, wielding dominion over men or dying in the attempt. But, alas! except in the dull, lifeless effigies on coins, we have no portraits of these terrible persons, no anecdotes of their tamer moments, no means of distinguishing one Cleopatra from the rest, amid the catalogue of parricides, incests, exiles, and bereavements.

The battle of Actium made Octavius master of the Mediterranean, and Egypt of course became a mere province of Rome, until it fell an easy prey to the rising Mohammedan power some six centuries later. The history of Egypt under Arab rule will form the subject of the next chapter.

CHAPTER III.

THE RULE OF THE CALIPHS.

THE period of some 650 years, from the fall of the Ptolemaic Empire (B. C. 30) down to the Mohammedan conquest in 638 A. D., need not detain us long. This age is an uneventful one for Egypt, now reduced to the position of a mere province of the Roman Empire, and then — on the disruption of the Empire and its partition in 395 A. D., when the two sons of the Emperor Theodosius, Arcadius and Honorius, ruled respectively over the Eastern and Western Empires — a portion of what may be conviently called the Byzantine Empire.

In the early part of the seventh century the great Semitic race of the Saracens begins to play a most important part in the world's history, and with little difficulty the army of the Caliph Omar under Amru wrests the province of Egypt from Rome.

We now enter upon a picturesque period of Egyptian history, though it is of more importance to lovers of the arts than to historians. It lasts for nearly nine hundred years, till the conquest of Egypt by the Ottoman Turks in 1517. The chief historical landmarks of this long epoch of Mohammedan rule are Ahmed Ibn-Tulun, El-Muizz, Saladin, and En-Nasr Mohammed.

Amru, fully alive to the suitability of the site of the Roman stronghold of Babylon, builds here his new capital, called Fostat (old Cairo). This is some two miles south of modern Cairo. The latter city is often erroneously attributed to Saladin. This enlightened monarch no doubt

THE RULE OF THE CALIPHS.

improved the new capital considerably, and fortified it; but the modern city dates from 969 A. D., when El-Muizz, the first of the Fatimite dynasty (Tunis), transferred the seat of the government, and we might also say of the Caliphate, from Kerouan (the "Holy City") to a site about two miles from Fostat. To this new city, Gohar, the Caliph's general, gave the proud title of Masr-El-Kahira (the Victorious), a name which was corrupted by Europeans into Cairo, though the natives still call it Masr. Gohar's design was, however, at first limited to a fortress and palace for his master, and for some time the new site was only the royal residence of the Caliph El-Muizz. Here lived the harem, the court, and the garrison, and in this enormous *enceinte* lived, so say the Arab chroniclers, over twelve thousand souls. It was not till the reign of the great Saladin that the walls of the palace were extended to include a city, which even then, in the twelfth century, occupied as large a site as intra-mural Cairo of to-day; that is, about three miles long, and a mile to a mile and a half wide.

"Most of these changes," remarks Mr. Stanley Lane-Poole, "can be traced in the present city. A small part of Fostat remains under the name of Masr-El-Atika (old Cairo), separated from the capital by the great mounds of rubbish which indicate vanished suburbs. Of Kahira the whole growth can readily be traced. The second wall still stands on the north side, though the magnificent Norman-looking gateway of the Bab-En-Nasr, or 'Gate of Victory,' with its mighty square towers and fine vaulting within, and the Bab-El-Futuh, or 'Gate of Conquests,' flanked with massive round towers, are not quite on their original sites. The cornice and frieze, adorned with fine Kufic inscriptions, which run along the face of the gateway and the faces and inner sides of the two towers half-way from the ground, no less than its solid and clean-cut masonry, distinguish the 'Gate of Victory' among Saracenic monuments.

"The second wall is still visible at the eastern boundary of the city, and its other sides may be traced by the *names* of demolished gates, as the Water Gate (Bab-El-Bar), the Bab-El-Luk, and the Bab-El-Khalak; while the Bab Zuweyla, still standing in the heart of the city, is one of the most striking buildings in Cairo, though its walls and inscriptions are daubed over with plaster, and its towers are lowered to make room for the minarets of the adjoining Mosque of El-Muayyad. The second wall, thus mapped out, must have run from near the present bridge over the Ismailiya Canal, along the western side of the Ezbekiya (where the wall was standing in 1842), to near the Abdin Palace, where it turned up to the Bab Zuweyla, and was prolonged to the eastern wall.

"Since it was built, the Nile has considerably changed its course, and now runs much farther to the westward. Saladin's wall was a restoration of this in part, but his addition (begun in 1170) round the citadel is in partial preservation, like the fortress itself, though the continuation round the site of Katai on the south is demolished. The names of the gates, however, show that the limits of the present city on the south are nearly what they were in Saladin's day, and this wall must have run from the Citadel to near the Mosque of Ibn Tulun, enclosed it, and turned north to meet the old wall near Bab-El-Luk.

"The limits of the modern additions are only too plain, but street improvements of the reigning dynasty happily do not extend to the old Fatima Quarter, and indeed scarcely affect Saladin's city, except in the prolongation and widening of the Mooski, the opening of the broad Boulevard Mehemet Ali up to the Citadel, and the laying out of the Rumayla Quarter and the Kara-Meydan in the usual European style. With these exceptions, the modern additions extend only from the Ezbekiya Quarter to the river, and consists of a number of parallel boulevards and *rondes places*, where ugly Western uniformity is partly redeemed by some cool, verandahed villas, and the grateful shade of trees."

In short, the three creators of modern Cairo are Saladin, Mehemet Ali, and Ismail. Saladin built it, Mehemet Ali enlarged it, and Ismail embellished and modernised it.

Under the Saracens Egypt was governed by no less than a hundred and forty-four rulers, some of whom were merely governors or viziers under the Damascus and Bagdad Caliphs respectively, while the more powerful of these dynasties, as we shall see later, claimed the title of Caliphs, and were virtually independent kings of Egypt.

These dynasties of Mohammedan rule, amounting to no less than ten, cover a period of history comparatively featureless and unimportant. Egypt under the Caliphs seems to have no external history to speak of, except during the reign of Saladin, and some of the Mameluke Sultans, such as El-Ashraf, who captured Acre, and Bursbey, who reconquered Cyprus. The only important dynasties are those of the Omayyades, Abbassides, Fatimites (Tunis), Ayyubides (Kurdish), and the two slave dynasties of the Mamelukes, — the Baharide and the Circassian. The most picturesque and interesting are the two latter.

This is a period which Mr. Stanley Lane-Poole has made his own, and for a graphic picture of the Mameluke days we must go to this author's " Arabian Society in the Middle Ages," " The Art of the Saracens," and other works dealing with mediaeval Egypt. An appreciable part of the history of this period is to be read in the Cairo mosques, for most of these magnificent shrines of Islam were built by the Mameluke sovereigns.

In order to understand, however, the course of events in Egypt from the fourth to the fifteenth century, it is necessary to bear in mind the involved question of the Caliphate and its succession. The first four Caliphs, Abu-Bekr, Omar, Othman, and Ali, were either kinsmen or principal adherents of the Prophet. Then we have the rule of the Omayyades, which lasted for nearly a hundred years. When the last of the race, Marwan II., was killed in battle, a descendant of Abbas, an uncle of Mohammed, founded the important dynasty of Abbassides, and the seat of the Caliphate is transferred from Damascus to Bagdad. In the tenth century the power of the Caliphate of Bagdad declined, and its claim to the temporal and spiritual sovereignty of Islam was only acknowledged in theory by the Egyptian Caliphate. In fact the Caliphs of Bagdad gradually fell under the control of their viziers or governors in Egypt, just as the Merovingian sovereigns had become subject to the "Mayors of the Palace." In the twelfth century we see the Fatimite dynasty of Tunis, who claimed descent from Fatima, the daughter of Mohammed, in possession of the Egyptian Caliphate, and members of this family succeeded in maintaining their rule for over a century, till in 1169 they were overthrown by the victorious Saladin, who founded the Ayyubides (Kurdish) dynasty.

This great sovereign does not at first claim the title of Caliph, but brings back Egypt nominally under the spiritual control of the Caliph of Bagdad. Saladin deservedly ranks as one of the greatest, and incontestably the most enlightened, of all the sovereigns of Egypt from Pharaonic days downwards, and under his rule Egypt is transformed from a small kingdom into a powerful empire. In fact, this period is closely bound up with the most important events in European history, and every one is familiar with Saladin's magnificent campaigns in Palestine, his conquest of Jerusalem, and the treaty with the English king, Richard I., and these are only a small part of his exploits. Saladin, too, combined in a marked degree the genius for war with the love of the beautiful, says Mr. Stanley Lane-

THE RULE OF THE CALIPHS. 47

Poole; and the walls of Cairo and the noble Citadel bear witness to his encouragement of architecture.

" Saladin's empire needed a strong hand to keep it united, and the number of relatives who demanded their share of his wide provinces rendered the survival of the Ayyuby dominion precarious. Saladin's brother controlled the centrifugal tendencies of his kindred for a while, and his son, El-Kamil, gloriously defeated Jean de Brienne on the spot where the commemorative city of El-Mansura (the Victorious) was afterwards erected by the conqueror. After his death in 1237, however, the forces which made for disintegration became too strong to be resisted; various petty dynasties of the Ayyuby family were temporarily established in the chief provinces, only to make way shortly for the Tartars, and in Egypt and in Syria notably for the Mamelukes, who in 1250 succeeded to the glories of Saladin."

The strict meaning of *Mameluke* is "owned," and the Egyptian Mamelukes were originally white slaves. They were first employed by the Sultan Es-Salih in the middle of the thirteenth century as mercenaries, and in many respects they resembled the Janissaries of the later Turks, a body first raised for a similar purpose by the Ottoman Sultans, about a century later. The Mamelukes soon obtained the control of the army and became an important factor in the body politic of Egypt, and in a few years gained the chief authority, by 1250 A. D. becoming sufficiently powerful to seize the throne.

The Sultans of this Mameluke dynasty offer remarkable contrasts. Slaves in origin, and warriors by trade as well as by inclination, bloodthirsty and ferocious, this dynasty of adventurers had an appreciation of art which would have done credit, as Mr. Lane-Poole aptly remarks, to the most civilised rulers that ever sat on a constitutional throne. " It is one of the most singular facts in Eastern history, that, wherever these rude Tartars penetrated, there they inspired a great and vivid enthusiasm for art. It was the Tartar Ibn-Tulun who built the first example of the true Saracenic mosque at Cairo; it was the line of Mameluke Sultans, all Turkish or Circassian slaves, who filled Cairo with the most beautiful and abundant monuments that any city can show. The arts were in Egypt long before the Tartars became her rulers, but they stirred them into new life, and made the Saracenic work of Egypt the centre and headpiece of Mohammedan art.

"Why this should be,—why the singularly tyrannical, bloodthirsty, and unstable rule of the Mamelukes should have fostered so remarkable a development of art,—remains, as we have said, a mystery; but the fact is indisputable that the period of Frankish and Circassian tyranny in Egypt and Syria was the age of efflorescence of the purest Saracenic art in all its branches.

"Wherever the Saracens carried their conquering arms, a new and characteristic style of art is seen to arise. In the mosques and private houses of Cairo, of Damascus, of Kairowân, of Cordova and Seville, throughout Egypt, Syria, Mesopotamia, Persia, North Africa, and Spain, and in Sicily and the Balearic Isles, we trace their influence in the thoroughly individual and characteristic style of architecture and ornament which is variously known as 'Arabian,' 'Mohammedan,' 'Moorish,' and 'Saracenic.' The last term is the best, because the most comprehensive. 'Arabian' seems to imply that the art owed its origin to Arabia and the Arabs, whereas it was only when the Arabs left Arabia and ceased to be purely Arabian, that the style of art miscalled Arab made its appearance. 'Mohammedan' indicates that the art was the work and invention of Muslims, which can hardly be maintained in the face of the fact that the first great monument of Saracenic architecture in Egypt was designed by a Christian, and that much of the finest work was produced by Copts and Greeks. 'Moorish' limits the art to the Mohammedan rulers of Spain, where indeed a singularly magnificent development of the style took place; but this was neither the earliest nor the most typical form. 'Saracenic' art includes all the work of the countries under Saracen rule, and, moreover, carries with it the perfectly accurate impression that the chief development of the art was at the time when the Saracens were a fighting power, and the name was a household word among the crusading nations of the West."

The famous collection in the National Museum of Arabic Art, which is described in a subsequent chapter, affords abundant proofs of the extraordinary development in the decorative arts attained by Egypt under the Mamelukes.

By some historians Melik-es-Salih is reckoned as the founder of the Mameluke dynasty. It is true that it was during his reign that the Mamelukes, whose influence and power had been steadily increasing after the death of Saladin, first became a factor of the greatest importance in the government of the country; but Melik was himself one of the Ayyubide Kurds, and was, in fact, a grandnephew of Saladin. On Melik's death and the accession of a weak and incapable sovereign, the Mamelukes, headed by El-Muizz-Ebek, seized the throne. Ebek, who had strengthened his position by marrying Melik's widow, was in fact the founder of the Mameluke dynasty.

The genesis of this dynasty of adventurers is well described by Mr. Stanley Lane-Poole:

"Before El-Salih's death, a certain number of his Mamelukes had risen from the ranks of common slaves to posts of honour at their master's court; they had become cup-bearers, or tasters, or masters of the horse to his Majesty, and had been rewarded by enfranchisement; and these freed Mamelukes became, in turn, masters and owners of other Mamelukes. Thus, at the very beginning of the Mameluke history, we find a number of powerful amurs, or lords, who had risen from the ranks of the slaves, and in turn became the owners of a large body of retainers, whom they led to battle, or by whose aid they aspired to ascend the throne. The only title of kingship among these nobles was personal prowess, and the command of the largest number of adherents. In the absence of other influences, the hereditary principle was no doubt adopted, and we find one family, that of Kalaun, maintaining its succession to the throne for several generations; but, as a rule, the successor to the kingly power was the most powerful lord of the day, and his hold on the throne depended chiefly on the strength of his following, and his conciliation of the other nobles. The annals of Mameluke dominion are full of instances of a great lord reducing the authority of the reigning Sultan to a shadow, and then stepping over his murdered body to the throne."

The great Sultan Bebars is a typical representative of the rulers of this military oligarchy which controlled the destinies of Egypt for over three centuries. In many respects Bebars resembled Saladin, and his romantic career has much in common with that of the founder of the present dynasty, Mehemet Ali. His wonderful force of character and diplomatic talents no doubt contributed to his strikingly successful career as much as his personal courage and capacity for governing men, qualities in which few of the Mameluke Sultans were deficient. These qualities, too, enabled this one-eyed slave not only to gain the throne, but to keep it for nearly twenty years, — an unusually long reign for a Mameluke, which averages five or six years only, — and to found an empire that endured for nearly three hundred years.

Bebars's reign is a fair sample of the history of this epoch, and in Marco Polo we glean many interesting details of this picturesque personality. Bebars was a native of Kipchak, a district between the Caspian Sea and the Ural Mountains. Of magnificent physique, he had one serious defect, from the slave-trader's point of view, — a cataract in one eye. On this account he only sold for £20. He

THE RULE OF THE CALIPHS.   51

eventually passed into the possession of the Sultan Es-Salih. In the war against the saintly Louis of France and his Crusaders, Bebars distinguished himself so markedly that he was given high command in the Mameluke army. Taking advantage of the dissensions and rivalry of the Mameluke generals, and the incapacity of the Sultan Ed-Mudhaffer, he seizes the throne with little difficulty, having won over the army to his side.

Thus begins that singular succession of Mameluke Sultans which lasted, in spite of special tendencies to dissolution, for two hundred and seventy-five years.

"The external history of these years is monotonous. Wars to repel the invasions of the Tartars, or to drive the Christians from the Holy Land, struggles between rival claimants to the throne, embassies to and from foreign powers, including France and Venice, the Khan of Persia and the King of Abyssinia, constitute the staple of foreign affairs. To enumerate the events of each reign, or even the names of the fifty Mamelukes who sat on the throne at Cairo, would be wearisome and unprofitable to the reader. But it is different with the internal affairs of the Mameluke period. In this flowering time of Saracenic art, a real interest belongs to the life and social condition of the people who made and encouraged the finest productions of the Oriental artist. History can show few more startling contrasts than that offered by the spectacle of a band of disorderly soldiers, to all appearance barbarians, prone to shed blood, merciless to their enemies, tyrannous to their subjects, yet delighting in the delicate refinements which art could afford them in their home life, lavish in their endowment of pious foundations, magnificent in their mosques and palaces, and fastidious in the smallest details of dress and furniture. Allowing all that must be allowed for the passion of the barbarian for display, we are still far from an explanation how the Tartars chanced to be the noblest promoters of art, of literature, and of public works, that Egypt had known since the days of the Ptolemies."

To resume our sketch of the most picturesque figure among all the Mameluke sovereigns:

"So well did Bebars organise his wide-stretching provinces, that no incapacity or disunion among his successors could pull down the fabric he had raised, until the wave of Ottoman conquest swept at last upon Egypt and Syria. To him is due the constitution of the Mameluke army, the rebuilding of a navy of forty war-galleys, the allotment of feofs to the lords and soldiers, the building of causeways and bridges, and digging of canals in various parts of Egypt.

"He strengthened the fortresses of Syria, and garrisoned them with Mamelukes; he connected Damascus and Cairo by a postal service of four days, and used to play polo in both cities within the same week."

In Marco Polo will be found an interesting example of the business hours of this famous Sultan. He arrived before Tyre one night; a tent was immediately pitched by torchlight; the secretaries, seven in number, were summoned with the commander-in-chief; and the adjutant-general (Anûr Alam), with the military secretaries, were instructed to draw up orders. For hours they ceased not to write letters and diplomas, to which the Sultan affixed his seal; this very night they indited in his presence fifty-six diplomas for high nobles, each with its proper introduction of praise to God. One of these letters has been preserved; it is a very characteristic epistle, and displays a grim and sarcastic appreciation of humour. It appears that Boemond, Prince of Antioch, was not present at the assault of that city by Bebars, and the Sultan kindly conveyed the information of the disaster in a personal despatch. He begins by ironically complimenting Boemond on his change of title, from prince to count, in consequence of the fall of his capital, and then goes on to describe the siege and capture of Antioch, sparing his correspondent no detail of the horrors that ensued. The letter winds up by an ironical felicitation on Boemond's absence: "This letter holds happy tidings for thee; it tells thee that God watches over thee, inasmuch as in these latter days thou wast not in Antioch! As not a man hath escaped to tell thee the tale, we tell it thee; as no soul could apprise thee that thou art safe, while all the rest have perished, we apprise thee!" It would seem that, not unnaturally, the unfortunate Prince of Antioch was highly incensed with the Sultan's sarcastic attentions.

The most ample details of the outward life of the Mamelukes may be gathered in the chronicles of the Arab historian, El-Makrizy; but if we seek to know something of the domestic life of the period, we must go elsewhere. We occasionally find, indeed, in this historian an account of the revels of the court on great festivals, and he tells us how, during some festivities in Bebars's reign, there was a concert every night in the Citadel, where a torch was gently waved to and fro to keep the time.

"But to understand the home life of the Mamelukes, we must turn to the 'Thousand and One Nights,' where, whatever the origin and scene of the stories, the manners and customs are drawn from the society which the narrators saw about them in Cairo in the day of the Mamelukes. From the doings of the characters in that immortal story-book, we may form a nearly accurate idea how the Mamelukes amused themselves; and the various articles of luxury that have come down to us — the goblets, incense-burners, bowls, and dishes of fine inlaid silver or gold — go to confirm the fidelity of the picture. The wonderful thing about this old Mohammedan society is that it was what it was in spite of Islam. With all their prayers and fasts and irritating ritual, the Moslems of the Middle Ages contrived to amuse themselves. Even in their religion they found opportunities for enjoyment. They made the most of the festivals of the faith, and put on their best clothes; they made up parties to visit the tombs, indeed, but to visit them right merrily on the backs of their asses; they let their servants go out and amuse themselves, too, in the gaily illuminated streets, hung with silks and satins, and filled with dancers, jugglers, and revellers, fantastic figures, the Oriental Punch, and the Chinese Shadows; or they went to witness the thrilling and horrifying performances of the dervishes."

Contemporaneous with the accession of the first Mameluke dynasty is the commencement of the great Ottoman Empire. The Ottoman Turks were so called from their first leader, Othman, who, towards the end of the thirteenth century, seemed likely to swallow up not only the Asiatic provinces of the Byzantine Empire, but all Christendom. The Turks were not, like the Saracens, a Semitic race, nor were they of Aryan descent, but of Mongolian or Tartar origin. Though the Turks and Arabs are often loosely described, as if they were of the same nationality, they have, in fact, nothing in common except their religion. In 1453 the capital of the Empire, Constantinople, was taken by Mohammed the Conqueror, after a siege which lasted several years. In 1517 the Ottoman Sultan Selim, known as the "Inflexible," who had already added Syria to the Ottoman Empire, conquered Egypt.

From the Ottoman conquest in 1517 till the French occupation in the last years of the last century, and the subjugation of the country to the famous adventurer Mehemet Ali, a sketch of whose reign is given later, the history of Egypt is entirely without interest.

CHAPTER IV.

THE MAKING OF EGYPT.

A BARE outline of the principal events of Egyptian history, from the end of Mehemet Ali's reign in 1848, to the suppression of Arabi's rebellion in 1882, will suffice to preserve the thread of the narrative in the sketch of Egyptian history which has been attempted in the previous chapters.

Mehemet's successor, Abbas, seems to indicate what biologists call a " throw-back " to the type of Oriental despot, of which some of the Mameluke sovereigns are examples. All that can be said for him is that he maintained the strictest authority over the army and his officials, and that the public security in Egypt was never greater than during his reign. He was followed by his uncle, Said, who had the same leaning towards Western civilisation as his father, Mehemet, and was, in many respects, an enlightened prince. To him is due, more than to any other sovereign, the great scheme of the maritime canal.

Many important public engineering schemes were carried on during this reign, including the partial restoration of the Barrage, the railway from Cairo to Alexandria, the building of the National Museum (since removed to Ghizeh). In spite of the crippled state of the finances, Said Pacha abolished monopolies and equalised the incidence of taxation, and inaugurated numerous other beneficial fiscal reforms. Unfortunately his reign was short, and in 1863 he was succeeded by Ismail, grandson of Mehemet Ali.

Ismail, in spite of his passion for European institutions and his exalted aims for the national development of Egypt, which he attempted to raise to the position of a European Power, was little more than a magnificent failure as a nineteenth century sovereign. Though he did much for the material progress of the country, and spent enormous sums in what, in the case of Egypt, can in an ironical sense only be termed " reproductive public works," such as roads, bridges, canals, railways, etc., he may be said to have done more harm to his country than any sovereign since the age of the Ptolemies. His prodigality, which will be referred to later, was proverbial, and the fact that the public debt on his accession was three millions, and by the end of his reign had increased to nearly *thirty-fold*, speaks volumes for the unfitness of Ismail to continue as the sovereign of a country in the last throes of financial embarrassment, and on the verge of bankruptcy.

"Ismail's mistake lay, not in the aim he set before him, but in his manner of trying to attain it. No one can doubt that he was right, as the great founder of his dynasty, Mehemet Ali, was right, in striving to bring Egypt into line with European civilisation. . . . Ismail failed for lack of patience and judgment. He tried to rush his transformation scene. He wanted, by a stroke of the pen, to turn the most conservative people on earth into a living embodiment of all the virtues of a progressive and enlightened civilisation. He had no patience for the slow conversion of a nation almost as stolid and immovable as their own Pyramids. Their whole system was to be changed in an instant by a *coup de théâtre*, with trap-doors, stage-thunder, and a shower of fireworks. It was not so to be done, as Ismail has by this time realised in his meditative seclusion at Stambul.[1]

"Inexhaustible patience, tact, and discretion are needed before the immemorial vices of Egyptian government and the time-honoured corruption of Egyptian society can be transformed."

In 1876, the European bondholders, fearing national bankruptcy and repudiation of the innumerable loans, in-

---

[1] This was written before Ismail's death in 1896.

duced their respective governments to interfere; and the revenue and expenditure were placed under the control of commissioners appointed by the Great Powers. Ismail, having placed insuperable difficulties in the way of the Financial Commission, the Porte, at the instigation of the Powers, dethroned Ismail, and placed his eldest son, Tewfik, on the throne.

Tewfik was virtually the protégé of the Powers, and this naturally lessened his prestige considerably in the eyes of his subjects. Egypt was, in fact, practically a big estate, with the Great Powers as landlord, and Tewfik as tenant.

The army, from the first, seemed to have got out of hand, and in 1881 the military leaders, combining with the heads of the so-called National movement, whose chief ostensible object was the freeing of Egypt from European influence and control, the disaffection of the people culminated in open rebellion under Arabi, the minister of war. In July, the English fleet went to the assistance of the Khedive by bombarding Alexandria, and in less than two months an English expeditionary force, under Sir Garuch (now Lord) Wolseley, stamped out the rebellion by a crushing defeat of Arabi's troops at Tel-el-Kebir. This practically marks the end of Egypt as an independent kingdom (except for the nominal allegiance due to the Porte), and from that date to the present the history of Egypt is the history of the development of the country under English influence.

At the very outset, Great Britain, in dealing with Egyptian reforms, had to contend with the serious external obstacles due to the peculiar position of the country through its dependence on the Porte, and to the international tutelage as regards finances to which she was subject. Obviously, with insufficient material the *morale* of government would be lessened. Under Ismail the suzerainty of Turkey was limited, to all intents and purposes, to the right to exact an annual tribute of some £700,000. But the accession of Tewfik was the Sultan's opportunity, and the new firman included one very serious restriction on the borrowing power of the vassal state. The sanction of the Porte was necessary, equally with that of the Powers, before Egypt could negotiate any fresh loan.

With this important exception, most of the powers and privileges of sovereignty could be exercised by the Khedive. Egypt was, indeed, far more hampered by the Great Powers, as guardians of the *caisse* (treasury), than by the Sultan of the Ottoman Empire. Another obstacle was the privileges granted to foreigners which are known as the Capitulations, of which the most important were the exemption from the jurisdiction of the local courts of justice, and immunity from taxation. These privileges, too, from the time of Mehemet Ali, had been notoriously abused by the large and powerful foreign colonies in Egypt.

This immunity from the local courts had, during the reign of Ismail, been particularly abused by the army of *concessionaires* who exploited Egypt at that period. Thousands of preposterous claims used to be brought against the Government by these adventurers, in the consular courts, — the only jurisdiction to which foreigners were subject, — who were naturally predisposed in favour of the claimant.

"Indeed, Egypt, in the sixties and seventies, was the happy hunting-ground of financiers and promoters of the shadiest description. An industrial or commercial enterprise might or might not be profitable to the persons undertaking it; but the man who was lucky enough to have a case against the Government could regard his fortune as assured. The same ruler, who could with impunity perpetrate acts of gross perfidy and injustice towards his native subjects, was himself mercilessly tricked and plundered by the foreign vampires that found such a congenial home upon Egyptian soil.

". . . If the personality of Ismail was an essential factor in the ruin of his country, it needed a whole series of unfortunate conditions to render that personality as it actually became. It needed a nation of submissive slaves, not only bereft of any vestige of liberal institutions, but devoid of the slightest spark of the spirit of liberty. It needed a bureaucracy which it would have been hard to equal for its combination of cowardice and corruption. It needed the whole gang of swindlers — mostly European — by whom Ismail was surrounded, and to whom, with his phenomenal incapacity to make a good bargain, — strange characteristic in a man so radically dishonest, — he fell an easy prey.

"A concession, nominally asked for to forward some useful enterprise or business, was actually sought simply in order to find an excuse for throwing it up, and then claiming compensation from the Government. When the Mixed Tribunals (international courts established to decide civil actions) were established, there were £40,000,000 of outstanding claims made by foreigners against the Government. The extravagant nature of these claims may be estimated by the fact that in one claim, where 30,000,000 francs had been demanded, the Mixed Courts awarded the plaintiff £1,000. Ismail himself was fully alive to the sharp practice of these European adventurers and concession-hunters, — convertible terms for the most part, — and with a genial cynicism used to rally these European *concessionaires* on their extortionate practices. During the interview with a famous *concessionaire*, Ismail told one of his suite to close the window, 'for if this gentleman catches cold it will cost me £10,000.'

"But in Egypt European influence was far too strong to permit of this solution of the financial difficulty, and the Powers embodied a kind of composition with Egypt's creditors by what is known as the Law of Liquidation, by which the country was freed from the threatened insolvency. The interest on the debt was immensely reduced, and Egypt was able once more to meet her liabilities, 'but tied hand and foot, unable to move, almost unable to breathe, without the consent of Europe.'"

The weak points in the position of Egypt are admirably summed up by Sir Alfred Milner:

"A Government which cannot legislate for, and cannot tax, the strangers resident in its dominions, — especially when those strangers form, by virtue of their numbers, wealth, and influence, a very important section of the community, — is lamentably shorn of its due measure of authority and of respect. But this weakness in the position of Egypt, springing from the Capitulations, has been greatly enhanced by the further disabilities and restrictions which she has brought upon herself by her unfortunate financial career. There is no country in the world to the position of which a policy of profuse expenditure and reckless borrowing was more ill-suited. Other states which have plunged in the same direction — though perhaps none ever went to such lengths — could at least fall back, in the last resort, on the desperate remedy of repudiation."

But the Egyptian Government was too much under the thumb of the Great Powers to adopt such an *ultima ratio*. Native creditors might, and indeed were, defrauded with impunity; but European influence was too powerful to permit of such a policy in the case of foreign bondholders.

To return to the condition of Egypt after the collapse of the National Party and the fall of Arabi Pacha.

With the crushing of Arabi's rebellion, England's work in Egypt had only begun, no doubt much to the surprise and disgust of the English Government, which had interfered with no other object than to "restore order." But the quick march of events, and the fearfully rapid spread of popular and religious excitement, were too much even for the most pronounced supporters of a *laissez faire* attitude, and a policy of simple temporary intervention was necessarily converted by the course of events into one of more or less permanent occupation.

"Here was a country, the very centre of the world, the great highway of nations, — a country which, during the last half-century, had been becoming ever more and more an appanage of Europe, — in which thousands of European lives and millions of European capital were at stake, and in which, of all European nations, Great Britain was, by virtue of its enormous direct trade and still more enormous transit trade, the most deeply interested. And this country, which the common efforts and sacrifices of all the Powers had just dragged from the verge of bankruptcy, was now threatened, not with bankruptcy merely, but with a reign of blank barbarianism."

The European Concert seemed as little able as Turkey, Egypt's nominal protector, to cope with this pressing emer-

THE MAKING OF EGYPT. 61

gency; and France, the partner of England, shirked her duties in a somewhat pusillanimous fashion. Consequently Great Britain was morally bound to " bell the cat." The difficulty of " restoring order," or, as it was officially worded, " restoring the authority of the Khedive," was enormously increased by the fact that not only had the whole machinery of government been upset by the revolutionaries who called themselves the National Party, but the whole fabric of government had rested on a rotten base. It had no moral or material force at its back, and the personal prestige of the Khedive Tewfik had been seriously impaired.

Two courses were open to the British Government. (1) They could have contented themselves with restoring order externally, and left the responsibilities for its maintenance to Turkish troops. Such a policy would not, however, be tolerated in a country which, " with its large number of European residents and swarms of foreign tourists, lives, so to speak, constantly under the eye of civilised mankind." In short, such a barbarous policy seemed out of the question. (2) If the welfare of Egypt was to be studied, and the country to be put in the way of governing itself according to the methods of civilised states, then the only course was to be prepared for an occupation of the country till the whole machinery of government could be reconstructed, and peace and justice secured to the Egyptians, and native administrators educated in the methods of orderly and honest government. This was the task which England entered upon; and it is this kind of veiled protectorate which she is still exercising.

This " veiled protectorate " was of course in the nature of a compromise; but for many reasons annexation, or even an absolute protectorate, was undesirable. The creation of this disguised protectorate was notified to the Great Powers, January 3, 1883, in the memorable despatch, quoted below, of Lord Granville.

"Although, for the present," says that document, "a British force remains in Egypt for the preservation of public tranquillity, her Majesty's Government are desirous of withdrawing it as soon as the state of the country and the organisation of proper means for the maintenance of the Khedive's authority will admit of it. In the meantime, the position in which her Majesty's Government are placed towards his Highness imposes upon them the duty of giving advice with the object of securing that the order of things to be established shall be of a satisfactory character, and possess the elements of stability and progress."

This constitutes one of the famous "pledges of withdrawal" with which England is twitted in season and out of season by the French press. In fact, in a leading French journal published at Alexandria, these pledges are *daily* printed in a prominent position on the front page.

In connection with this memorable "Note" may be quoted the important despatch — a corollary of the first — sent by Lord Salisbury to the English envoy to the Porte in 1887:

"The Sultan is pressing the Government of Great Britain to name a date for the evacuation of Egypt, and in that demand he is avowedly encouraged by one, or perhaps two, of the European Powers. Her Majesty's Government have every desire to give him satisfaction upon this point; but they cannot fix even a distant date for evacnation, until they are able to make provision for securing beyond that date the external and internal peace of Egypt. The object which the Powers of Europe have had in view, and which is not less the desire of her Majesty's Government to attain, may be generally expressed by the phrase, 'The neutralisation of Egypt;' but it must be neutralisation with an exception designed to maintain the security and permanence of the whole arrangement. The British Government must retain their right to guard and uphold the condition of things which will have been brought about by the military action and large sacrifice of this country. So long as the Government of Egypt maintains its position, and no disorders arise to interfere with the administration of justice or the action of the executive power, it is highly desirable that no soldier belonging to any foreign nation should remain upon the soil of Egypt, except when it may be necessary to make use of the land-passage from one sea to the other. Her Majesty's Government would willingly agree that such a stipulation should, whenever the evacuation had taken place, apply to English as much as any other troops; but it will be necessary to restrict this provision, as far as England is concerned, to periods of tranquillity. England, if she spontaneously and willingly evacuates the country, must retain a treaty right of intervention, if at any time either internal peace or external security should be seriously threatened. There is no danger that a privilege so costly in its character will be used unless the circumstances imperatively demand it."

These documents are such important landmarks in England's Egyptian policy, that no excuse need be offered for quoting them at some length.

It is proverbially easy to be wise after the event; but there is little doubt that an uncompromising protectorate, albeit merely temporary, would have been the most satisfactory course.

"It is certain that if we had grasped the Egyptian nettle boldly, if we had proclaimed from the first our intention of exercising, even for a time, that authority which, as a matter of fact, we do exercise, we could have made the situation not only much more endurable for the Egyptians, but much easier for ourselves. Had we seen our way to declaring even a temporary protectorate, we might have suspended the Capitulations, if we could not have got rid of them altogether, as France has done in Tunis. Had we been willing to guarantee the debt, or a portion of the debt, not only could the interest have been at once reduced, and the financial burdens of the country enormously lightened, but Europe would no doubt have agreed to free the Egyptian Government from the network of restrictions which had been imposed upon it for the protection of the bondholders. In order to have Great Britain as surety for their bond, the creditors would have abandoned with alacrity all their minor safeguards."

And now we will consider the more important reforms and improvements carried out by England during this virtual protectorate of the country. They may conveniently be divided according to the great State departments,—the army, finance, public works, and justice. But in order to understand the significance and value of her great reforms in the internal government of Egypt, it is necessary to have a clear comprehension of the peculiar difficulties—a maze of obstacles both external and internal—which England had to contend against; and, therefore, in the preceding pages we have attempted to indicate the peculiar nature of these difficulties.

The delicate diplomatic relations between the Egyptian and English Governments constitute one of the gravest difficulties of England's position as the virtual protector and guardian of Egypt; and the presence of an English army of occupation in an autonomous province of a friendly Power,—for that is the nominal relation of Egypt to Turkey,—is not the least of these difficulties.

The British troops have, of course, no sort of status in the country. They are not the soldiers of the Khedive, nor foreign soldiers invited by the Khedive. They are not the soldiers of the protecting Power, since there is in theory no protecting Power. In theory their presence is an accident, and their character that of simple visitors. At the present moment they are no longer, from the military point of view, of vital importance, for their numbers have been repeatedly reduced; and for several years past they have not exceeded, and do not now exceed, three thousand men.[1] It is true that their presence relieves a certain portion of the Egyptian army from duties it would otherwise have to perform, and that if the British troops were altogether withdrawn, the number of Egyptian soldiers might have to be somewhat increased. But its value as part of the defensive forces of the country does not, of course, constitute the real importance and meaning of the British army of occupation. It is as the outward and

---

[1] This was written in 1892. Since that date the numbers have been increased, and the full strength of the army is now nearer four than three thousand.

THE MAKING OF EGYPT.

visible sign of the predominance of British influence, of the special interest taken by Great Britain in the affairs of Egypt, that this army is such an important element in the present situation. Its moral effect is out of all proportion to its actual strength.

The most pressing of all the reforms so imperatively needed in Egypt was the remodelling and the reorganisation of the discredited and distinctly non-effective Egyptian army. The first step was simple enough, viz., to get rid of the existing army. This was done by the historic Decree of December, 1882,—" The Egyptian Army is disbanded." But Sir Evelyn Wood, to whom the task of creating a new army was intrusted, did not despair of converting the fellah into a useful fighting machine; and his faith in what, after the miserable show the native troops had made in the recent rebellion, looked like very poor material, has in the last campaign been thoroughly justified.

The fellaheen are no doubt wanting in initiative power and individuality, but when intelligently led they fight well. In fact, as is the case with Turkish soldiers, good leadership is simply everything in the field. Moreover, the Egyptian soldiers are not wanting in the useful quality of insensibility to danger, which is a tolerable substitute for true courage.

Hitherto, not only had the native soldiers been badly led in battle, but they were constantly defrauded of their pay, and treated with harshness and cruelty by their officers. Now, under the new régime, they are properly fed and clothed, and, though discipline is strict, they are treated as sentient beings by the new English officers. Moreover, they are properly looked after when ill: under the old régime a military hospital did not exist. Perhaps the conduct of the English officers, when cholera was raging in 1896, did more han anything else to gain the confidence and respect of the new army. The twenty or thirty "accursed" Christians nursed these men day and night, and never shrank from doing the most menial offices for them.

The British officers, as Mr. Moberly Bell aptly remarks, are also an educational force of immense value: six thousand natives taught obedience and discipline, and encouraged to take a pride in themselves and their work, are a solid gain to Egypt. The result is, that, on one occasion when six soldiers were required for the Soudan, — formerly regarded by the fellahs as a place of exile for life, — the whole battalion volunteered.

While a native army was all very well, it required to be "stiffened" by English troops. Besides, it was obvious that without the moral support afforded by the presence of an English army of occupation it would be hopeless to carry out any lasting projects of reform.

Those responsible for the reform in the army had, of course, within wide limits, a free hand. Very different was the case of those responsible for placing on a sound basis the Egyptian finances. From the outset they were met by the fact that the representatives of the Powers on the Commission of the *caisse* regarded the Egyptian financial administration as the mere bailiff of the bondholders, and were inclined to starve the public services for their benefit. The cardinal principle of Egyptian finance involved, in fact, a perpetual struggle between the *caisse* and the Government. The interest on the debt being the first charge on the *caisse*, all the revenue is paid first to the treasury, but the Government can draw upon any surplus up to the limit of the "authorised" annual expenditure.

So fettered was Egypt by the Powers in financial matters, that nothing in the nature of a variable budget was allowed. A certain fixed sum (about six millions) is allowed her annually for all the expenses of government. If, however, there still remains a surplus in the *caisse* after the interest on the debt and the authorised expenditure have been met, half goes to the reduction of the debt, and half to the Government. In the event of there being no surplus, and an extra sum is yet required by the Government for a public work of undoubted utility, it must raise *double that sum* from the taxpayers, because of the stringent rules which insist on half of all the revenue (after interest and authorised expenditure are paid) being devoted to the reduction of the debt.

This, in a nutshell, was the condition of Egypt's financial position when England entered upon the task of bringing the revenue and the expenditure into a state of stable equilibrium. The results have exceeded the most sanguine expectations. The chief features of the new fiscal policy are a more equitable distribution of the taxes, the suppression of the corvée (the forced labour of the peasants for the dredging and repair of the canals, the most grievous of all the burdens of the people), greater outlay on reproductive works, and less expenditure on " non-effective " objects. All this has been accomplished without any increase in the annual expenditure; and the increase in the revenue, which has been remarkably uniform and steady since 1886 to the present year, has been concurrent with lightened taxation. This has been possible, owing to the careful economy in the administration and improved methods of collection. Under Ismail an enormous proportion of the taxes, actually wrung from the overburdened fellaheen, never reached the treasury at all, but was absorbed by the officials and the farmers of the taxes.

" Two great factors have combined to bring about the financial recuperation of Egypt, — the prevention of waste on the part of the administration, and the development of the productive powers of the country. As far as the prevention of waste is concerned, the first essential was a proper system of accounts. Accounts are the foundation of finance. You may have good accounts and a bad financial administration, but you cannot have good finance with bad accounts.

There was nothing more fatal in the financial chaos of the days of Ismail than the manner in which the private property of the Khedive was jumbled up with the property of the State. This mischievous confusion was put an end to when Ismail's vast estates were surrendered to his creditors, and a regular civil list substituted for the multifarious revenues which at one time flowed into the coffers of the sovereign of Egypt."

The creation of a solvent Egypt has, indeed, been mainly the work of Sir Edgar Vincent and his successors in the office of financial adviser to the Khedive. This reëstablishment of solvency is directly traceable to increased production.
The material wealth of Egypt is far from being exhausted; and if proper measures are taken to economise her potential productiveness, there is no reason why, in less than a generation, she should not attain "a degree of prosperity as undreamt of now, as her present position of solvency was undreamt of only ten years ago."
It is all a question of *water*. The cultivable area might be enormously extended if the water supply, which for many months of the year is practically unlimited, could be properly utilised on a large scale by means of canals and reservoirs.
From the time of the Caliphs downwards, this truth seems to have been recognised by the more enlightened Egyptian sovereigns and statesmen. It was the Caliph Omar who gave the following advice to his viceroy: "Beware of money-lenders, and devote one-third of thy income to making canals." Had Ismail taken this counsel of perfection to heart, the regeneration of Egypt need not have been left to Great Britain and the other Great Powers.
Except in abnormal cases, the Egyptian cultivator can afford to pay his taxes if he receives a proper supply of water for his crops. From time immemorial, Egyptian law has recognised the intimate connection between land tax

THE MAKING OF EGYPT. 69

and water supply. The land which in any given year gets no water, is for that year legally exempt from all taxation whatever. As soon as it gets water its liability is established. But it is evident that the mere fact of receiving some water, though it may set up the liability of the cultivator to pay, does not necessarily insure his capacity to do so. In order to insure that, he must get his water in proper quantities and at the proper times. But this is just what, in thousands of instances, he could not get, as long as the irrigation system remained in that state of unutterable neglect and confusion into which it had fallen in the period preceding the British occupation.

Of the long catalogue of beneficent measures by which the tax-paying power of the Egyptian people has been increased, the greatest and most essential is the reform of the irrigation system.

It would not be easy to exaggerate the enormous importance of irrigation in Egypt. An adequate and sound system of irrigation implies, in fact, not only its commercial and agricultural prosperity, but its very existence as a civilised and solvent State.

In many respects, as we have shown, Egypt is a unique country, but only Government officials are able to realise fully the deep significance of Herodotus's epigram, which attempts to sum up the one great feature of this "Land of Paradox" in the pregnant aphorism, "Egypt is the gift of the Nile."

To understand even the very $A. B. C$ of the Egyptian system of agriculture, two great facts must be borne in mind. The first is that the country is watered, not by rain, but by the river. In Upper Egypt rain practically never falls. Even in Lower Egypt it is a negligible quantity. The second great fact is that the river is not only the irrigator, but the fertiliser of the soil. The fine, reddish-brown mud, which the Blue Nile washes down from the volcanic plateaus of Abyssinia, mixed with organic matter from the swamp region of the White Nile, does more than manure can do for the annual renovation of the land.

Having grasped these essential facts, we are able to understand the reason of there being two systems of agriculture in Egypt. In Upper Egypt the natural inundation is not supplemented by a subsidiary system of irrigation canals (except the flood canals) and reservoirs, and the methods are absolutely the same as those sculptured on the walls of Pharaonic temples. After the spring harvest, the land lay idle till the next inundation. This primeval system answered, no doubt, for cereals, but not for cotton and sugar, two of the most profitable of the earth's products for which the Egyptian climate is admirably suited. But perennial irrigation is reserved for these crops, and they must be watered, not drowned.

The important distinction between the two kinds of irrigation must always be borne in mind. In the Upper Nile Valley, the aim of the cultivator is to cover as much land as possible with the Nile water and its deposit of fertilising mud. In the more scientific farming of the Delta, the efforts of the cultivator were mainly confined to controlling the Nile inundation, — to keep it away during high flood, and to retain as much as possible of the water during the period of low Nile. To Mehemet Ali is due the credit of inventing this system of perennial irrigation and encouraging the cultivation of those more valuable crops, cotton and sugar, in the Delta, which has given Egypt a high position in the markets of the world for these commodities. But Mehemet Ali's scientific methods were too advanced for the times, and depended for success upon the continuous personal supervision of his French engineers. This was not given; and local prejudices being against these "new-fangled notions," Mehemet's admirable conception was a failure.

Of the specific works of reform in this department, the Barrage was one of the most important. This great dam, however, forms the subject of a separate chapter.

Irrigation on the Delta has now been put on a proper footing. There is a complete network of main and subsidiary canals designed on scientific principles, with the Barrage as the starting-point.

Great importance has also been given, as will be seen from the following extract from Lord Cromer's last report (February, 1897), to the important work of drainage:

"Including the cost of pumping out Lake Mareotis, about £52,000 was spent upon drainage works in 1896. For this sum, 180 kilometres of new drains were dug. The irrigation service is now extending the drainage system into the higher and more highly cultivated tracts, where water is abundant, and where the soil would in time deteriorate if drains were not constructed. Although about £500,000 have already been spent on drains in Lower Egypt, a further large expenditure of money will be required before it can be said that the drainage system is complete.

"It may safely be asserted that funds could hardly be applied to a more necessary work, or to one which would bring in a quicker return on the capital expended. In Egypt, exhausted soil recovers its productive power very rapidly. Whenever a drain is dug, the benefit caused is quickly apparent in the shape of increased produce.

"For some years past, the Department of Public Works has devoted all its available credits to the improvement of the drainage system. In 1897 nearly all the budget allotment for new works will be spent on those specially connected with the removal of the water from the subsoil.

"For in every part of the country drainage projects are in course of preparation. If, however, in order to complete the system of drainage, the Government relies wholly upon such sums as can be granted annually out of the resources at its disposal, a long time must elapse before the work is completed. Advantage has therefore been taken of the fact that large sums of money are held in the special Reserve Fund, to apply to the Commissioners of the Debt for a grant of £250,000 to be spent on drainage in 1897. I am glad to be able to report that the Commissioners have complied with this request."

Very different in character have been the irrigation operations in Upper Egypt, where reservoirs take the place of canals. The chief work here has been the reclamation of the *Sharaki* districts. This is the term given to lands which, owing to their receiving no water, are relieved of all taxation. Obviously, few public works could be more directly and more immediately remunerative to the State than this. For instance, in the year of low Nile, £300,000 of taxes had to be abandoned.[1]

What is imperatively required in the Upper Nile Valley is not a great dam like the Barrage, but a large reservoir for retaining the superfluous flood-water for distribution during the summer. This need is admitted on all hands, but the burning question of Egyptian irrigation was for many years narrowed to the comparative merits of the proposed sites. As, however, Assouan has now been definitely selected by the Government for the site of this reservoir, it is unnecessary to discuss the rival projects for a storage reservoir at Wady Halfa, Kalabsheh, or Wady Rayan in the Fayyum. It goes without saying, that, with an increased supply of water, the amount of crops could be enormously increased in the Delta and Upper Egypt. But while in Lower Egypt the increase would be in additional reclaimed land, in Upper Egypt, where the cultivated area cannot be extended, increased cultivation simply means summer as well as winter crops.

Experts estimate that a reservoir capable of storing about two thousand millions cubic metres a year, and providing one hundred thousand acres with summer irrigation, would add between £2,000,000 and £3,000,000 annually to the produce of the country; and as Sir Colin Scott Moncrieff's estimate of the cost is not more than £2,600,000, the profit on this capital would obviously be enormous.

The English engineers, mostly trained in the Indian

[1] In average seasons the remission amounts to about £50,000.

Public Works Department, did not fall into the error of attempting to carry out the various undertakings connected with irrigation from the headquarters at Cairo. Personal supervision was the key-note of the policy of the new department. The country was divided into five circles of irrigation (three in the Delta, and two in Upper Egypt), of which four were intrusted to the newcomers from India. This plan of localising the engineering talent, which it had been found desirable to import into the country, proved a complete success.

"Viewed as a whole, there can be no question that the Irrigation Department is, of all the branches of the Egyptian service managed by British chiefs, the one upon which, from first to last, it has been possible to look with the most unmixed pride. With men of this calibre stationed in every quarter of the country, seeing with their own eyes, and intrusted with a wide discretion to act to the best of their judgment, the work of improvement marched as rapidly as the limited amount of money at the disposal of the Irrigation Service would permit. While a great deal was left to the initiative of the individual inspectors, and the methods of each of them presented considerable diversity, there was still a general harmony of purpose running through their work."

Nothing, perhaps, illustrates more forcibly the confidence the natives have in the engineers than an incident quoted by Sir Alfred Milnes in his invaluable study of modern Egypt. He had asked a native statesman, who was bitterly opposed to the English occupation, what Egypt would do without the engineers. The reply was to the effect that the sooner England retired the better, but that the engineers would certainly not be allowed to go.

The engineer in the remote country district is, indeed, not only an indispensable official, but may be regarded as a useful educational and civilising force. "The people recognise in him the great benefactor of their district, and, with a childlike simplicity, they turn to him for help and counsel even in concerns the least related to his actual functions."

The following amusing anecdote illustrates this attitude of the fellaheen towards these officials.

In one year of exceptionally low Nile, a certain district was threatened with a total failure of the crops, owing to the canal being too low to irrigate the fields. A cry of despair arose from the whole populace, who, as usual, implored the aid of one of the English inspectors of irrigation who happened to be on the spot. This official promptly determined to throw a temporary dam across the canal. The idea was a bold one. The time was short. The canal was large, and, though lower than usual, it was still carrying a great body of water at a considerable velocity. Of course no preparations had been made for a work the necessity for which had never been contemplated. Labour, at any rate, was forthcoming in any quantity, for the people, who saw starvation staring them in the face, needed no compulsion to join gladly in any enterprise which afforded them even the remotest chance of relief. So the inspector hastily got together the best material within reach. *He brought his bed on to the canal bank*, and did not leave the scene of operations, night or day, till the work was finished. And the plan succeeded. To the surprise of all, the dam was somehow or other made strong enough to resist the current. The water was raised to the required level, and the land was effectually flooded. The joy and the gratitude of the people knew no bounds. It was decided to offer thanksgivings in the mosque of the chief town of the district, and the event was considered of such general importance that even that exalted functionary the Minister of Public Works, himself made a special point of attending the ceremony.

In the Department of Justice and Police — using the word "justice" in its narrow but conventional sense as meaning all that appertains to courts of law — less progress has been made towards reform than in other State departments.

And yet there is no doubt that in the whole administrative field of Egypt, in no department is the cardinal principle which underlies all British intervention,—viz., not merely governing, but teaching the Egyptians how to govern themselves,—more necessary to be kept in view. One reason for the slow development of law and justice is, that this is a branch of government which has been less under the influence of the English. In fact, we were late in the field. No effective interference took place till about 1889, when Sir John Scott was appointed with the title of Judicial Adviser to the Khedive, who virtually undertook the functions of minister, though there was a native statesman bearing that title.

There is not one judicial system in Egypt, but four. There is the old Koranic system, worked by the Mehkennehs, or courts of the religious law, which are now mainly confined to dealing with the personal status of Mohammedans. There is the system of the mixed courts, which deals with civil actions between foreigners of different nationalities, or between foreigners and natives, and, in a small degree, with the criminal offences of foreigners. There is the system, or no system, of the consular courts, which deals with the great body of foreign crime. Finally, there is the system of the new native courts, which deals with civil actions between natives, or crimes committed by them. Of all these, it is only the native courts which the English have taken in hand, and that not till within the last few years.

The native courts are, in one sense, though ranking only as courts of first instance, the most important of all as affecting the greatest number of people; but the English were, at first, chary of doing more than giving advice. The original *personnel* of the native court was very unsatisfactory, and jobbing and nepotism was rife. Mr. Scott entered upon the delicate work of reform in a judicious and moderate spirit. He wisely contented himself with modifying the judicial system without radically altering the procedure and machinery of the law.

By a series of important changes of detail Sir John has modified the judicial system which he found existing, and rendered it vastly more suitable to the conditions of the country; but he has never attempted to revolutionise it. No doubt, if he had the work to do *de novo*, he would prefer something more like the Indian system, which experience has proved to be so well suited to the wants of a backward country, where most of the litigants are poor, and most of the cases simple. He recognised, however, that the Egyptian codes and procedure, such as he found them, were the only ones which the native judicial body knew how to work, or to which the people were accustomed. He therefore wisely decided not radically to alter the actual administration of justice, but simply to improve it in the points where it was most imperfect.

It is curious that, at first, the chief fault in the administration of justice by these lower courts was the dilatoriness of the proceedings. Now, according to the last report of the Judicial Adviser to the Khedive, the chief defect of these courts was the hasty manner in which the actions were tried, and the old charge that " Justice long delayed is no justice," certainly cannot now be brought against the native tribunals. The natural result of this tendency to haste on the part of the judges, who must, however, be given full credit for the zeal in which they set their faces against arrears of cases, is to give an unnecessary amount of work to the courts of appeal. Good authorities are, however, of opinion that, taken collectively, the native tribunals give every sign of working admirably, with a judicious leaven of European judges.

In the organisation of the police mistakes have avowedly been made by the English officers responsible for the reconstruction, owing mainly to a lack of continuity in the policy of reconstruction and reorganisation. The first chief, Gen. Valentine Baker, who was sent out to command the police soon after the English occupation, though an admirable cavalry officer, was totally unfitted for the office of inspector-general of police. Besides, he started on a wrong tack. "His whole management of the police was influenced, from the first, by the conviction that they would sooner or later be converted into a military reserve."

After General Baker's death, Mr. Clifford Lloyd tried his hand at the work of police organisation. Under this energetic reformer, the police were made an independent body, and free from the control of the mudirs (governors of provinces). This proved a short-sighted policy, and lessened the prestige of these provincial authorities, on whom the whole internal administration of their respective provinces depended. Ultimately, through the efforts of Nubas Pacha, a compromise was arrived at, which is still in force.

The police of each province, as matters are now arranged, are under the authority of the mudir; but, on the other hand, his orders must be given to them through their own local officers. He has no power of interference with the discipline and organisation of the force, nor can he make use of it except for the legitimate purposes of maintaining order and repressing crime. If he has cause of complaint against the conduct of the police, his remedy lies in an appeal to the ministry of the interior, which, through the inspector-general at headquarters, deals with the case. This is as it should be; but, of course, the success of the system depends on a spirit of give and take on both sides, and on friendly relations between the mudirs and the chiefs of the police.

In the Department of the Interior important reforms

in the maintenance of public security, in addition to the police force, have been effected since the establishment of a responsible English official, who bears the title of Adviser on Internal Affairs. Mr. J. L. Gorst, appointed in 1894, was the first to occupy this important post; and he is still the virtual head of the Department of the Interior, though a native statesman is the titular chief. The principal work has been the reorganisation of the village watchmen (ghaffirs), who serve as a supplementary police force in the country districts. This unwieldy body was much reduced in numbers, but put into a state of efficiency, and placed under the control of the respective omdahs, or village sheiks.

These omdahs were answerable to the mamurs, or governors of districts, and the latter were under the control of the mudirs, who, in turn, were responsible to the Minister of the Interior. Thus a regular series of authorities was effected in the machinery of government, by which the central authority in Cairo was in touch with the fellahs in the remotest district of the Upper Nile Valley.

The above is an epitome of the development and results of the more important reforms in the administration of Egypt under British influence; but without wearying my readers with a catalogue of reforms suggesting a diluted Blue Book, it will be well to note briefly a few more improvements in other branches of the public services.

In the matter of sanitation and sanitary reform, the attention of the Egyptian Government has only of late years — prompted, doubtless, by the serious epidemics of cholera in 1883 and 1896 — been directed to the pressing need of reform in matters affecting the public health; and till recently the Department of Public Health remained one of the least satisfactory in the public service. This is largely due, no doubt, to the paucity of the funds available for sanitary reform on a large scale. The department was, in short, for many years after its establishment in 1885, shelved and starved. This is virtually admitted by Lord Cromer in his report for 1897:

"It is, however, the misfortune that the sums of money required to execute the very necessary reforms proposed by Rogers Pacha, the head of the Health Department, are large. During the fourteen years which have elapsed since the British occupation of the country commenced, Egyptian finance has passed through several distinct phases. During the first period, which lasted from 1882 to the close of 1886, there could be no question either of fiscal reform, or of increasing expenditure save on such subjects as irrigation, which were distinctly and directly remunerative. The aggregate deficits of these years amounted to £2,751,000. The whole attention of the Government was, during this period, directed to the maintenance of financial equilibrium. When, at last, a surplus was obtained, fiscal relief was, very wisely in my opinion, allowed to take precedence of increased expenditure, even on the most necessary objects. During the next period, which may be said to have lasted till 1894, large reductions were made in indirect taxation, and direct taxes to the extent of about £1,000,000 were remitted.

"It is only since 1894 that the Egyptian Government has been able to turn its attention seriously to those numerous reforms which involve increased expenditure on any considerable scale. Amongst the objects which most nearly concern the general welfare of Egypt, it cannot be doubted that the reconquest of some portion, at all events, of the Soudan, takes a very high place. It is to the accomplishment of this object that the attention of the Egyptian Government must, for the time being, be mainly directed.

"More than this, the development of the system of irrigation should not be long delayed, more especially as the returns to be obtained from money spent on irrigation will certainly in the end provide funds for expenditure in other directions.

"No government, and certainly not the semi-internationalised government of Egypt, can afford to embark at once and at the same moment in a number of expensive and difficult operations. I do not doubt that the day of the Egyptian sanitary reformer will come; but under the circumstances to which I alluded above, I fear, though I say it with regret, that some little while must yet elapse before the question of improved sanitation in Egypt can be taken seriously in hand."

A great deal must be allowed for the ingrained horribly unsanitary habits of the natives. Though personally clean and not averse to the use of water, — in fact, their religion enjoins frequent and regular ablution, — the huts of the fellaheen are indescribably filthy. The canals, which in the remote districts are the only source of water, are subject to every kind of pollution. Near most villages there are *birkas*, or stagnant ponds, which are as malarious as they are malodorous. Even in the principal cities there is absolutely no system of drainage. In the case of Cairo, as will be shown later, this reproach will, however, soon be removed. In short, the observant traveller only wonders that the awful cholera epidemic of last year is not repeated annually. Then, besides, there are special difficulties in addition to the ignorance and apathy and unsanitary customs of the people, which the sanitary reformer has to confront. These are the religious prejudices of the Moslems. The mosques are the principal offenders against the laws of health, and the latrines attached to every one of these buildings are often centres of infection. Injudicions interference might easily excite a fanatical opposition, which would stand seriously in the way of all sanitary reform. However, the judicious handling of this sanitary work by Rogers Pacha resulted in placing, in one year (1896), over one hundred and fifty mosques in a proper sanitary condition.

In connection with this subject some reference should be made to the cholera epidemic of last year, already referred to. The following extracts from Rogers Pacha's Report are instructive:

"There can be little doubt that the disease was originally introduced, in August or September, 1895, by pilgrims returning from Mecca. It was at first limited to sporadic cases which did not attract attention. By the first of February the disease was completely stamped out in the provinces.

THE MAKING OF EGYPT. 81

" Unfortunately, Alexandria had become infected on the 28th of December. In the month of January, 1896, twenty-one cases, and in February forty-eight cases, occurred in that town. In April the number of cases once more rose to fifty, and in May the disease assumed an epidemic form in the town. Cases imported from Alexandria soon began to occur all over the country, and by the middle of May it was evident that a general infection was imminent.

"From the 1st of May to the 22d of October, 703 villages were infected. In all these villages inspection was carried out, generally, by one of the four very capable English inspectors who were available for provincial work. In each village a cholera hospital was established.

"By the end of October the disease had practically disappeared. During the winter epidemic, 1,018 deaths were recorded. From the 1st of April to the 31st of October the number of deaths was 17,087, making a total of 18,105 deaths out of 21,693 cases notified or detected.

"The reduced mortality in 1895-6, as compared to 1883, is due to two causes; namely, (1) to the fact that in the interval of thirteen years a great advance has been made in medical science, with the result that the proper methods for arresting the propagation of cholera are now more fully understood than was formerly the case ; (2) to the fact that the Medical and Sanitary Departments of the Egyptian Government are now far better organised than was the case in 1883."

The scheme for a thorough system of drainage for Cairo shows that the revival of interest in sanitation is beginning to take a practical form.

" This is a tremendous undertaking, estimated to cost at least £500,000. The necessity has long been recognised, but it has been put off from year to year, owing to want of money, — not so much absolute want of money, as want of power to apply money that actually existed to the desired object, owing to the usual and ten-times explained necessity of obtaining the consent of the Powers, or, more properly, the consent of France, for none of the others made any difficulty. France was finally appeased last year by the appointment of an International Commission to examine the various competing schemes. This Commission, composed of an Englishman, a Frenchman, and a German, sat last winter, and ended by proposing a scheme of its own, for which preliminary investigations are at present being made. So in two or three years we may hope to see Cairo drained, in which case that city, or at any rate the European quarter of it, will very likely be one of the healthiest places of residence in the world."

It may reasonably be expected that this important sanitary reform will have some effect in reducing the deplorable high death-rate of Cairo, — forty-six per one thousand, which is actually double that of many European capitals; the average death-rate of Paris being twenty-three, and London nineteen, per one thousand. It must, however, be remembered that this abnormally heavy bill of mortality is to some extent factitious. For Cairo is regarded by the Egyptians in the light of a sacred city, and they are accustomed to crowd into it from the villages of the Delta, when they feel their end approaching, simply to die in Cairo.

Till the last few years, the educational system seemed little affected by the spirit of reform which was influencing Egypt and its national institutions. No department has borne richer fruit of late. But though there has lately been a remarkable increase in the number of schools and scholars, only a small minority of the latter belong to the Mohammedan religion.

Previous to 1884, the few Government schools were also boycotted by parents of the dominant faith, the religious influence of the Ulemas, who controlled the El-Azhar University and the innumerable schools attached to the mosques, being too strong to be combated. The famous El-Azhar University — " a petrified university, which rests like a blight upon the religious and intellectual life of the country " — has moulded all the religious training in Egypt.

The better class of the Mohammedans are now, however, beginning to tolerate the Government foundations; and there are now nearly eight thousand scholars in the primary schools, while there are about fifteen hundred in the secondary schools and the eight higher professional schools or technical colleges (Law, Military, Medicine, Engineering, Agriculture, etc.).

Hitherto, the educational vote has made a poor show in the Egyptian budget, and some critics maintain that education is the " Cinderella " among the Egyptian departments of state. This, no doubt, will be rectified in future budgets. It must of course be remembered that —

"People must live before they can be taught. Famine is worse than ignorance. What the Egyptian Government had to fight for, six or seven years ago, was the very existence of the people. Essential as education is, the provision of education is not such a primary duty of government as the defence of personal property, the maintenance of justice, or, in a country like Egypt where human life depends upon public works, the careful preservation of these works upon which life depends. And, in the next place, it would have been no use simply to augment the budget of the Education Department, so long as the schools were being conducted on unintelligent methods."

To come to a higher form of public education, — the art of government, — it cannot be said that much progress has been made in developing representative institutions in the machinery of government. It is true that there is a Legislative Council, but its powers are inconsiderable, being mainly confined to proposing amendments to proposed laws affecting the administration. As the Council cannot initiate legislation, and as the Ministry need not accept the amendments, the Legislative Councils are not of great importance in the body politic.

Then there is the General Assembly, — which is simply the Council, enlarged by a popular element. This has one important function, for no *new* taxes can be imposed without its consent. As, however, this assembly only meets once every two years, it cannot play a very considerable part in Egyptian politics.

The time, in fact, has not yet come for applying the principle of representative government, in any great degree, to the national affairs of Egypt. It would be sounder policy to begin by introducing it into the management of local business, and even then tentatively and with caution.

The only local representative institution having administrative powers, which at present exists, is the municipality of Alexandria. That city, by virtue of its large European population, has probably more of the elements requisite for the success of local self-government than any other town in Egypt. On the other hand, the mixture of Europeans and natives in this municipality gives rise to certain special difficulties.

The attitude of England in this policy of Egyptian intervention, since the Arabi revolt, is simple and comprehensive. It was natural that the British Government should suppose that their task, when France, in 1882, threw all responsibility for Egypt on their hands, was a simple one; namely, to crush a military rising. Only actual experience taught England that the rebellion was a very small matter, and that the real difficulty lay in the utter rottenness of the whole fabric of government. Naturally, then, the pledges England made, being based on a total misapprehension, were impossible of fulfilment. But to the spirit of these pledges England has been faithful. It is indisputable that England has derived no pecuniary or other benefit from her occupation of Egypt. As a matter of fact, among the foreign employees in the Egyptian civil service there are nearly twice as many of French or Italian nationality as of English. In 1895, for instance, there were 348 Italians, 326 French, and 174 English in the Khedive's service.

No nation is able to say that any legitimate right or privilege which it once possessed in Egypt has been infringed by any action of England. Such right or privilege remains absolutely untouched, even where it would be just and reasonable that it should be modified. And, on the other hand, what European people, having any interests in Egypt, has not benefited by the fact that that country has been preserved from disorder and restored to prosperity? That this is the true view of the character of British policy is shown by the willing acquiescence, if not the unspoken approval, of the majority of civilised nations.

As for the attitude of the French Government, it is natural enough that France should feel some resentment at England holding the position in Egypt, among all European nations, that she herself once held, and foolishly resigned when, in 1882, she shirked at the last moment, and left England to " face the music " alone. Then in 1887, at the time of the Constantinople Conference, it was France who put obstacles in the way of the withdrawal of England. In short, logically, France is mainly answerable for the British continued occupation in Egypt. But yet it must be allowed that France has many reasons for being hurt and disappointed, considering the enormous value of her services to Egypt in the past.

"It was France who supported Egypt in her struggle for independence from Turkey, when all the other Powers were against her, and when by this opposition they prevented that independence from becoming complete; it was to France that Mehemet Ali turned for aid in his attempt to civilise Egypt, as he understood the meaning of civilisation. For something like half a century, French lawyers, French engineers, French men of learning, were engaged in doing their best — often under most discouraging circumstances — to deluge Egypt with the fruits of European culture.

"In short, Frenchmen may claim to have been the pioneers of European influence. Whatever Egypt borrowed from Europe, whether in the material or intellectual sphere, came to her first through French channels. Her upper classes, if educated at all, were educated by Frenchmen in French ideas. French even became an official language, side by side with Arabic. To this day, the English in the Egyptian service write official letters to one another in halting French."

Then there is the Canal. This stupendous work is of course purely French in conception and execution, and was (see a later chapter) undertaken in face of the continued and bitter hostility of England. There is, then, some excuse for France making all the capital she can out of the unfortunate engagements, or "pledges," of England, published and reiterated *urbi et orbi*, in 1883 and 1887.

It is necessary, however, to look at the other side of the question. France has, no doubt, been of great service to this erstwhile "distressful country;" but her services are counterbalanced by her tendency to exploit and make money out of Egypt, which seems to have been a cardinal principle of her Egyptian policy, from the death of Mehemet Ali to 1882.

"In the days prior to the establishment of the Mixed Tribunals, — which France resisted with all her might, — French adventurers exploited Egypt in the most merciless fashion, and they frequently enjoyed the support of French diplomacy in their nefarious game. No Great Power has clung with such tenacity as France to all the advantages, however indefensible and galling, bestowed on its subjects by the Capitulations. She has shown no consideration for the weakness of Egypt. She has never hesitated to use her immense superiority of power to push the interests of French traders, French contractors, and French financiers. In the years immediately preceding the Arabist revolution, when England and France were acting in concert in the Egyptian affairs, it was France who was for getting the last pound of flesh out of the Egyptian debtor. It was England who was in favour of showing some consideration for the people of Egypt, and not of treating the question purely as one of pounds, shillings, and pence."

The withdrawal of England on the understanding that France should never occupy the country — if such a pledge could be enforced, for circumstances might easily arise in which France would be wrong to keep this pledge — has been suggested as one way out of the Egyptian difficulty. A settlement of this vexed international question by means of such a self-denying ordinance on the part of France and England is not likely to be advantageous, or even anything but a temporary shelving of the difficulty.

"Can any man," says an old resident, who has held high office in the Egyptian civil service, and had peculiar opportunities for observing and judging impartially the results of English influence in Egypt, "knowing the social and political condition of the country, maintain with confidence that if Egypt were left to herself to-morrow favouritism and corruption would not once more raise their heads; that justice would not once more be venal; that the administration would not once more gradually fall back into disorder; and that, as a consequence of such disorder, financial equilibrium would not again be jeopardised? And then should we not have the old story: the embarrassment of the treasury, causing the impoverishment of the people,—such impoverishment leading to discontent and agitation; that agitation directed not only against the Government, but, under the inspiration of mischief-making fanatics, against all progressive elements of society,—another Arabi, another revolution? And if, in prospect of a fresh cataclysm threatening every European interest, after all diplomatic means had been exhausted France were to declare that she could stand it no longer; if she were to take the line which we took in 1882,—what moral right should we have to say her nay? Could we fight or restrain her from interfering?"

The withdrawal, however, of Great Britain, if it is not to end in disaster, can only be a gradual process. An intàngible influence made up of many elements, like that of England in Egypt, cannot be withdrawn any more than it can be created at a certain hour or by a certain act.

One of the most absurd suggestions for the cutting of this Gordian knot is neutralisation. In the case of small but well-governed and highly civilised States, such as Belgium and Switzerland, neutralisation and a strict principle of non-intervention by the Great Powers is all very well; it would, however, be difficult to conceive anything more unlike than the internal condition of those well-governed countries and that of Egypt. A neutral policy on the part of the Powers would scarcely be likely to insure the internal good government and the peace of Egypt. It would be simply evading the main object of all foreign interference, whether by the six Powers, or England and France jointly, or by England alone. However, Great Britain is hardly likely to adopt so weak and cowardly a policy, which would " simply mean that, from unwillingness to allow any one of their number to do the work in which all are interested, the Powers should determine that that work must be left undone." Such, indeed, stripped of all diplomatic highfalutin, is the meaning of the specious word " neutralisation " applied to Egypt. Besides, how would the various foreign interests, which undoubtedly exist in Egypt, be safeguarded if Egypt was neutralised?

Another suggestion by political theorists is that Egypt's natural guardian the Porte, as its suzerain, should be the protector of Egypt, which should be neutral as regards all other European powers. Turkey, in short, would be the policeman of Egypt, and be responsible for order and firm internal government. There is something almost ludicrous in this proposal. "The idea of intrusting Turkey with the maintenance of reforms the chief aim of which has been to differentiate Egypt from Turkish administration, is like substituting the wolf for the sheep-dog as the guardian of the flock."

Then there are many who advocate what they are pleased to call "internationalisation." This is going backwards with a vengeance. In other words, Egypt would be " put into commission," and fettered by the Great Powers in her administrative and internal policy, as she is already in her financial measures. For Egypt has indeed suffered already from a certain amount of internationalism. It is the bondholders who have the power of the purse, and the *raison d'être* of the sanction of the Powers in measures affecting the finances is the fact that they represent the creditors of Egypt. Then, too, the veto of the Powers which already exists on the legislative authority of the Egyptian Government, might be supposed to give sufficient European influence. When the political chaos of the last years of Ismail, when Egypt was tied hand and foot by Europe, — each country having a right to a finger in the pie, and each disdaining responsibility, — gave way to the dual control, it was a great step in advance, and results have shown that the single control has benefited Egypt still more. It might naturally be supposed, then, by all unbiassed and disinterested observers, — by all, in short, who are not confirmed Anglophobists, — that the retention of the guardianship by England, so long as any foreign intervention is necessary, is the one sensible solution of the Egyptian question.[1]

[1] For most of the facts and a great deal of the information in this chapter, I have laid under contribution Sir Alfred Milner's invaluable study of contemporary Egypt, entitled "England in Egypt."

CHAPTER V.[1]

ALEXANDRIA AND THE NILE DELTA.

THE traveller, reaching the Land of the Pharaohs by the direct sea-route viâ Alexandria, must be prepared for a certain sense of disappointment when the bleak and barren shores of the Nile Delta are first sighted. The monotonous ridges of desolate sand-hills, varied by equally unattractive lagoons, are a melancholy contrast to the beautiful scenery of the North African littoral farther west, which delighted his eyes a few days before, as the vessel skirted the Algerian and Tunisian coasts. If the expectant traveller is so disillusioned by his first glimpse of Egypt from the sea, still keener is his disappointment when the ship enters the harbour. But for an occasional palm-tree or minaret standing out among the mass of shops and warehouses to give a faint suggestion of Oriental atmosphere, this bustling and painfully modern-looking city might be mistaken for some flourishing French seaport, say a Marseilles or a Havre, plumped down on the Egyptian plain. It is difficult to realise that this is the city of Alexander the Great, and the metropolis of Egypt under the Ptolemies.

Alexandria, though a much modernised and hybrid sort of city, is not without interest. It has, no doubt, been rather neglected by writers of Egyptian travel, and, cousequently, ignored by tourists, who do not as a rule strike

---
[1] This chapter (and a portion of the following one) is reprinted from an article contributed to the " Picturesque Mediterranean," by kind permission of the publishers, Cassell & Company, Limited, London.

out a line for themselves. It has been regarded too much as the most convenient landing-place for Cairo, and visitors usually devote but a few hours for a hasty inspection of its curiosities before rushing off by express-train to the City of the Caliphs.

It would, of course, be absurd to compare Alexandria, essentially the commercial capital of Egypt, in point of artistic or historic interest with Cairo; though, as a matter of fact, the capital is a modern city in comparison with the Alexandria of Alexander, while Alexandria itself is but of mushroom growth contrasted with Heliopolis, Thebes, Memphis, or other dead cities of the Nile Valley of which traces still remain. It has often been remarked that the Ptolemaic capital has bequeathed nothing but its ruins and its name to the Alexandria of to-day. Even these ruins are deplorably scanty, and many of the sites are purely conjectural. Few vestiges remain of the architectural splendours of the Ptolemaic dynasty. Where are now the four thousand palaces of which the conquering general Amru boasted to his master, the Caliph Omar? What now remains of the magnificent Temple of Serapis towering over the city on its platform of one hundred steps? But though there are scarcely any traces of the glories of ancient Alexandria, the traditions of the golden age of the Egyptian Renaissance cannot be altogether forgotten by the classical student; and to the thoughtful traveller imbued with the *genius loci*, this city of memories is not without a certain charm. Here Saint Mark preached the gospel and suffered martyrdom, and here Athanasius in warlike controversy did battle with the Arian heresies. Here, in this centre of Greek culture, were for many centuries collected the greatest intellects of the age. Here Cleopatra, *vainqueur des vainqueurs du monde*, held Antony a willing captive while Octavius was preparing his legions to crush him. Here Amru conquered, and here

Abercrombie fell. Even those whose tastes do not incline them to historical or theological researches are familiar, thanks to Kingsley's immortal romance, with the story of the noble-minded Hypatia and the crafty and unscrupulous Cyril, and can give rein to their imagination by verifying the site of the museum where she lectured, and of the Cæsareum where she fell a victim to the atrocious zeal of Peter the Reader and his rabble of fanatical monks.

Just as Alexandria has been ignored by the Egyptian tourist, so has it been persistently neglected by antiquaries and Egyptologists, and no systematic excavation on the sites of ancient buildings has been undertaken. It is true that of recent years some attempt has been made by the Egyptian Exploration Fund to discover some of the architectural spoils of the Ptolemaic dynasty buried beneath the accumulation of rubbish of centuries; but the splendid opportunity for the excavation and exploration of the conjectural sites of the Serapeum, Cæsareum, and other famous monuments, afforded in 1882, when a great portion of the city lay in ruins after the bombardment, was allowed to pass by this learned society. In 1895 Mr. Hogarth carried out a series of experimental borings, but the results were not encouraging, as water was found under the twenty to thirty feet of the deposit of rubbish, and only a few poor specimens of Roman and Byzantine architecture rewarded the trouble of the explorer. Mr. Hogarth explains the remarkable disappearance of the many palaces and temples, which studded the city during the age of the Ptolemies, by the subsidence of the soil and the encroachment of the sea. Some authorities, among them Professor Mahaffy, do not, however, consider that any definite conclusions should be drawn from this partial and superficial probing of the soil. Very possibly Mr. Hogarth was unfortunate in tapping the low-lying parts of the city, and it would be advisable that future excavations should be carried on in the elevated ground near Pompey's Pillar, which most antiquaries agree in regarding as the site of the Serapeum. But in a crowded city like Alexandria all scientific excavation is particularly costly, owing to the difficulty of disposing of the excavated soil.

The peculiar shape of the city, built partly on the Pharos island and peninsula, and partly on the mainland, is due, according to the ancient chroniclers, to a patriotic whim of the founder, who planned the city in the form of a chlamys, the short cloak or tunic worn by the Macedonian soldiers. The modern city, though it has pushed its boundaries a good way to the east and west, still preserves this curious outline, albeit, to a non-classical mind, it rather suggests a starfish. Various legends are extant to account for the choice of this particular spot for a Mediterranean port. According to the popular version, a venerable seer appeared to the Great Conqueror in a dream, and recited those verses in the Odyssey [1] describing the one sheltered haven on the Egyptian coast. Acting on this supernatural hint, Alexander decided to build his city on this part of the coast, where the Pharos isle acted as a natural breakwater, and where a small Greek fishing-settlement called Rhacotis was already established. It is, however, hardly necessary to fall back on a mythical legend to account for the selection of this site. The two great aims of Alexander were the creation of a centre for trade and the development of commerce, and the fusion of the Greek and Roman nations. To attain these objects it was necessary to build a seaport near the mouths of the Nile, — the great highway of Egypt. A site west of the Nile mouths was probably chosen because of the eastward set of the tide, as the alluvial soil brought down by the Nile would soon choke a harbour excavated east of the river, as had already

---

[1] "A certain island called Pharos, that with the high-waved sea is washed, just against Egypt," etc.

happened at Pelusium. It is this alluvial wash which has also rendered the harbours of Rosetta and Damietta almost useless for vessels of any draught, and at Port Said the accumulation of sand necessitates continuous dredging in order to keep clear the entrance of the Suez Canal.

A well-known writer on Egypt has truly observed that there are three Egypts to interest the traveller, — the Egypt of the Pharaohs and the Bible, the Egypt of the Caliphates and the "Arabian Nights," and the Egypt of European commerce and enterprise. To which he might have added, the Egypt of the Ptolemies and the Roman Empire. It is to this last stage of civilisation that the fine harbour of Alexandria bears witness. Not only is it of interest to the engineer and the man of science, but it is also of great historic importance. It serves as a link between ancient and modern civilisation. The port is Alexander's best monument, — "*si quæris monumentum, circumspice.*" But for this, Alexandria might now be a little fishing-port of no more importance than the little Greek fishing-village Rhacotis, whose ruins lie buried beneath its spacious quays. The harbour was originally formed by the construction of a vast mole (Heptastadion) joining the island of Pharos to the mainland; and this stupendous feat of engineering, planned and carried out by Alexander, has been supplemented by the magnificent breakwater constructed by English engineers in 1872, at a cost of over two-and-a-half millions sterling. After Marseilles, Malta, and Spezia, it is perhaps the finest port in the Mediterranean, both on account of its natural advantages as a haven, and by reason of the vast engineering works mentioned above.

The western harbour (formerly called Eunostos, "good home-sailing"), of which we are speaking,— for the eastern, or so-called New Harbour, is choked by sand and only used by small native craft,— has, however, one serious drawback in a dangerous bar at the entrance, which should, of course, have been partially blown up before the breakwater and the other engineering operations were undertaken. Owing to this obstruction, large vessels seldom attempted, till recently, to cross the bar in rough weather, and never at night. In the course of the last few years, however, a wide and deep channel has been cut through this reef, and now the entrance to the harbour is practicable at all hours of the day and night. In fact, during 1896 over four hundred vessels entered Alexandria harbour in the night-time. These improvements have naturally tended to make Alexandria more resorted to than formerly by travellers as the port of entry for Cairo, instead of Port Said or Ismailia.

During the period of Turkish misrule — when Egypt under the Mamelukes, though nominally a *vilayet* of the Ottoman Empire, was practically under the dominion of the Beys — the trade of Alexandria had declined considerably, and Rosetta had taken away most of its commerce. When Mehemet Ali, the founder of the present dynasty, rose to power, his clear intellect at once comprehended the importance of this ancient emporium and the wisdom of Alexander's choice of a site for the port which was destined to become the commercial centre of three continents.

Mehemet Ali is the creator of modern Alexandria. He deepened the harbour, which had been allowed to be choked by the accumulation of sand, lined it with spacious quays, built the massive forts which protect the coast, and restored the city to its old commercial importance by putting it into communication with the Nile through the medium of the Mahmoudiyeh Canal. This vast undertaking was only carried out with great loss of life. It was excavated by the forced labour of 250,000 peasants, of whom some twenty thousand died from the heat and the severe toil. The whole canal was completed in one year (1819) and cost £300,000.

The great thoroughfare of Alexandria — a fine street running in a straight line from the western gate of the city to the Place Mehemet Ali — is within a few minutes' walk of the quay. A sudden turn, and the strange mingling of Eastern and Western life bursts upon the spectator's astonished gaze. This living diorama, formed by the brilliant and ever-shifting crowd, is in its way unique.

The Place Mehemet Ali, usually called for the sake of brevity the Grand Square, is close at hand. This is the centre of the European quarter, and round it are collected the banks, consular offices, hotels, and principal shops. This square, the focus of the life of modern Alexandria, is appropriately named after the founder of the present dynasty, and the creator of the Egypt of to-day.

To this great ruler, who at one time bid fair to become the founder not only of an independent kingdom, but of a great Oriental empire, Alexandria owes much of its prosperity and commercial importance. The career of Mehemet Ali is interesting and romantic. There is a certain similarity between his history and that of Napoleon I., and the coincidence seems heightened when we remember that they were both born in the same year. Each, rising from an obscure position, started as an adventurer on foreign soil, and each rose to political eminence by force of arms. Unlike Napoleon, however, in one important point, Mehemet Ali founded a dynasty which still remains in power, in spite of the weakness and incapacity of his successors. To Western minds, perhaps, his chief claim to hold a high rank in the world's history lies in his efforts to introduce European institutions and methods of civilisation, and to establish a system of government opposed to Mohammedan instincts. He created an army and navy which were partly based on European models, stimulated agriculture and trade, and organised an administrative and fiscal system which did much towards putting the country on a sound financial footing. The great blot of his reign was, no doubt, the horrible massacre of the Mameluke beys; and this has been the great point of attack by his enemies and detractors. It is difficult to excuse this Oriental example of a *coup d'état;* but it must be remembered that the existence of this turbulent and rebellious element was incompatible with the maintenance of his rule, and that the peace of the country was as much endangered by the Mameluke beys as was that of the Porte by the Janissaries a few years later, when a somewhat similar atrocity was perpetrated.

In the middle of the square stands a handsome equestrian statue of Mehemet Ali, which is in one respect a remarkably singular monument. The Mohammedan religion demands the strictest interpretation of the injunction in the decalogue against making "to thyself any graven image," and consequently a statue to a follower of the Moslem faith is rarely seen in a Mohammedan country. The erection of this particular monument was much resented by the more orthodox of the Mussulman population of Alexandria, and the religious feelings of the mob manifested themselves in riots and other hostile demonstrations. Not only representations in stone or metal, but any kind of likeness of the human form is thought impious by Mohammedans. They believe that the author will be compelled on the Resurrection Day to endow with life the sacrilegious counterfeit presentment. Tourists in Egypt who are addicted to sketching, or who dabble in photography, will do well to remember these conscientious scruples of the Moslem race, and not let their zeal for bringing back pictorial mementoes of their travels induce them to take "pot shots" at mosque interiors, for instance. In Egypt, no doubt, the natives have too wholesome a dread of the Franks to manifest their outraged feelings by physical violence; but still it is ungenerous, not to say unchristian, to wound people's religious prejudices, however superstitious they may appear to us. In some other countries of North Africa, notably in the interior of Morocco or Tripoli, promiscuous photography might be attended with disagreeable results, if not a certain amount of danger. A tourist would find a kodak camera, even with all the latest improvements, a somewhat inefficient weapon against a mob of fanatical Arabs.

For the best view of the city and the surrounding country we must climb the slopes of Mount Caffarelli (now generally called Fort Napoleon) to the fort which crowns the summit, or make our way to the fortress Kom-el-Deek on the elevated ground near the Rosetta Gate. Alexandria, spread out like a map, lies at our feet. At this height the commonplace aspect of a bustling and thriving seaport, which seems, on a closer acquaintance, to be Europeanised and modernised out of the least resemblance to an Oriental city, is changed to a prospect of some beauty. At Alexandria, even more than at most cities of the East, distance lends enchantment to the view. From these heights the squalid back streets of the native quarter, and the modern hausmannised main thoroughfares, look like dark threads woven into the web of the city, relieved by the white mosques, with their swelling domes curving inward like fan-palms towards the crescents, flashing in the rays of the sun, and their tall, graceful minarets piercing the smokeless and cloudless atmosphere. The subdued roar of the busy streets and quays is occasionally varied by the melodious cry of the muezzin. Then, looking northward, one sees the clear blue of the Mediterranean, till it is lost in the hazy horizon. To the west and south the placid waters of the Mareotis Lake, in reality a shallow and insalubrious lagoon, but to all appearance a smiling lake, which, with its waters fringed by the low-lying sand-dunes, reminds the spectator of the peculiar beauties of the Norfolk Broads.

Beyond Lake Mareotis lies the luxuriant plain of the Delta. The view of this plain may not be what is called picturesque, but to the artist the scenery has its special charm. It is no doubt flat and monotonous, but there is no monotony of colour in this richly cultivated plain, once the granary of the Roman Empire. Simplicity is, in short, the predominant "note" in the scenery of Lower Egypt, but, as Mr. H. D. Traill has well observed, here the artist finds "the broadest effects produced by the slenderest means." In the description of this North African Holland innumerable pens have been worn out in comparison and simile. To some this huge market-garden, with its network of canals and ditches, simply invites a homely comparison with a chess-board. Others, with a gift for fanciful metaphor, will liken the landscape to a green robe or carpet shot with silver threads, or to a seven-ribbed fan, the ribs being, of course, the seven mouths of the Nile. One may, however, differ as to the most appropriate metaphors, but all must agree that there are unique elements of beauty in the Delta landscape. Seen, as most tourists do see it, in winter or spring, the green fields of waving corn and barley, the meadows of watermelons and cucumbers, the fields of pea and purple lupin one mass of colours, interspersed with the palm-groves and white minarets which mark the site of the almost invisible mud-villages, and intersected thickly with countless canals and trenches that in the distance look like silver threads, and suggest Brobdignagian filigree work or the delicate tracery of King Frost on our window-panes, the view is impressive, and not without beauty.

In the summer and early autumn, especially during August and September, when the Nile is at its height, the view is still more striking, though hardly so beautiful. Then it is that this Protean country offers its most impressive aspect. The Delta becomes an inland archipelago studded with green islands, each island crowned with a white-mosqued village, or conspicuous with a cluster of palms. The Nile and its swollen tributaries are covered with huge-sailed dahabiyehs, which give life and variety to the watery expanse.

Alexandria can boast of few "lions," as the word is usually understood, but of these by far the most interesting is the column known by the name of Pompey's Pillar. Every one has heard of this famous monolith, which is as closely associated in people's minds with Alexandria as the Coliseum is with Rome, the Alhambra with Granada, or the Kremlin with Moscow. It has, of course, no more to do with the Pompey of history (to whom it is attributed by the unlettered tourist) than has Cleopatra's Needle with that famous queen, the "Serpent of old Nile" or Joseph's Well at Cairo with the Hebrew patriarch. It owes its name to the fact that a certain prefect named after Cæsar's great rival erected on the summit of an existing column — in the opinion of Professor Mahaffy one erected by Ptolemy II. in memory of his favorite wife, Arsinoe — a statue in honour of the horse of the Roman emperor Diocletian. There is a familiar legend which has been invented to account for the special reason of its erection, which guide-book compilers are very fond of. According to the story, this historic animal, through an opportune stumble, stayed the persecution of the Alexandrian Christians, as the tyrannical emperor had sworn to continue the massacre till the blood of the victims reached his horse's knees. Antiquarians and Egyptologists are, however, given to scoffing at the tradition as a plausible myth.

In the opinion of many learned authorities, the shaft of this column was once a portion of the Serapeum, that famous building which was both a temple of the heathen god Serapis and a vast treasure-house of ancient civilisation. In order to account for its omission in the descriptions of Alexandria given by Pliny and Strabo, who had mentioned the two obelisks of Cleopatra, it has been suggested that the column had fallen, and that the Prefect Pompey had merely reërected it in honour of Diocletian, and replaced the statue of Serapis with one of the emperor, — or of his horse, according to some chroniclers. This statue, if it ever existed, has now disappeared. As the column stands, however, it is a singularly striking and beautiful monument, owing to its great height, simplicity of form, and elegant proportions. It reminds the spectator a little of Nelson's column in Trafalgar Square; and perhaps the absence of a statue is not altogether to be regretted, considering the height of the column, as it might suggest to the irrepressible tourists, who scoff at Nelson's statue as the " Mast-headed Admiral," some similar witticism at the expense of Diocletian.

With the exception of this monolith, which, " a solitary column, mourns above its prostrate brethren," only a few fragmentary and scattered ruins of fallen columns mark the site of the world-renowned Serapeum. Nothing else remains of the famous library, the magnificent portico with its hundred steps, the vast halls, and the four hundred marble columns of that great building, designed to perpetuate the glories of the Ptolemies. This library, which was the forerunner of the great libraries of modern times, must not be confounded with the equally famous one which was attached to the Museum, whose exact site is still a bone of contention among antiquarians. The latter was destroyed by accident when Julius Cæsar set fire to the Alexandrian fleet. The Serapeum collection survived for six hundred years, till its wanton destruction through the fanaticism of the Caliph Omar. The Arab conqueror is said to have justified this barbarism with a fallacious epigram, which was as unanswerable, however logically faulty, as the famous one familiar to students of English history under the name of Archbishop Morton's Fork. " If these writings," declared the uncompromising conqueror, " agree with the Book of God, they are useless, and need not be preserved; if they disagree, they are pernicious, and ought to be destroyed." Nothing could prevail against this flagrant example of a *petitio principii*, and for six months the three hundred thousand parchments supplied fuel for the four thousand baths of Alexandria.

Hard by Pompey's Pillar is a dreary waste, dotted with curiously carved structures. This is the Mohammedan cemetery. As in most Oriental towns, the cemetery is at the west end of the town, as the Mohammedans consider that the quarter of the horizon in which the sun sets is the most suitable spot for their burying-places. In this melancholy city of the dead are buried also many of the ruins of the Serapeum, and scattered about among the tombs are fragments of columns and broken pedestals. On some of the tombs a green turban is roughly painted, strangely out of harmony with the severe stone-carving. This signifies that the tomb holds the remains of a descendant of the Prophet, or of a devout Moslem who had himself, and not vicariously as is so often done, made the pilgrimage to the sacred city of Mecca. Some of the headstones are elaborately carved, but most are quite plain, with the exception of a verse of the Koran cut in the stone. The observant tourist will notice on many of the tombs a curious little round hole cut in the stone at the head, which seems to be intended to form a passage to the interior of the vault, though the aperture is generally filled up with earth. It is said that this passage was made to enable the Angel Israfel, at the Resurrection, to draw out the occupant by the hair of his head; and the custom which obtains among the lower-class Moslems of shaving the head, with the exception of a round tuft of hair in the middle — a fashion which suggests an incipient pigtail or an inverted tonsure — is as much due to this superstition as to sanitary considerations.

Of far greater interest than this comparatively modern

cemetery are the cave cemeteries of El-Meks. These catacombs are some four miles from the city. The route along the extended low ridge of sand-hills is singularly unpicturesque; but the windmills (built by Napoleon I. to grind corn for his troops when he occupied the country) which fringe the shore give a homely aspect to the country, and serve at any rate to break the monotony of this dreary and desolate region. We soon reach Said Pacha's unfinished palace of El-Meks, which owes its origin to the mania for building which helped to make the reign of that weak-minded ruler so costly to his overtaxed subjects. One glimpse at the bastard style of architecture is sufficient to remove any feeling of disappointment on being told that the building is not open to the public.

The catacombs, which spread a considerable distance along the seashore, and of which the so-called Baths of Cleopatra are a part, are very extensive, and tourists are usually satisfied with exploring a part. There are no mummies, but the niches can be clearly seen. The plan of the catacombs is curiously like the wards of a key.

There are few "sights" in Alexandria of much interest besides those already mentioned. In fact, Alexandria is interesting more as a city of sites than sights. It is true that the names of some of the mosques — such as that of the One Thousand and One Columns, built on the spot where Saint Mark suffered martyrdom, and the Mosque of Saint Athanasius — are calculated to arouse the curiosity of the tourist; but the interest is in the name alone. The Mosque of Many Columns is turned into a quarantine station, and the Mosque of Saint Athanasius has no connection with the great Father except that it stands on the site of a church in which he probably preached.

Then there is the Coptic Convent of Saint Mark, which, according to the inmates, contains the body of the great evangelist, — an assertion which would scarcely deceive the most ignorant and most credulous tourist that ever intrusted himself to the fostering care of Messrs. Cook, as it is well known that Saint Mark's body was removed to Venice in the ninth century. The mosque with the ornate exterior and lofty minaret, in which the remains of Said Pacha are buried, called Mosque Nebbi Daniel, is the only one besides those already mentioned which would be worth visiting. This is interesting to Egyptologists as being the reputed site of the tomb of Alexander the Great. As, however, no Christians are admitted to this khedivial mausoleum, no antiquarian researches or excavations can be undertaken in order to verify this traditional site. The stone sarcophagus in the British Museum, which was thought to have been that of Alexander, is now known to be erroneously attributed to this monarch. It was made for an earlier king of the thirtieth dynasty, B. C. 378–358.

CHAPTER VI.

THE STORY OF THE SUEZ CANAL.

THE coast between Rosetta and Port Said is, like the rest of the Egyptian littoral, flat and monotonous. The only break in the dreary vista is afforded by the picturesque-looking town of Damietta, which, with its lofty houses, looking in the distance like marble palaces, has a striking appearance seen from the sea. The town, though containing some spacious bazaars and several large and well-proportioned mosques, has little to attract the visitor, and there are no antiquities or buildings of any historic interest. The traveller full of the traditions of the Crusades, who expects to find some traces of Saladin and the Saracens, will be doomed to disappointment. Damietta is comparatively modern, the old Byzantine city having been destroyed by the Arabs early in the thirteenth century, and rebuilt — at a safer distance from invasion by sea — a few miles inland, under the name of Mensheeyah. One of the gateways of the modern town, the Mensheeyah Gate, serves as a reminder of its former name. Though the trade of Damietta has, in common with most of the Delta seaports, declined since the construction of the Mahmoudiyeh Canal, it is still a town of some commercial importance, and consular representatives of several European powers are stationed here. To sportsmen Damietta offers special advantages, as it makes capital headquarters for the wild-fowl shooting on Menzaleh Lake, which teems with aquatic birds of all kinds. Myriads of wild duck may be seen feeding here, and "big game," — if the expression can be applied to birds, — in the shape of herons, pelicans, storks, flamingoes, etc., is plentiful. In the marshes which abut on the lake specimens of the papyrus are to be found, this neighbourhood being one of the few habitats of this rare plant.

Soon after rounding the projecting ridge of low sandhills, which fringe the estuary of the Damietta branch of the Nile, the noble proportions of the loftiest lighthouse in the Mediterranean come into view. It is fitted with one of the most powerful electric lights in the world, its penetrating rays being visible on a clear night at a distance of over twenty-five miles. Shortly afterwards the forest of masts, apparently springing out of the desert, informs the passenger of the near vicinity of Port Said. There is, of course, nothing to see at Port Said from a tourist's standpoint. The town is little more than a large coaling station, and is of very recent growth. It owes its existence solely to the Suez Canal, and to the fact that the water at that part of the coast is deeper than at Pelusium, where the isthmus is narrowest.

The town is built partly on artificial foundations on the strip of low sand banks which form a natural sea-wall, protecting Lake Menzaleh from the Mediterranean. In the autumn, at high Nile, it is surrounded on all sides by water. An imaginative writer once called Port Said the Venice of Africa, — not a very happy description, as the essentially modern appearance of this coaling station strikes the most unobservant visitor. The comparison might for its inappositeness rank with the proverbial one between Macedon and Monmouth. Both Venice and Port Said are landlocked, and that is the only feature they have in common.

The sandy plains in the vicinity of the town are, however, full of interest to the historian and archæologist.

THE STORY OF THE SUEZ CANAL. 107

Here may be found ruins and remains of antiquity which recall a period of civilisation reaching back more centuries than Port Said (built in 1859) does in years. The ruins of Pelusium (the Sin of the Old Testament), the key of northeastern Egypt in the Pharaonic period, are only eighteen miles distant, and along the shore may still be traced a few vestiges of the great highway — the oldest road in the world of which remains exist — constructed by Rameses the Great in 1350 B. C., when he undertook his expedition for the conquest of Syria.

To come to more recent history, it was on these shores that Cambyses defeated the Egyptians; and here, some five centuries later, Pompey the Great was treacherously murdered when he fled to Egypt after the battle of Pharsalia.

To the southwest of Port Said, near the little fishing-village of Sais, on the southern shore of Lake Menzaleh, are the magnificent ruins of Tanis (the Zoan of the Old Testament). These seldom-visited remains are only second to those of Thebes and Memphis in historical and archæological interest. The ruins were uncovered at great cost of labour by the late Mariette Bey, and in the Great Temple were unearthed some of the most notable monuments of the Pharaonic age, including over a dozen gigantic fallen obelisks. This vast building, restored and enlarged by Rameses II., dates back over five thousand years. As Thebes declined, Tanis rose in importance, and under the kings of the Twenty-first Dynasty it became the chief seat of government. Mr. John Macgregor (Rob Roy), who was one of the first of modern travellers to call attention to these grand ruins, declares that of all the celebrated remains he has seen, none impressed him "so deeply with the sense of fallen and deserted magnificence" as the ruined temple of Tanis.

The Suez Canal is admittedly one of the greatest undertakings of modern times, and has perhaps effected a greater transformation in the world's commerce, during the twenty years that have elapsed since its completion, than has been effected in the same period by the agency of steam.

It was emphatically the work of one man, and of one, too, who was devoid of the slightest technical training in the engineering profession. Monsieur de Lesseps cannot, of course, claim any originality in the conception of this great undertaking, for the idea of opening up communication between the Mediterranean and the Red Sea by means of a maritime canal is almost as old as Egypt itself, and many attempts were made by the rulers of Egypt, from Sesostris downwards, to span the isthmus with " a bridge of water." Most of these projects proved abortive, though there was some kind of water communication between the two seas in the time of the Ptolemies, and it was by this canal that Cleopatra attempted to escape after the battle of Actium. When Napoleon the Great occupied Egypt, he went so far as to appoint a commission of engineers to examine into a projected scheme for a maritime canal; but owing to the ignorance of the commissioners, who reported that there was a difference of thirty feet in the levels of the two seas, — though there is really scarcely more than six inches,— which would necessitate vast locks and involve an enormous outlay of money, the plan was given up.

The Suez Canal is, in short, the work of one great man, and its existence is due to the undoubted courage and indomitable energy, to the intensity of conviction and to the magnetic personality, of M. de Lesseps, which influenced every one with whom he came in contact, from the viceroy down to the humblest fellah. This great project was carried out, too, not by a professional engineer, but by a mere consular clerk, and was executed in spite of the most determined opposition of politicians and capitalists, and in the teeth of the mockery and ridicule of practical engineers, who affected to sneer at the scheme as the chimerical dream

THE STORY OF THE SUEZ CANAL. 109

of a vainglorious Frenchman. The canal, regarded from a purely picturesque standpoint, does not present such striking features as other great monuments of engineering skill, — the Forth Bridge, the Mont Cenis Tunnel, the Brooklyn Bridge, or the railway which scales the highest peaks of the Rocky Mountains. This " huge ditch," as it has been contemptuously called, has not, indeed, " been carried over high mountains, nor cut through rock-bound tunnels, nor have its waters been confined by Titanic masses of masonry." In fact, technically speaking, the name " canal," as applied to this channel, is a misnomer. It has nothing in common with other canals, — no locks, gates, reservoirs, nor pumping engines. It is really an artificial strait, — a prolongation of an arm of the sea. We can freely concede this; yet to those of imaginative temperament there are elements of romance about this colossal enterprise. It is the creation of a nineteenth-century wizard, who, with his enchanter's wand — the spade — has transformed the shape of the globe, and summoned the sea to flow uninterruptedly from the Mediterranean to the Indian Ocean. Then, too, the most matter-of-fact traveller who traverses it can scarcely fail to be impressed with the peculiar *genius loci*. Every mile of the canal passes through a region enriched by the memories of events which had their birth in the remotest ages of antiquity. Across this plain Abraham wandered from distant Ur of the Chaldees, some four thousand years ago. Beyond the placid waters of Lake Menzaleh lie the ruins of Zoan, where Moses performed his miracles. On the right lies the Plain of Pelusium, across which the hosts of Persian, Greek, and Roman conquerers successively swept to take possession of the riches of Egypt. In passing through the canal at night,— the electric light serving as a " pillar of fire " to the steamer, as it swiftly but silently ploughs its course through the desert,— the strange impressiveness of the scene is intensified. " The Suez Canal links together, in striking contrast, the great Past and the greater Present, pointing to a future which we are as little able to divine as were the Pharaohs or Ptolemies of old to forecast the wonders of the nineteenth century."

The history of the enterprise from 1855, when the concession was granted by Said Pacha, to the inauguration of the canal in November, 1869, reads like a romance. The main difficulties were political, for the physical obstacles were not serious, considering the magnitude of the task. Indeed, the very simplicity of the undertaking from an engineering point of view — for the cutting of the Isthmus of Suez was merely a question of time, money, and a sufficiency of native labour in the crudest form — no doubt contributed not a little to wreck M. de Lesseps's subsequent enterprise, as it led him to underestimate the serious nature of his task in the western hemisphere, in which the physical obstacles were almost insuperable in comparison. Then, in the case of Panama, there were no predecessors from whose mistakes M. de Lesseps might profit, as was the case in Egypt, where previous projectors were seriously handicapped through accepting Napoleon's engineers' erroneous calculation of the Red Sea being thirty feet higher than the Mediterranean as a hydrographical axiom. Then, too, there seemed to be a kind of tradition among them that no canal could be a success which did not depend upon the Nile for its water supply. It was the political aspect of the canal which gave rise to so much opposition; and the political significance of the exclusive control, by a French company, of the great highway to India and the Australasian colonies was appreciated at its full value by Great Britain.

In short, the Suez Canal project was regarded by diplomatists as an international question involving serious issues, and it was certainly a powerful factor in European politics. The neutrality of the canal in times of war was felt to be a matter of great importance; for, as it was destined to be

the great gate between the eastern and western hemispheres, it was essential that it should be kept open. In fact, to look ahead a few years, one reason for the intervention of the English, in helping to crush the military revolution in 1882, was the necessity of maintaining a free waterway in the canal, which was menaced by Arabi's troops. Lesseps's chief difficulty lay in the determined opposition of Lord Palmerston, whose influence with the Porte at this time was considerable. The British Government succeeded in getting the imperial firman sanctioning the concession of the Viceroy withheld for a considerable time, by suggesting that it would tend to increase the independence of Egypt. Lord Palmerston's commercial objections to the canal certainly showed a striking lack of appreciation of the economical conditions of the world's commerce. His argument was based on the ill-founded assumption that England would lose her supremacy as a great carrying nation if this new maritime route were thrown open to the world. Yet by reducing the voyage to India almost one-half England would, of course, benefit more than any other nation. The absurdity of Palmerston's contention is sufficiently demonstrated by the fact that, in 1895, seventy per cent. of the tonnage of ships which passed through the canal carried the English flag.

There was, however, some sound reason in Lord Palmerston's objection to the canal, as a statesman. In the original concession of Said Pacha, the territory stretching for several miles on either side of the canal, and extending its whole length, was granted to the Canal Company. Cousequently, the British Government contended that in time of war France's control of the isthmus would be a menace to England. But Lord Palmerston might have made his sanction and approval contingent on the amendment of this dangerous clause, instead of irritating a friendly Power by uncompromising opposition.

Had England joined the other Powers in furthering M. de Lesseps's scheme, and not placed itself out of court by its persistent hostility, in all probability the actual neutrality of the canal would not have been delayed till 1887.

M. de Lesseps, whose faith in the project was not shaken by the hostility of the English Government and the apathy of the Porte, started operations in 1859, himself cutting the first sod in the narrow strip of sand between Lake Menzaleh and the Mediterranean, on April 25.

Till 1864, progress was steady but slow, as the actual excavation was done by manual labour, over twenty-five thousand fellahs being supplied by the *corvée* for this work. In this year, difficulties arose which threatened to wreck the enterprise. The new Khedive, Ismail, was alarmed at the continual drain on his subjects by the concession of his predecessor, which compelled him to supply so large a number of workmen to the Canal Company, and threatened to stop the supply of native labourers. The dispute was submitted to the Emperor Napoleon III., as arbitrator, who decided that the Egyptian Government should pay an indemnity of one and one-half million pounds for the withdrawal of the native labourers. This misfortune proved, however, a blessing in disguise. The Company was compelled to use machinery for excavating and dredging, which proved far more efficacions and, eventually, more economical than native labour, and enabled the contractors to complete the undertaking within a few months of the stipulated time.

By November, 1869, all was ready for the inauguration ceremonies, which were carried out by the Khedive on a scale of unparalleled magnificence. At these festivities all the Powers of Europe were officially represented: France and Austria by the Empress Eugénie and the Emperor Francis Joseph, respectively, and other countries by members of the royal family or special envoys. Even England forgot her old political jealousy, and was adequately repre-

THE STORY OF THE SUEZ CANAL. 113

sented. But then, it must be remembered that the *crux* of the objection of the English Government had been removed in 1864, when Ismail bought back from the Canal Company the territorial rights over the lands abutting on the canal, for £3,360,000.

In order to impress his royal guests, whom Ismail had personally invited in a tour which he made round the European courts the year before, the Khedive, who seemed to have a perfect genius for spending, seized the opportunity of renovating and haussmannising Cairo, and attempted to turn this unique Oriental city into a feeble copy of a third-rate European capital. Parks and public gardens were planted, palaces restored, and boulevards built, and gas was laid in the chief streets. Among the entertainments provided for visitors were concerts and theatrical performances, for which the chief stars of Paris and Vienna were engaged. Even a new opera was " commanded " for the occasion, Verdi composing the Egyptian opera "Aida" to entertain the Khedive's guests. It has been computed that the expenses attendant on the inauguration of the Suez Canal cost the Khedive, or rather Egypt, fully four millions; and, no doubt, this lavish expenditure materially contributed to bring about Ismail's financial collapse and virtual bankruptcy a few years later.

Honours of all kinds were subsequently showered upon M. de Lesseps, who was eulogised by the press of Europe as a benefactor to mankind, ennobled by his grateful sovereign, and made the recipient of decorations and orders from most of the sovereigns of Europe. Finally, to crown all, a place was found for the national hero among the "Immortal Forty." Nor was England behindhand in making up for its former neglect, and Comte de Lesseps was created a K. C. S. I., and presented with the freedom of the City of London.

CHAPTER VII.

CAIRO AS A RESORT FOR INVALIDS.

CAIRO itself cannot be unreservedly recommended as a health-resort pure and simple. The Egyptian climate is undeniably admirably suited for a winter residence, and in most respects it is superior to that of any health-resort in the south of France, — the world's great winter sanatorium. But the city of Cairo possesses too many factitious drawbacks, which militate against its use as a climatic health-station. Now that other health-resorts, such as Luxor, Assouan, Helouan, etc., are getting better known and developed, medical men are beginning to realise that, hygienically speaking, Cairo is not Egypt. Its enormous population and limited area, for one thing, does not commend it to medical men as a winter residence for their patients. An overcrowded city of nearly half a million inhabitants, with its unsatisfactory hygienic conditions and appallingly primitive and unsanitary system of drainage, — if system it can be called, — the annual summer visitation of cholera, etc., seems, indeed, the last place to which the health-seeker, as distinct from the mere tourist or pleasure-seeker, should be sent. It is true that the sanitation of the Continental, Shepheards, Ghezireh Palace, and other fashionable hotels is beyond reproach, but the visitor is not likely to spend all his time in the hotel. Besides, the innumerable urban amusements and social gaieties and dissipations of this fashionable winter-city offer too many temptations to the invalid to neglect his health.

Twenty or thirty years ago, no doubt, the invalid had no choice: a winter in Egypt necessarily meant spending that season in Cairo. But now, thanks mainly to the enterprise of the great tourist-agents, Luxor, Assouan, and the Nile have been rendered available for serious invalids. The above remarks apply, of course, to the genuine invalid, as distinct from the large class of valetudinarians or quasi-invalids. For this class of visitors, and especially over-worked persons and those suffering from worry and "nerves," who require mainly change of scene and rest, Cairo, with its innumerable resources and varied interests, is an ideal wintering-place. The above-mentioned objections to Cairo in the case of real invalids apply, however, to those contemplating spending the whole winter in the city, and not merely a few weeks. In many cases a whole winter on the Nile would be found monotonous, so the best disposal of time would be to spend the early winter months at Luxor or on a Nile voyage, and postpone the return to Cairo till the beginning of February. November, December, and January are the least suitable months for Cairo, owing to the risk of malaria from the moisture arising from the subsiding inundation of the Nile. Then, when Cairo gets too hot, Ramleh, near Alexandria, will be found an excellent intermediate health-resort for a few weeks before leaving Egypt.

Helouan-les-Bains, within half an hour of Cairo by train, or Mena House, at the foot of the Pyramids, would, however, be a better residence than Cairo itself. Helouan is, in fact, the oldest health-resort in the world. There are about a dozen sulphur springs similar to those of Aix-les-Bains, but rather stronger. Those who have undergone a course at Aix can continue their "cure" here during the winter and spring, when the Aix establishment is closed. The atmosphere is remarkably pure and salubrions, and the electrical tonic influence of the desert climate is felt here to a striking degree. There are good hotels here, two resident doctors, and several pensions. The Administration have shown themselves thoroughly alive to the requirements of modern tourists by providing lawn-tennis courts, laying down golf links, etc. The chief drawback is that, at present, the English and American guests are rather swamped by the Teutonic element, the baths belonging to a German directorate.

Another resort, which is strongly recommended by Dr. F. M. Sandwith, Dr. Hermann Weber, and other eminent climatologists, is Mena House, at the Pyramids. Its advantages are thus summed up by Dr. Sandwith:

"Life at the large hotel here, numbering some 120 bedrooms, is for those who wish for purer air than that of crowded Cairo, but who desire to be within driving distance of their friends, and who dread the somewhat sombre monotony of Helouan. The Sphinx and the Pyramids, besides many attractions of their own, insure a constant stream of visitors during the winter months. The air at both suburbs is probably equally pure and equally dry. For the comfort of the guests, there are provided a resident English doctor and chaplain, a chapel, a noble dining-room for 250 people, European chambermaids, swimming bath, excellent conservancy arrangements, drinking water from a special well in the desert, steam laundry, a stringed band, books and magazines, billiard-tables, and photograph-rooms. There are desert-carts for driving, horses and camels for riding, occasional races, golf and lawn-tennis, and capital shooting from November to April. The climate of Helouan and the Pyramids is much the same as in Cairo, except that the air is fresher, purer, and drier."

Whole volumes have been written by meteorologists and medical experts on the climatology of Egypt, but its chief characteristics can be summed up in a few words: a remarkably pure and salubrious atmosphere, almost continuous sunshine, rainlessness (the rainfall of the Upper Nile Val-

CAIRO AS A RESORT FOR INVALIDS. 117

ley is practically *nil*), genial warmth (which, owing to its lack of moisture, is not oppressive), and highly tonic qualities; but, to counterbalance these good points, great lack of equability. The great difference between day and night temperature is, no doubt, a very serious drawback. This lack of uniformity is, of course, inevitable in all countries where a high temperature and immunity from rain are combined. In short, it is a meteorological axiom that equability cannot exist with a very dry atmosphere and a high temperature. *Equability implies, of course, a certain amount of humidity.* An ideal climate would combine the equability and softness of Madeira, the warmth and dryness of Upper Egypt, and the chemically pure atmosphere of Biskra in Algeria.

The following summary of the climatic conditions of Cairo, by Dr. F. M. Sandwith, prepared for my work on the health resorts of South Europe and North Africa (3d ed., 1896), may be conveniently inserted here:

"To save space, it is only necessary here to consider the seven winter months from November 1 to May 31. The barometer seldom varies, though there is a steady fall from 29.99 in December to 29.82 in April. Rain amounts to one inch and a quarter, the number of days upon which drops or showers fall being about fifteen. Clouds during January and February reach a maximum of 4 upon a scale from 0–10. The prevalent wind is from the north or northwest, and is never sufficiently fierce to keep patients within doors. The Khamseen blows from the southwest desert during March and April, seldom for more than two days in a week. It is unpleasantly hot and dusty while it lasts, and drives many visitors away from Cairo. The following table, drawn up from my own observations, shows the temperatures to which patients may be exposed. It is based on the principle that a sick man need not concern himself with the minimum *outdoor* temperature of a place, for that is always at an hour when he ought to be safe in bed. The vital information for him is the average maximum shade temperature out of doors, together with the average minimum bedroom heat, and the daily range between them. It will be noticed that there is no very serious range until the hot weather begins. My bedroom records have purposely been taken in a north room with door wide open, never visited by the sun, unoccupied at night, and unwarmed by artificial light. This, therefore, gives the greatest cold to which a patient can be subjected, unless he opens his bedroom windows. A prudent invalid would, of course, eschew a north room, and would warm the air by lamp or candles on going to bed. Thus he would raise my minimum results some four degrees, and reduce the range of temperature considerably. It is interesting to note that my minimum results, within two or three degrees, correspond with the mean temperature of the month. During April and May it is, of course, easy to refrain from going out at the hottest time of the day. Thus it is evident that patients can spend six months in Cairo in a temperature which need only vary from 63° to 80°.

"The shortest days in December give us ten hours daylight, or three hours longer than in England."

	Temperature, Fahr.		Rain.	Khamseen Wind.
	Maximum in Shade.	Minimum in Bedroom.		
	deg.	deg.		
November	75	. . .	. . .	. . .
December	69	60	4 days	. . .
January	67.4	59.8	Showers 4 days	. . .
February	68.3	59.7	Showers 2 days	2 days
March	76	63.2	Drops 1 day	3 days
April	84.5	67.6	Drops 2 days	7.5 days
May	91.7	72	. . .	5.5 days

The mere fact, that, for one absolutely cloudless winter day in the British Islands — even in the sunniest region of the South Coast — there are ten or a dozen in Upper Egypt, means more, however, to the non-scientific reader than whole columns of meteorological readings and climatic statistics. In short, the Upper Nile boasts of the most wonderful and salubrious climate of any known winter resort in the world available to phthisical patients. There is, of course, no ideal climate on the surface of the globe,—no hygienic Utopia where "the consumptive can draw in healing influence with every breath;" but the climate of Upper Egypt is the nearest approach, within ten days of London, to Tennyson's legendary land of Avilion,

"Where falls not rain, or hail, or any snow,
Nor ever wind blows loudly."

Though the weather is popularly supposed to be the Englishman's staple topic of conversation, the ignorance of the veriest a, b, c of meteorology found among ordinarily well-informed and observant travellers is extraordinary. In Egyptian books of travel and magazine articles one occasionally finds the very quality in which the climate of Egypt is so deficient — equability of temperature — singled out, along with its undeniable dryness, for special praise.

Messrs. Hermann Weber, Burden Saunderson, F. M. Sandwith, and other physicians who have devoted considerable attention to the hygienic and climatological aspects of Egypt are agreed that Egypt is particularly suitable for most forms of lung disease, for incipient pulmonary consumption, chronic bronchitis, asthma, anæmia, chronic rheumatism, and, speaking generally, convalescents from acute diseases. But patients suffering from advanced heart disease, or, in short, very advanced disease of any organ, or from fever, should not be sent to Egypt. Persons subject to obstinate insomnia will also find the climate unsuitable.

With regard to the best way of reaching Egypt, though most travellers arrive by way of Port Said or Ismailia, this route is less preferable than *via* Alexandria for those who are wintering abroad for their health. The Egyptian tourist traffic is of slight importance compared with that of India and Australia, in the eyes of the directors of the great liners; and passengers who have rashly decided to disembark for Cairo at Ismailia often find themselves landed at this half-way house in the middle of the night, with no means of reaching the capital till the next day. What is merely a passing inconvenience to the robust traveller might naturally be a serious matter for the invalid. The light railway which now runs from Port Said to Ismailia can, no doubt, be made use of if the steamer arrives early in the day at Port Said; but the service is slow and infrequent. Though dignified by the name of railway, it is little more than a miniature steam tramway with a gauge of no more than two feet six inches. What is wanted is a railway from Port Said to Damietta, only forty miles west, whence there is direct railway communication to Cairo and Alexandria. There are no physical difficulties in the construction of this much-needed railway. The real difficulty is the jealous opposition of Alexandria. Then, too, the Egyptian Government is not inclined to regard the scheme favourably, as the increased harbour dues would fall into the coffers of the Suez Canal Company, and not into the Government treasury. The fact remains, that, as an ordinary commercial harbour, Port Said is of trifling importance. It is mainly an international port and coaling station. Though Alexandria should be the port of arrival for delicate persons, unfortunately the great passenger steamship companies, such as the Peninsular and Oriental, Orient, and North German Lloyd, make Port Said and not Alexandria, their port of call in their through services. Since 1895, however, an Egyptian service *via* Constantinople and Alexandria has been established by the Sleeping Car Company, in connection with the weekly Orient express. By this service, Alexandria can be reached from London, *via* Ostend, in five and a half days, with only *one change be-*

CAIRO AS A RESORT FOR INVALIDS. 121

tween Ostend and Alexandria. But this route is only for those to whom expense is no object, costing, with extras, about thirty pounds. Health seekers of moderate means would have to be content with the services of the Messageries Maritimes, the Austrian Lloyd, or the Italian Navigation Company, sailing from Marseilles, Trieste, and Genoa, respectively.

CHAPTER VIII.

CAIRO IN ITS SOCIAL ASPECT.

IN some respects, so far as concerns the permanent residents as distinct from the mere *hivernants*, — to use a convenient gallicism to describe those dwellers in Northern climes who winter in the South, for which we have no exact equivalent, — Cairo society resembles that of Simla, Naini Tal, and other fashionable haunts of Indian society, so large is the infusion of the official and military element. For society here has a decidedly official tone, and introductions are advisable if English or American visitors wish to take part in the social life of the place, with its innumerable gaieties and entertainments of all kinds, — from moonlight donkey-rides to the Pyramids, to bicycle gymkhanas at Ghezireh, and fancy-dress balls at Shepheard's and the Continental. In Cairo, however, the visitors at the principal hotels form a society of their own.

The hotel element, too, in Cairo is a factor of greater importance in the social life of the foreign community (for the obvious fact that the Anglo-American winter colony are foreigners is too often ignored) than at Cannes, Monte Carlo, Beaulieu, Pau, Algiers, Florence, and other fashionable winter resorts, partly because the class of visitors who at these stations would be inclined to live haughtily aloof from the cosmopolitan crowd who throng the hotels in isolated villas, at Cairo frequent the fashionable hotels. Villas, indeed, at Cairo are so scarce as to be practically unobtainable, as the only available ones are, as a rule,

CAIRO IN ITS SOCIAL ASPECT. 123

occupied by the families of the corps diplomatique, English officers stationed at Cairo, high government officials, etc. In Egypt, indeed, the aristocratic dahabiyah may almost be said to take the place of the villa.

In a sketch, then, of fashionable Cairo in the nineties, more prominence must be given to the hotels than would be necessary in most foreign watering-places. The most fashionable are, undoubtedly, the Continental, Shepheard's, and Ghezireh Palace, whose visitors' lists almost suggest a page out of the "Almanac de Gotha." Yet, as regards the *clientèle*, each has a distinct character of its own; and if I may attempt a somewhat invidious task, I should be inclined to say that the Continental is more peculiarly exclusive and aristocratic, while Shepheard's is smarter, and the note of modernity here is more insistent. As for the Ghezireh Palace Hotel, it is of too recent date to have acquired any distinct social characteristics. The salient features of these establishments may, perhaps, be better understood by comparison with London hotels. The Continental, then, may be compared with the Alexandra or the Albemarle, Shepheard's with the Savoy, and the Ghezireh Palace with the Cecil.

The leading hotels of Cairo can certainly compare favourably with the best hotels of the most fashionable Riviera watering-places. Leaving the United States out of the question, it is, perhaps, hardly going too far to say that no extra-European city of the same size offers such a wide choice of high-class and well-appointed hotels, so well adapted to meet the demands of English travellers, as the City of the Caliphs.

The historical Shepheard's has a world-wide reputation. It must, however, be remembered that not a stone remains of the old Shepheard's, with its world-renowned balcony, its garden containing the tree under which General Kleber was assassinated, its lofty rooms, and terraces. The new

Shepheard's, completely rebuilt in 1891, lacks these historical adjuncts; but the high reputation for comfort remains, and certainly, in point of luxury and refinements of civilisation, in the form of electric lights, lifts, telephones, etc., there can be no comparison. No doubt there was a touch of Oriental romance, and a suggestion of the "Thousand and One Nights" in the time-honoured practice which formerly obtained at Shepheard's, of summoning the dusky attendants by clapping the hands; but to the matter-of-fact latter-day traveller the prosaic, but reliable, electric bell is an infinitely preferable means of communication.

Shepheard's is *par excellence* the American hotel, while the Continental is more exclusively English. The latter, too, partakes more of the character of a high-class residential hotel, its numerous elegantly appointed suites of private apartments (some twenty sets) being one of its leading features.

Shepheard's *clientèle* is distinctly cosmopolitan. Cairo being the starting-point for the Desert, the Nile, and Palestine, and not far off the highroad to India and Australia, and also being one of those cities which no self-respecting globe-trotter can afford to omit in his round, it is much visited by passing travellers. Those purposing to spend the whole season in Cairo would be more likely to go to the Continental. Perhaps the great objection to Shepheard's lies in its situation. It is undoubtedly very central and easy of access, but, fronting the main road, it is unpleasantly noisy and dusty. In the old days there were no doubt compensations in the moving panorama of Oriental life which this crowded thoroughfare presented, — a kaleidosocopic procession of Bedouin Arabs from the Desert, camels, tattooed negroes, Turks, jewelled pachas ambling past on richly caparisoned mules, mysterious veiled figures, and other fascinating aspects of Eastern life, with a very slight admixture of the vulgarising (artistically speaking)

European element. Now, instead of these picturesque, motley crowds, the modern lounger on the famous terraces looks down upon a yelling crowd of donkey boys, guides, porters, interpreters, dragomans, itinerant dealers in sham antiques, and all the noisy rabble that live on the travelling Briton.

The Continental Hotel is comparatively new, while the New Hotel is one of the oldest hotels in Cairo; but this instance of erratic hotel nomenclature is not confined to Egypt. The Continental is most sumptuously decorated, and the appointments are, perhaps, as luxurious as those of the leading hotels at the fashionable watering-places on the opposite shore of the Mediterranean. Special mention should be made of the excellence of its sanitary arrangements. It is situated in a quiet part of the fashionable Ezbekiya quarter, near the English church, and it is a little out of the way compared with Shepheard's and the New Hotel; but it must be confessed that this comparative remoteness of its locality is regarded as an additional recommendation by many of its patrons.

The Ghezireh Palace, the newest of the Cairo hotels, formerly known as "Ismail's Folly," was one of the palaces of the late Khedive Ismail, whose mania for building palaces was as pronounced as that of the unfortunate King of Bavaria. It was bought by a syndicate from the creditors of the late ex-Khedive, and is now one of the International Palace Hotels — a commercial enterprise which is a worthy rival of the Gordon Hotels ring — belonging to the International Sleeping Car Co. It rivals the Continental or Shepheard's in the costliness of its decoration and the luxury of its appointments. From a medical point of view, its strong points are its delightfully rural and at the same time readily accessible situation, and its sheltered position, which effectually protects visitors from the occasional Khamseen winds, — rare, no doubt, but still to be reckoned with during the Cairo season. The chief drawback to this ambitious establishment is the presence of mosquitoes in the beginning of the season, owing to the proximity of the Nile. This tends to make the commencement of the season at this hotel somewhat later than at the intra-mural hotels. As regards its visitors, the Ghezireh Palace is rather more cosmopolitan in character than the Continental, or even Shepheard's.

Certainly there is room for an extra-mural hotel at Cairo, with its swarms of invalids increasing year by year, who invade Egypt for the winter; and it should appeal not only to this numerically important class, but also to sportsmen, owing to its vicinity to the race-course and the Sporting Club grounds.

So much, then, for the three leading Cairo hotels. We now come to another first-class hotel. The New Hotel was the favourite *caravanserai* of the ex-Khedive Ismail, and it occupies by far the best situation of any in Cairo, facing the Grand Opera House. It has had vicissitudes, but has recovered and stood the test of time; and not being so popular as Shepheard's and the Continental, which are often overcrowded in the height of the season, it might be preferred by invalids and those in need of rest and quietness. Its numerous sets of upper rooms, each furnished with an alcoved balcony, might also recommend it to this class of visitors.

Mena House, at the foot of the Pyramids, is a large and expensive establishment, which has found favour with our compatriots. No doubt those with the artistic sense highly developed will enlarge on the enormity of building a huge modern hotel in the midst of such incongruous surroundings, in the close vicinity of the immortal Pyramids and the mystic Sphinx; but it must be admitted, if I may be allowed to act as *advocatus diaboli*, that if the Pyramids had to be vulgarised, they could not have been vulgarised better (or less) by the English capitalist who is responsible for the undertaking. The origin of Mena House (called from Menes, the quasi-mythical earliest king of Egypt) is curious. Some seven years ago an Englishman in delicate health came to Egypt. He built a tiny house under the shadow of the Pyramids. Finding the air beneficial, he began to erect a small sanatorium, hoping that invalids like himself might resort there, and gain a longer lease of life. But before the plan was matured he died. Then Mr. Locke-King bought the property, and determined to start a hotel. The undertaking grew under his hands, and now Mena House may be considered to rank as one of the leading hotels in Egypt. Mr. Locke-King, however, no longer owns the Mena House, having transferred his interest therein to an English syndicate. It is well spoken of, and the rooms are furnished in good taste. It is well appointed, and is furnished with a large swimming-bath, English billiard-table, library, etc. Golf links are also duly advertised among its numerous attractions for visitors, though considering the general lay of the desert surrounding the Pyramids, "sporting bunkers" must be too plentiful even for the most determined devotee of the " royal and ancient game," and the laying out of anything approaching to a putting-green must have presented almost insuperable difficulties. There is a resident chaplain and physician.

The Hotel d'Angleterre is a favourite resort of English and Americans. It is a particularly comfortable and well-managed house, and is under the same proprietorship as the Continental. It has recently been rebuilt, and is furnished with all modern conveniences, — lift, electric light, etc.; in fact, it is a second Continental on a more modest scale, and may be regarded as a *succursale* or *dependance* of the parent establishment.

The Hotel Royal may be said to have some claims on the gratitude of Englishmen. During Arabi's rebellion, all the hotel keepers, save the landlord of the Royal, decamped. Thus, after the victorious campaign, the English officers would have fared badly had not the doors of the Royal been open to them. This hotel has a good reputation for its *cuisine* and moderate charges. There remains the well-known old established Hotel du Nil, handicapped a little, however, by its situation close to the malodorous street known as the Muski. This hotel, well-known to scholars, literary men, and Egyptologists, boasts of a famous garden, one of the most beautiful and striking in Cairo. In the opinion of many of its guests, this lovely pleasure-ground, which shuts off all noises from the crowded streets, quite compensates for its proximity to the native quarter.

So much for Cairo as a great hotel centre.

The City of Victory is, no doubt, a many-sided city, and might be described under many aspects did space permit. It is a famous historical city, an official capital and seat of government, an important garrison town, and a great Oriental metropolis, — in population the second city in the Turkish Empire. But by most visitors it is regarded merely as a fashionable health and pleasure resort, and it is with Cairo in its social aspect that we are in this chapter mainly concerned.

Its vogue as an aristocratic winter residence for Europeans may be said to date from the opening of the Suez Canal in 1869, when Cairo was boomed, to use a modern phrase, by the Khedive Ismail for all it was worth. This prodigal ruler spent literally millions in his effort to make known to Europeans the attractions and potentialities of his semi-Oriental capital. Yet compare Cairo of to-day as a fashionable tourist-centre with Cairo of a quarter of a century ago. Then the unfinished European quarter had the appearance of a hastily run-up suburb. It was thought a wonderful achievement to light the Ezbekiya quarter with gas. Now many of the streets, and all the large hotels, are lit with electricity, and electric tramcars run through the main thoroughfares. It is even proposed to drain the picturesque but highly insalubrious and malodorous Khalig Canal, which runs through the heart of the city from Old Cairo to Abbasieh, and lay an electric tramway along its bed. No doubt æsthetic tourists will rave at this utilitarian and vandalistic transformation, but the more thoughtful will not regret that what is virtually an open sewer should be converted into a broad highway calculated to benefit the teeming Cairene population. The Egyptians, it may be remarked, take very kindly to the new method of locomotion, — so much so that in the electric trams already running, Europeans are quite crowded out by natives.

Visitors to Cairo may be roughly divided into three classes, — sightseers and tourists; winter residents and society people generally, akin to the fashionable crowds who gravitate annually to Cannes, Monte Carlo, Mentone, and other Riviera towns; and invalids, — the latter class, however, less numerous in Cairo itself than formerly. To these may be added a leaven of artists, literary people, Egyptologists, students, etc.

The first class is numerically of most importance; but tourists, as a rule, have little time, and probably less inclination, for taking part in the social life of the Anglo-American colony, and are not ambitious of being thought to be "in the movement." The winter residents, along with the official community, — English officers attached to the army of occupation and the Egyptian army, government officials and their families, etc., — form the Anglo-American colony. Cairo is indeed emphatically a society place, and, of late years especially, as an aristocratic winter-resort it ranks with Cannes or Monte Carlo. Perhaps the tone of society more nearly resembles Nice or Monte Carlo than the ultra-aristocratic and exclusive Cannes, smartness being the prevalent note of its winter residents. From January to April there is one unceasing round of balls, dinner parties, picnics, gymkhanas, and other social functions.

Intelligent sightseeing or the study of Egyptian antiquities is, no doubt, apt to be undertaken in a decidedly perfunctory manner by the winter residents. The Necropolis of Memphis, for instance, is regarded mainly as a convenient site for a picnic, and the Pyramids or Heliopolis as a goal for a bicycling or riding excursion. Bicycling is now a particularly popular amusement in the City of the Caliphs; and the sight of an American or English girl bicycling down the Mooski, preceded by a running footman (*syce*) to clear the way, may perhaps provoke a smile from her compatriots at the startling incongruity. This is only one instance, however, of the strange contrasts between the latest development of European civilisation and fashionable culture and the old-world Orientalism so constantly seen in Cairo of to-day.

After all, in the Cairo season " distractions " and social dissipations of all kinds, not to speak of the ordinary urban amusements in the form of concerts, theatres, and promenades, follow so unceasingly that there is some excuse for the neglect of the regulation sights and antiquities. When it is the case of a bicycle gymkhana, a polo match at the Turf Club ground, or a lawn-tennis tournament at the Ghezireh Palace, or a visit to a gloomy old temple, it is perhaps only natural with young people that the ancient monuments should go to the wall.

The official balls and receptions at the Khedivial Palace or the British Agency are functions which demand more than an incidental notice. The British Agent gives at least a couple of large balls during the season, and the same hospitality is offered by the Khedive. In addition to these official entertainments, several important semi-official dances are given by the British officers quartered at Cairo. The invitations to the Khedive's ball are invariably sent to the foreign visitors through their Ministers or Consuls; and as everybody in Cairo seems to regard a ticket almost as a right, there is occasionally a certain amount of friction between the accredited representatives of the different Powers and the Khedive's officers.

It cannot be said that the present Khedive, or the officers of his household entrusted with the delicate task of issuing the invitations, always manifest the possession of *savoir faire* or a nice sense of diplomacy. According to a well-authenticated story, the Khedive once returned the United States Consul-General's list of visitors to whom he proposed invitations to be sent, with an observation to the effect that only those of noble birth were eligible. The Consul promptly replied that every American citizen considered himself a king in his own right. This brought the autocratic Khedive to his bearings, and not only was the list passed, but it is said that invitations were sent besides to all the guests at Shepheard's Hotel *en bloc*.

The season in the fashionable world is a short one, extending from January to April. The flight of the European visitors in this month is soon followed by the exodus of the official colony, and other permanent residents, to Ramleh and other summer refuges. The Khedive and his court leave for Alexandria usually about the beginning of May, and this departure of the titular sovereign marks formally the close of the Cairo season.

CHAPTER IX.

THE BAZAARS AND STREET LIFE.

A VISIT to the bazaars is one of the most instructive and entertaining, as well as the pleasantest, forms of killing time which Cairo offers to visitors. But the great charm of this excursion is lost, if it is simply regarded as one of the items in the day's programme of sightseeing. The only way to appreciate the native bazaars, and to get some insight into Cairo street-life, is to form no fixed plan for the disposal of time, and to make no itinerary, and certainly to dispense with a guide or dragoman. It is, however, decidedly advisable, before starting, to get some idea of the confusing topography of the bazaar quarter from a good map. The boundaries of the bazaar region can, however, easily be mastered; and there need be no fear of losing one's way, even in the apparently inextricable labyrinthine maze of narrow lanes and alleys which make up the native quarter, for it is intersected by two main thoroughfares, and has fairly well-marked boundaries. One of these, generally known as the Suk-en-Nahhassin, from its principal bazaar, is called by different names, according to the bazaar which abuts on it. It is one of the narrowest and oldest, but most important, of the Cairo streets, and extends north and south from the El-Hakim Mosque, near the Bab-en-Nasr, to the Boulevard Mehemet Ali, the modern highway which runs direct from the Ezbekiya Square to the Citadel. The other main street is the Rue Neuve, a continuation of the Mooski, and usually called by the name of the latter.

THE BAZAARS AND STREET LIFE. 133

The Mooski was the old Frankish quarter before Ismailia built the modern European district, radiating from the Ezbekiya Square. Some of the bazaars cluster round large covered market-places called khans, of which the Khan Khalil and Khan Ghamaliyeh are the most important. As I have said, the best way of exploring the bazaars is to have no prearranged plan or programme. Hurried tourists, however, who might naturally consider this a counsel of perfection, will find that the most satisfactory and expeditious method of doing the bazaars is to make the Suk-en-Nahhassin street a kind of movable base, and proceed northward or southward from its intersection with the Mooski.

The bazaars are considered by some travellers to be less Oriental in aspect, and to have less of the Eastern atmosphere and local colour about them than those of Damascus; and Bædeker considers them inferior even to those of Constantinople.

As in all Oriental cities, each bazaar is confined, as a rule, to the sale of one class of goods, or products of a certain district. There are, for instance, the bazaars of the Soudan, Tunis, Red Sea Littoral, Morocco, etc.

The Khan Khalil was built in 1292, by the famous Mameluke Sultan, El-Ashraf, the conqueror of Acre. It is on the site of the Tombs of the Caliphs. This is the chief emporium for carpets, rugs, and embroidered stuffs. Open-air auctions take place on the mornings of Monday and Thursday, which are very amusing to watch, — the *dellalin* (appraisers), the prototypes of the porters of modern sales by auction, carrying among the crowd the articles put up, and crying out the bids as they are made. In one part of the khan is a place reserved for dealers in brass and copper goods.

Crossing the street Suk-en-Nahhassin, we come to the Suk-es-Saigh (gold and silversmiths' bazaar), a much-frequented resort of tourists. The workmanship and quality of the trinkets have greatly deteriorated of late. In fact, old Cairo residents among the foreign colony declare that many of the jewels have a Palais Royal or Birmingham origin.

Continuing northwards, and turning to the right, we reach the Gamaliyeh (camel-drivers') quarter. Here are the shops of the Red Sea traders. Very inferior goods are usually only obtainable here, the chief commodities being incense, perfumes, spices, mother-of-pearl, and attar of roses. The latter is so much diluted that it is almost worthless, a small flask being sold for a franc or so, which would cost at least a pound if pure. The northern continuation of the street forms the coppersmiths' bazaar; and here are also booths for the sale of pipes, cigar-holders, amber, uarghilehs, chibouques, and other articles for smokers. Retracing our steps to the starting-point, and crossing the Rue Neuve, — as absurdly named as New College at Oxford, for it is one of the oldest streets, — we reach the once flourishing Suk-es-Sudan, which, though mentioned in the guide-books, no longer exists, since the Soudan has been practically closed to traders. In this quarter are also the booksellers' bazaar, of little interest, and the Suk-el-Attarin (spices, perfumes, etc.), one of the most characteristic bazaars.

Unfortunately, the articles in the bazaars mostly visited by strangers are often either inferior imported goods from Europe, — jewelry from Birmingham, carpets from Brussels, haiks and silk goods from Nîmes or Lyons, cotton stuffs from Manchester, etc., — or cheap and showy bric-à-brac and sham curios, manufactured to meet the factitious demand of tourists. In fact, many of the shops bear a striking resemblance to the Oriental stalls at international exhibitions. Genuine Oriental goods can, however, be bought at the picturesque Suk-el-Fahhamin, behind El-Ghuri Mosque, a favourite haunt of artists and others appreciative of local colour. Here are to be found rugs,

THE BAZAARS AND STREET LIFE. 135

bernouses, Fez caps, saddle-bags, and other articles, from Tunis, Algeria, and Morocco.

With regard to purchases, bargaining is, of course, necessary. Even if the tourist is inexperienced and ignorant of the value of Oriental wares, he might better trust to his own powers of bargaining than allow a guide or interpreter to intervene. The seller, it must be remembered, has a different price for each customer, as a rule. Seasoned travellers in the East lay down the axiom that the prospective buyer should, as a rule, offer half what is asked, when a bargain can be struck midway between the two prices. The objection to this "splitting the difference" is that the dealers are fully aware of this rule, and raise the original price to cope with it. Real bargains can, however, still be obtained by a visitor who is making a long stay in Cairo, and has the necessary patience to go through the tedious preliminary negotiations. The winter resident who makes several visits to the bazaar quarter, and is not in a hurry to spend his money, will, sooner or later, get the refusal of really valuable articles at not very much more than their market value. When purchasing jewelry, the buyer should see that it has the Government stamp, indicating number of carats. Genuine Mushrabiyeh work (carved wooden latticework) is very costly. Most specimens sold are imitations, the pieces being turned out in one uniform size by a lathe. In the real article (the most characteristic Cairo industry) each piece is irregular, and is cut by hand. The best days for the bazaars are the market-days, Mondays and Thursdays, and the hours early in the morning or late in the afternoon.

Even now, in this tourist-ridden native quarter, which is apt to be regarded by most strangers in the light of an Oriental spectacle conveniently arranged for the benefit of European visitors, at the threshold of New Cairo in the Ezbekiya (the hausmannised Cairo of Ismail), in bargaining for the more costly wares, the time-honoured Oriental methods prevail. The negotiations are hedged round with a certain amount of ceremony which recalls the stately fashion in the Arabian Nights, when the purchase of a brass tray or an embroidered saddle-cloth was a solemn treaty, and the bargain for a lamp a diplomatic event not to be lightly undertaken or hurriedly concluded by either of the high contracting parties. Those who are anxious to imbibe the Oriental "atmosphere" will, no doubt, be more inclined to tolerate the long and tedious process of chaffering, considered an indispensable preliminary to a purchase, than the ordinary, matter-of-fact tourist. Native manners and customs, and the multifarious phases of Cairene life — for, as in all Oriental countries, the inhabitants live and carry on their various occupations and avocations in the open air as much as possible, and the Cairene is as great a sun-worshipper as the Neapolitan — are, of course, best observed in the region of the bazaars. The El-Muayyad Bazaar, behind the mosque of that name, is a particularly good field for the searcher after local colour. This is peculiarly a native mart, and less of a tourist resort than most of the bazaars.

But, for broad spectacular effects, the visitor must betake himself to the Mooski, the most characteristic thoroughfare of Cairo. Here a strange amalgam of Eastern and Western life bursts upon the spectator's astonished gaze; and here, indeed, the "East shakes hands with the West." This living diorama, formed by the brilliant and ever shifting crowd, is, in its way, unique. A greater variety of nationalities is collected here than even in Constantinople, the most cosmopolitan city, in a spectacular sense, in Europe; and in this great carnival one seems to meet every costume of Europe, Asia, and Africa. Let us stand aside and watch this motley throng of all races and nationalities pouring along this busy highway. The kaleidoscopic variety of brilliant colour and fantastic costume is a little bewildering to the stranger. Solemn and impassive-looking Turks, gently ambling past on gaily caparisoned mules, grinning negroes from the Soudan, melancholy-looking fellahs in their scanty blue kaftans, cunning-featured Levantines, green-turbaned Shereefs, and picturesque Bedouins from the desert, stalking past in their flowing bernouses, make up the mass of this restless throng. A sakkah, or water-carrier, carrying his picturesque goatskin filled with Nile water, still finds a sale for his drinks in spite of the public fountains; while among other *dramatis personæ* of the Arabian Nights are the vendors of sweets and all kinds of edibles. Interspersed, and giving variety of colour to this living kinetoscope, are gorgeously arrayed Jewesses, fierce-looking Albanians, their many-coloured sashes bristling with weapons, and petticoated Greeks. Then, as a restful relief to this blaze of colour, appears a white group of Egyptian ladies, — "a bevy of fair damsels richly dight," no doubt, but their faces, as well as their rich attire, concealed under the inevitable yashmak and voluminous haik. Such are the elements in this mammoth masquerade which make up the brilliant and varied picture of Cairene street-life.

These are, no doubt, the aspects which force themselves on the notice of the most unobservant tourist, and are among the impressions of every scribbling globe-trotter. Less obvious is the "charm of endless contrasts, — not chromatic alone, but contrast of race, feature, form, costume, attitude, occupation, movement, mood. This it is that makes the magic of the marvellous Eastern city for the Western eye. Nor is the medley of manners less striking than the hotch-potch of races and the tangle of tongues." The Oriental justifies the popular Western conception of gravity and impassiveness of demeanour. Plenty of these types abound, but there are others, — *souvent homme varie*. "In one form he treads the roadway with the majesty of

Haroun Alraschid; in another, he scampers through the streets like a Parisian gamin. The features of that venerable pipe-merchant are as unemotional as a Red Indian's; but if the purchaser, who is haggling with him for the abatement of a piastre, were pleading for the life of his only child, the passionate, suppliant expression of his countenance would more than satisfy the dramatic requirements of the situation." Thus are the salient features of the Cairo streets amusingly and cleverly hit off by Mr. H. D. Traill, in his "Impressions de Voyage," recently published under the title "From Cairo to the Soudan Frontier."

CHAPTER X.

THE MOSQUES.

IT must be admitted that mosques are not of great interest, from the casual sight-seer's point of view, owing to their uniformity and severe simplicity of design, which, however, harmonises well with the almost complete absence of ritual in Moslem worship. The chief features are an open court (sahn) with a fountain or cistern in the middle, surrounded by a covered cloister (liwan). The more sacred part of the building (maksura), corresponding to the choir of an English cathedral, is often screened off from the rest of the building. Here the tomb of the founder is usually placed. In the centre of this sanctuary is the niche (mihrab or kibla) showing the direction of Mecca, and the pulpit (mimbar).

The visitor should remember the names of these principal portions of a Mohammedan temple, if he wishes to obtain an intelligent grasp of Moslem ecclesiastical architecture. Archæologically speaking, the most correct mosque in Cairo is Amru, which will be described later in the chapter devoted to Old Cairo and the Coptic churches. This is the original and normal type of mosque, the best example of which must not, however, be sought in Cairo, but in Cordova, the mosque cathedral there being considered to be the most perfect and best-preserved specimen of this form of Saracenic art in existence. In Cairo the only mosques, besides Amru, which strictly follow the orthodox pattern, are Ihn Tulun and the University Mosque, El-Azhar.

There are over three hundred mosques in Cairo, — indeed, it is said by the Arabs that, as in the case of the churches of Rome, there is one for every day of the year, — but most are in ruins; a large number have been devoted to secular purposes, and there remain scarcely over a score that even the most conscientious sight-seer would care to explore. In some of the larger mosques, such as the Kalaun, a whole group of public buildings are comprised. Besides the mosque proper, there will be found a hospital, school, court of justice, monastery, library, etc. In short, the mosque may be said to serve as a kind of embodiment of the national life.

One of the largest mosques in Cairo is Muristan-Kalaun. It is not strictly a mosque, but a hospital, and is now in a ruinous condition. The mosque-tomb of the founder, adjoining, is a much-frequented shrine of the poorer classes, who firmly believe in the curative properties of the columns of the prayer-niche, which they are accustomed to lick. Certain relics of the Sultan are preserved here, which, of course, possess equally miraculous powers in the eyes of the devout. These antiquities — a turban and sash of the Sultan Kalaun — cannot, it need hardly be said, be shown to strangers.

The adjoining mosque is comparatively uninteresting; but the next one (Barkuk), which contains the tombs of the wife and daughter of the Mameluke Sultan Barkuk, should be visited, if only to see the exquisite workmanship in bronze of one of the doors. The tomb of the Sultan himself, whose body would be thought to be desecrated if placed in the same building as that of his wife, is buried in the Tomb Mosque Barkuk, in the Eastern Cemetery.

In one of the most striking features of the Kalaun may be seen a trace of Gothic influence introduced by the Crusaders. This is the beautiful arched doorway, which was brought from a Christian church at Acre built by the

Crusaders. This archway is a fine specimen of early English architecture, and Mr. Stanley-Poole pertinently observes that it would not be out of place in Salisbury Cathedral.

For beauty of decoration this mosque must, however, yield the palm to the twin mosques of Kait Bey, especially the one in the Eastern Cemetery (usually, but erroneously, known as the Tombs of the Caliphs). The exterior is unequalled among the monuments of the Arabic art of Cairo for richness and variety of decoration. The delicate scrollwork and tracery of the fawn-coloured dome, and the graceful pagoda-like minarets, are familiar to every traveller. The interior has little decoration of any kind. Possibly this was intentional, to mark a place of sepulture, for Kait Bey is buried here. In the sister mosque within the walls, the highly elaborate decoration of the interior offers a strong contrast. This mosque, owing, probably, to its not being prominently mentioned in the guide-books, — for the average tourist rarely strikes out an independent line for himself, — or perhaps because it is a little difficult to find, is seldom visited. Yet this mosque is one of the most characteristic in Cairo, and should on no account be neglected. It has been restored in good taste by the Commission for the Preservation of Arabic Monuments.

This admirable Society, which receives an annual subsidy of no more than £4,000 from the State, has done excellent work since its institution by the late Khedive Tewfik in 1881. It carries out all necessary renovations under the old established, but somewhat cumbrous, Wakfs Administration, the Department which has the charge of all the mosques, corresponding in some respects to the Ministry of Public Worship in the French Republic, or to the Ecclesiastical Commissioners in Great Britain. This body depends for its income, apart from the State convention, on the entrance fee of two piastres, which is levied on strangers for each mosque. In this ancient corporation is vested all ecclesiastical property in Egypt; in fact, next to the Khedive, the Church, if such a word may be used in connection with a heathen faith, was the richest landlord in Egypt. If a man died without immediate issue, his property went to the nearest mosque, — in practice to the Wakf; and if his next of kin claimed it, he would have to pay an enormous percentage of the value to the Administration in order to redeem his inheritance. Then a tithe was obligatory on every head of a family. Consequently, as Mr. Richard Davey observes, in his exhaustive work on "The Sultan and his Subjects," Mohammedanism, though it had no regularly endowed priesthood, was as richly furnished with this world's goods as the Church in England before the Reformation. In theory, the Church devoted her vast wealth to the poor, to education and charity, the service and preservation of the mosques, and to the maintenance of the preachers, attendants, and other officials of the mosques. But the practice was far worse than the worst which Henry the Eighth's Visitors discovered in the monasteries before the old order was swept away, as may be seen by a visit to most of the mosques whose restoration has not been taken in hand by the Commission for the Preservation of Arabic Monuments. Now, of course, since the removal of Ismail from the viceroyalty by the Sultan, at the demand of the Great Powers, and the appointment of an English Comptroller of the Exchequer, under the title of Financial Adviser to the Khedive, the powers of the Wakf corporation have been much curtailed, and the collection, and to a large extent the expenditure, of this revenue is controlled by the State.

After visiting the Kalaun, it is worth while to turn aside into one of the picturesque alleys branching off from the Sharia (street) en-Nahhassin, — the great mosque thor-

THE MOSQUES. 143

oughfare, though a narrow street, according to modern notions, — and make one's way to a small but beautifully decorated mosque, called Abu Bekr. As the guide-books barely mention it, the ordinary tourist misses it; but a visit will be well repaid. The exquisite marble mosaics are almost unequalled in Cairo. Great pains have been taken in the restoration of this mosque by Herz Bey, the architect of the Wakfs Administration, who has carried out the work with the most scrupulous fidelity to the original plan. The result is an architectural gem, as pleasing to the eye as it is archæologically correct.

El-Ghuri, near the Attara Bazaar, is another mosque which is not visited as much as it deserves. The restorations carried on here by the Ancient Monuments Commission also reflect considerable credit on this body.

The mosque known as El-Hassanen is dedicated to the two sons (Hasseen and Hassan) of Ali, the son-in-law of Mohammed, and in the eyes of devout Moslems it consequently possesses peculiar sanctity. It has been entirely rebuilt, and in modern style, and lighted throughout with gas, to the dismay of artists and archæologists. In spite of this aggressive note of modernity, this mosque, as the burial-place of the head of Hasseen (one of the most venerated saints in the Mohammedan calendar), is much frequented by the Cairenes, and the Festival of the Molid (birthday) of the two saints celebrated here is the most important after that of the Prophet. The Khedive visits the mosque in state, followed by thousands of the populace, who throng the building till midnight. The illuminations of the mosque and surrounding bazaars are magnificent. "There is no scene in Cairo which reminds one more forcibly of the Arabian Nights," says that high authority, Murray. In the Mosque Siti Zenab, generally known as the "Women's Mosque," at the other end of the city, is buried Zenab, the sister of the Hassanen. It is elaborately decorated and has a great wealth of coloured glass; but the restorations have not been tastefully carried out, and "the mixture of Turkish decoration with the modern style of architecture does not produce a pleasing effect."

The Ihn Tulun Mosque, like the mosque in the Place du Gouvernement at Algiers, and the Agia Sofia (St. Sophia), of Constantinople, was designed by a Christian architect, and is said to be a copy of the Kaaba at Mecca. The original idea of Sultan Tulun (the founder of the Tulunide dynasty, A. D. 868 to 895) was to build a mosque which should vie with that of Kerouan (Tunisia) in the number of its columns, taken, as was usual with the Arab mosque-builders, from the ruins of Greek and Roman temples. Fortunately, he renounced this vandalistic scheme. The columns of the arches which form a colonnade skirting the sides of the court are of brick instead of stone. The pointed arches recall the Norman style of architecture, and Mr. Lane-Poole declares that this mosque constitutes the first example of the employment of pointed arches throughout a whole building, for their adoption in England did not take place till some three hundred years later. An absurd number of traditions are attached to the building, which, according to some chroniclers, is built on the site of the "Burning Bush," where the Almighty conversed with the Patriarch Moses, as well as the site of Abraham's sacrifice, and the landing-place of the Ark. The fact that Ihn Tulun is, next to Amru Mosque, the oldest in Cairo, perhaps explains the wealth of legendary lore which clusters round this venerable ruin. Owing to its ruinous state, the mosque is of more interest to the historian or Egyptologist than the ordinary traveller. Its exterior view bears a curious resemblance to a dismantled fortress.

The Mosque El-Azhar is unique among the Cairene mosques. It is the largest Moslem university in the world, and perhaps the oldest of any university, Christian or

Mohammedan, the old mosque having been set apart for purposes of study towards the end of the tenth century. Over eleven thousand students, drawn from every Mohammedan country, are said to be "inscribed on the books," and the professors number over three hundred. The educational methods might, in the present-day vernacular, be termed undenominational, for all the chief Moslem sects are represented in this truly catholic institution. Innumerable chambers are partitioned off among the colonnades of the Great Court, which correspond to the side chapels in a Christian cathedral, each of which serves as the lecture-hall of natives of a particular country; these represent the colleges of the university. On Friday, the Mohammedan Sabbath, no teaching takes place; and as this is its most salient feature, travellers should take care to choose some other day for their visit. The authorities do not encourage the presence of strangers, and, *pace* the guide-books, admittance is not always practicable. Some of the sects are decidedly fanatical, and strangers will be well advised to abstain from any overt expression of amusement at the extraordinary spectacle of some thousands of students, of all ages, repeating verses of the Koran in a curious monotone, while swaying their bodies from side to side, — supposed to be an aid to memory.

The Mosque Sultan Hassan is a magnificent building of the palmy days of Arab art, and, on account of its grand proportions and splendid decorations, is called by the Cairenes the "superb mosque." It is said to have cost over £600,000. The mosque may, in a sense, be considered the national mosque of Cairo, and is attended by the Khedive on the occasion of any great religious function. The building, too, has often served as a kind of meeting-place of the natives, in times of public disturbance, and has always been the rallying-place of demagogues and opponents of the Government, notably at the time of the Arabi revolt in 1881. The body of the Sultan, who was assassinated in 1361, lies in a mausoleum which is crowned with a magnificent dome one hundred and eighty feet high.

The Mameluke sovereigns were great mosque-builders, and it will be noticed that many of the most interesting mosques date from the end of the thirteenth century to the beginning of the sixteenth (when the Ottoman sultan, Selim II., conquered Cairo), which synchronises with the golden age of the two Mameluke dynasties.

The following description of this majestic building will give an idea of its enormous proportions:

"The outer walls of this stately mosque are nearly a hundred feet in height, and they are capped by a cornice thirteen feet high, projecting six feet, formed of stalactite, which has ever since been a marked feature in Arabian architecture. The arches of the doorways and of the numerous windows, and even the capitals of the columns, are similarly enriched. The great doorway in the northern side is situated in a recess sixty-six feet in height. The minaret, gracefully converted from a square at its base to an octagon in its upper part, is the loftiest in existence, measuring two hundred and eighty feet." [1]

Unfortunately, this noble fabric is in a very ruinous condition, and instead of restoring it, the late Khedive devoted his energies and his purse to the building of a new mosque adjoining, which was intended to rival the other. So far as can be judged at present, — for it is still a long way from completion, — the Sultan Hassan Mosque is not likely to be eclipsed by the new one, known as the Mosque of the Rifaiya, a particularly fanatical order of dervishes, corresponding in some respects to the Aissoua sect of Algeria.

Perhaps one of the most attractive mosques is that popularly known as Ibrahim Agha, or by tourists, "The Blue-tiled Mosque." Its official title is Kher-bek, as it was built by this renegade Mameluke, who afterwards (1517)

[1] The Art Journal, 1881.

became the first Pacha of Egypt under the Ottoman sultans. On this account it is not surprising that the Cairenes have not wished to perpetuate the name of this traitor, and prefer to call the mosque after Ibrahim Agha, who enlarged and restored it in 1617. The interior is well described by Colonel Plunkett in his slight but charming little brochure, " Walks in Cairo."

The vaulted colonnade on the east side rests on massive piers, and between them glows the rich blue of the tiles which cover the wall; they are set in panels, though somewhat irregularly, and with some serious gaps, where, doubtless, unscrupulous collectors have obtained valuable specimens by the aid of dishonest guardians. The effect depends greatly on the light by which the mosque is seen, but is always rich and striking; the open court, too, with its little garden of palms and other trees in the centre, and the graceful minaret rising above the crenelated wall, is very attractive, and has, especially towards sunset, a pecnliarly quiet and beautiful appearance.

El-Hakim is one of the largest mosques of Cairo, as well as the oldest (after Amru, Tulun, and El-Azhar), but it is in a deplorably ruinous condition. The mosque is unique, as being the sole one provided with a makhara (an external platform, not to be confounded with a minaret), on which incense is burned on important festivals. It is visited chiefly as the temporary house of the Museum of Arabic Art.

In most cases, the best movable decorations and fittings of the mosques, such as the carved mihrab, bronze doors, enamelled lamps, woodwork, etc., have been removed from the mosques and preserved in the Arab musuem. Most visitors would, no doubt, prefer to see these objects *in situ*, but the authorities are certainly justified in their action; for there is no doubt that most of the more artistic objects in the mosques would have been sold, sooner or later, to strangers and collectors by the mosque guardians, and what escaped their rapacity would soon have been spoiled by neglect. ˙ For, many years the objects in this unique collection were stowed away in one of the mosque buildings, without any attempt at systematic or chronological arrangement, and were lost to most visitors; but recently the authorities have had the objects carefully arranged and scientifically catalogued. In a subsequent chapter this magnificent collection will be described at some length.

Though, next to the bazaars, the mosques are, in the opinion of the guides and dragomans, the chief sights of Cairo, it must be allowed that the ordinary visitor will find a whole day devoted solely to these Moslem temples somewhat tedious. It is certainly advisable to combine the excursion to the mosques with some other kind of sightseeing. However, whatever the tastes of the traveller, I think the mosques described above are fairly representative specimens of Moslem architecture.

I have said nothing of the mosques of the Citadel, but these will be treated of in the chapter in which I propose to describe the Cairene Acropolis.

CHAPTER XI.

THE TOMBS OF THE CALIPHS.

THE Tombs of the Caliphs are a remarkably interesting group of mausolea, strictly mosque-tombs, situated outside the walls, a little north of the Citadel. They are easily reached by the Mooski and Rue Neuve. These tombs have no connection with the Caliphs, but as the guides invariably employ this designation, it has naturally been adopted by visitors. The Caliphs have no separate burial-place, and, in fact, most of their tombs in the various mosques of the city have been destroyed. As the tomb-mosque of Kait Bey is the most important in this necropolis, it is often called by Cairenes the Cemetery of Kait Bey. It also goes by the name of the Eastern Cemetery. The Sultans buried here belong to the Circassian Mameluke dynasty, and most of the tombs date from the fifteenth century. They are, for the main part, in a terribly dilapidated condition; the Wakfs Administration seem to have recognised the impossibility of restoring them properly with the funds at their disposal, and have, perhaps wisely, made no attempt at restoration, except in the case of one or two of the more important ones.

The title Caliph, in connection with the various Mohammedan dynasties in Egypt, is often used loosely by those who have written their history. Cairo was never, according to the orthodox view of Mohammedans, the seat of the Caliphate, though some of the Arab rulers, who were strictly viziers, or viceroys, usurped the title itself as well as its functions. Up to 750 A. D., Damascus was the seat of the Caliphate. Then Bagdad, under the Abbasside dynasty; and finally, on the conquest of Egypt by the Ottoman Turks under Sultan Selim, Constantinople became the titular city of the Caliph, and has remained so down to the present time. It is true, however, that during the *later* Arab dynasties in Egypt the actual Caliph was occasionally under the virtual protection of the Egyptian Sultan, and Cairo was the residence of this *fainéant* Commander of the Faithful. The last of these nominal Caliphs died in Egypt about 1537 A. D.

It is important, then, to distinguish between those who were Caliphs *de facto* merely, and those who were both *de facto* and *de jure* successors of Mohammed, which is the strict interpretation of the much-abused term Caliph.

What might be called the historical instinct would be required for a clear comprehension of the intricate succession of dynasties who controlled the destinies of Egypt, from its conquests by Amru, the general of the Caliph Omar (a genuine Caliph), in 1638, down to the invasion by the Turks in 1517, when Egypt was reduced to a mere pachalic of the Ottoman Empire. The most important of these dynasties were the Abbassides, Fatimites, Ayyubides, and the Mamelukes. Perhaps the former is the most familiar to the general reader, as it was to this dynasty that our old friend Haroun-Al-Raschid belonged. The Fatimites form a highly important landmark in our rapid survey of Mohammedan Egypt, as the first of these sovereigns founded the city of Masr-El-Kahira (modern Cairo), transferring the seat of government from Fostat to the "City of Victory."

The Ayyubide dynasty is noteworthy from its founder, Salah-Ed-Deen, known to us as Saladin, who at first ruled in the name of the then incapable Caliph. In 1169 Saladin usurped the supreme authority of the Caliphate, though by the orthodox Mohammedans this was considered to be still vested in the representative of the deposed sovereign of the Abbasside dynasty, whose throne had been usurped by the famous Ibn Tulun. The dynasty of the Ayyubides, founded by this twelfth century Napoleon, lasted nearly a century, — a respectable age for a mediæval Egyptian dynasty; and during this period the Caliphs of Bagdad, who were still reckoned as the spiritual heads of Islam, were unable to exercise even a show of sovereignty in temporal affairs. The era of Saladin, during which Egypt was transformed from a vassal province into an empire, is, of course, familiar to all of us. But though best known on account of the long struggle with the Crusaders and the conquest of Jerusalem, these are only a part of Saladin's achievements. "He made his power felt," writes Mr. Stanley Lane-Poole, " far beyond the borders of Palestine; his arms triumphed over hosts of valiant princes to the banks of the Tigris; and when he died, in 1193, at the age of fifty-seven, he left to his sons and kinsmen, not only the example of the most chivalrous, honourable, and magnanimous of kings, but substantial legacies of rich provinces, extending from Aleppo and Mesopotamia to Arabia and the Country of the Blacks."

With the rise of the Mameluke Sultans, who established their rule over Egypt for the unprecedented period of two hundred and seventy-eight years, we enter upon a kind of renaissance in art and literature, in spite of the perpetual wars and internecine struggles between rival claimants to the throne.

The question of the Caliphate during this troublous time is, however, rendered comparatively free from difficulty, as, possibly with the view of conciliating the orthodox Moslems, the Mameluke Sultans protected the successive representatives of the Abbasside dynasty (named from Abbas, the uncle of Mohammed), and formally recognised them as nominal Caliphs. On the conquest of Egypt by the Ottomans, in 1517, the Turkish Sultan confirmed the claim of the then Abbasside Caliph, and on his death assumed the title. This title has since been claimed by every successive Sultan of Turkey.

Let us now visit the most interesting of these sepulchral monuments.

Kait Bey, Burkuk, and El-Ashraf are considered the show-mosques, and are the only ones visited by the majority of tourists. To visit the latter special permission is necessary. Those fond of architecture are, however, strongly recommended not to confine their attention to the three principal ones.

The mosque of Kait Bey, whose beautiful dome is so familiar in sketches and photographs, is not only incomparably the finest mosque in this cemetery, but for beauty ranks high among all the innumerable mosques of Cairo. Fergusson, in his famous architectural text-book, speaks in enthusiastic terms of the elegance of the building:

"Looked at externally or internally, nothing can exceed the grace of every part of this building. Its small dimensions exclude it from any claim of grandeur, nor does it pretend to the purity of the Greek and some other styles; but as a perfect model of the elegance we generally associate with the architecture of this people, it is, perhaps, unrivalled by anything in Egypt, and far surpasses the Alhambra, or the Western buildings of its age."

Two slabs of red and black granite, with a depression of about the size of a man's foot, will be shown by the guide. Naturally a legend attaches to these curiously formed stones, and they are said to have been brought from Mecca by Kait Bey, and the depression is said to be the impress of the Prophet's foot.

Not far from the Kait Bey Mosque is the large and more imposing tomb-mosque of Burkuk, the first of the Circassian Mameluke dynasty who flourished towards the end of

THE TOMBS OF THE CALIPHS.

the fourteenth century. This mosque can easily be recognised by its magnificent twin domes, which mark respectively the burial-place of the male and female members of the Sultan's family.

This style of architecture is unusual in Egypt, and, indeed, certain features of the building are quite unique among the Cairo mosques. The court is surrounded by loggia, which form very picturesque cloisters. Though a great part of the building is in ruins, the remains give one an idea of its magnificent proportions. "The symmetrical plan of the edifice, its massive masonry, and the symmetrical disposition of the rows of pilasters with domes constitute this mosque one of the most perfect examples of Arabian architecture in existence." One of the most interesting objects is the beautifully chiselled stone-pulpit, perhaps the best specimen of its kind in Cairo; while next to the domes the most noticeable external features are the splendid minarets, the roof decorated with chevron mouldings.

A striking feature of this mosque is the remains of buildings which served as temporary dwellings of relatives and friends of the deceased, the residence of the custodian, etc. This group of buildings (called Hosh), which corresponds to the precincts in English cathedrals, are sometimes, as in this case, almost as extensive as the mosque itself.

Another mosque worth visiting is the tomb of the Sultan Barsbey, or in full El-Ashraf Barsbey, a Sultan who earned the unusual distinction of dying a natural death. It is smaller than the two mosques described above, and is in a ruinous state. The dome, with its intricate pattern of stone lace-work, is very striking. A mosaic pavement in coloured stones is much admired by connoisseurs of Arabian art. The ornamentation of the dome, with its network of arabesques, is very graceful.

Many other mosques are scattered around, but they usually serve more as a subject for the artist than as goals for tourists, owing to their ruinous condition. The same may be said of the tombs of the Mamelukes south of the Citadel, which are even more in need of repair at the hands of the Wakfs Commission. " Many of these tombs present admirable examples of dome architecture in, perhaps, its greatest perfection, and are models of beauty as regards both form and decoration." The sculpturing of the exterior is in some cases exquisite. Several are enriched by bands of porcelain, containing inscriptions in white letters upon a coloured ground. In others, discs of blue porcelain figure among the interstices of the variegated moulding. None of the monuments, situated in what has often been a battle-ground, have remained intact, and time is making sad havoc with some of the most beautiful, as every traveller notes with regret.

Between the Tombs of the Caliphs and the walls of Cairo stretches the extensive Mohammedan cemetery, which should be visited if only to see the grave of Burckhardt, the celebrated Eastern traveller, who died in Cairo in 1817. Like the ill-fated Professor Palmer, he was best known to the Arabs under a native name, and many stories of the old traveller, known all over the East as Sheik Ibrahim, are told by the Arab guides. His tomb for many years was unknown to travellers, but in 1870 it was restored by Rogers Bey.

The next group of mausolea to be visited are those popularly known as the Tombs of the Mamelukes. Owing to the comprehensive nature of this title, which would equally apply to the tombs in the Eastern Cemetery (Tombs of the Caliphs), it is a little misleading. Practically nothing remains of these tombs but the minarets, domes, and some portions of the outer walls. There does not appear to have been any systematic or thorough antiquarian exam-

THE TOMBS OF THE CALIPHS. 155

ination of the ruins, — the science of Egyptology not being supposed to concern itself with monuments of later date than the Roman period, — so that hardly anything is known of the builders. The most important of these Moslem mortuary chapels belong to the period of the Baharide Mameluke Sultans, making them about a century older than those in the Kait Bey Cemetery. This may account for their more ruinous condition. " The whole of this region," Baedeker informs us, "is still used as a Moslem burial-ground, and in some cases the ancient mausolea have been converted into family burial-places."

South of this ruined necropolis, which, however, at a distance, with its lofty and elegant carved minarets, does not prepare the spectator for the scanty ruins remaining of the mosques themselves, — in some cases the minarets alone being erect, — are the group of mausolea containing the tombs of the Khedivial family. The tomb of the well-meaning but somewhat weak sovereign Tewfik — the nearest approach to a constitutional ruler, perhaps, that Egypt has ever had — will probably be the most interesting to sight-seers.

On the occasion of the funeral, a large number of buffaloes formed part of the procession, for the widow of the Khedive had given orders that a thousand poor persons should be fed daily for forty days at the tomb-side. This was quite in accordance with Oriental customs, and in its object it bears a strong analogy to the Roman Catholic practice of bequeathing sums of money to pay for masses for the repose of the testator's soul.

The curious custom is well described by Mr. Pollard in his " Land of the Monuments." This writer had witnessed the characteristic funeral banquet a few days after the ceremony. A large space near the tomb had been covered in for the crowd of poor Cairenes who were to take part in this commemorative banquet. In the centre was a small tent, which enclosed the royal tomb, which was covered with dark crimson cloth. Six imaums (Moslem priests) sat on the floor chanting, or rather droning, a ritual in a low monotone. The European visitors who were attracted by the strange spectacle, on leaving their cards with one of the attendants, were supplied with coffee and cigarettes, and then conducted to a large courtyard adjoining, where about five hundred poor people were seated on the ground in circles or messes of about a dozen. There were a few police, but the huge crowd of hungry and expectant diners was remarkably orderly. Soon appeared a procession of men bearing on their heads large trays piled up with pieces of coarse bread cooked with rice, followed by others carrying trays of buffalo beef boiled. A tray being placed in the centre of each little circle, the group at once helped themselves with all the eagerness of those to whom meat was a rarity, only indulged in on important festivities. After the meal, water was handed round in small brass bowls. Then another detachment of natives took their places after the courtyard had been cleared, were quickly formed into messes, and the meal was served as before. " It was a picturesque, interesting, and impressive scene, singularly Oriental, and certainly one never to be forgotten. There was in it a suggestion of the scene recorded in the Gospels of the feeding of the multitudes, in external appearance, orderly and regular disposition of rows on the ground, and the manner in which they fed themselves with the hand, — a custom which is still general in the East."

CHAPTER XII.

THE NATIONAL MUSEUM.

> Antiquity appears to have begun
> Long after thy primeval race was won.
> Thou couldst develop, if that withered tongue
> Might tell us what those sightless orbs have seen,
> How the world looked when it was fresh and young,
> And the great Deluge still had left it green;
> Or was it then so old that History's pages
> Contained no record of its early ages?
> *Address to a Mummy.* — HORACE SMITH.

THE Palace of Ghizeh, the old Haremlik (Palace of the Harem) of Ismail Pacha, has been, since 1889, when the antiquities were removed from Boulak, the home of the National Museum of Antiquities. The building, huge rambling structure that it is, with nearly one hundred rooms, is scarcely large enough to hold this vast collection. The Egyptian Government has long felt the urgent necessity of having a building specially constructed for a museum for this invaluable collection of antiquities. Not only is the Ghizeh Palace too small, but the danger from fire is a very serious one. The foundations of a new Egyptological Museum, which is to be thoroughly fire-proof, have recently (1897) been laid, and the building will probably be completed by the year 1900.

The museum contains, not only the largest, but the most valuable collection of Egyptian antiquities in the world. It is also considered by scholars and Egyptologists that in point of arrangement and classification of the objects collected here, the museum may serve as a model to most of the great museums of Europe. As a preliminary to the study of Egyptology, or even for an intelligent understanding of the monuments of the Upper Nile, a course of visits here is almost indispensable.

Since 1892 the museum has been much enlarged, and now contains some ninety rooms, arranged, for the most part, according to chronological order. This book is not intended as a guide-book, so it will suffice to say that I shall not attempt to convoy the visitor through the collection on any fixed plan.

The origin, scope, and inestimable value of this museum is so admirably summed up by Murray, in the latest edition of his Handbook, that his observations are worth quoting *verbatim et literatim:*

" This museum contains, with the exception of historical papyri, of which it does not possess any at all equal to those in the British Museum," — and we might add, to those in the Turin Egyptological Museum, — " the most instructive and valuable collection of Egyptian antiquities in the world; the result, with very few exceptions, of the indefatigable labours and researches of Mariette Pacha and his successors, who have spent many years in studying and excavating the old monuments and ruins of Egypt. At the accession of the Khedive Ismail, in 1863, everything connected with old Egyptian history was placed under the charge of Mariette Pacha, and all digging and excavating by others forbidden; and, as a result, the objects which formerly would have enriched foreign museums or private collections, are exhibited together in the most appropriate place for their study and examination, in the capital of the country whose ancient history they illustrate. Apart from the richness and number of the articles it contains, one great superiority enjoyed by this museum over all others is, that the places whence every object comes are accurately known; and, moreover, any fragment, however small, which seems to possess any historic or scientific interest, has been preserved."

Even to visit one-tenth of the rooms which compose this magnificent collection of antiquities means a whole day's hard work; and in attempting to give the most superficial

THE NATIONAL MUSEUM. 159

sketch of its principal contents, one is overwhelmed by the appalling magnitude of the task. The mere fact that there are not far short of one hundred rooms, loaded with the art treasures of all the dynasties down to the Ptolemies, is alone staggering to the ordinary visitor, who makes no claim to Egyptological lore. One is tempted to reiterate the reminder that the " City of the Caliphs " is not meant as a substitute for the standard guide-books. And yet, even the erudite Murray recognises the difficulty of serving as a *vade-mecum* to this vast treasure-house of early Egyptian civilisation, and devotes barely a page to what the more conscientious Baedeker dedicates nearly forty pages of his erudite, but somewhat stony, prose.

Let us, however, cast a hasty glance at some of the more striking features of the Museum. We have scarcely begun our pilgrimage, when a remarkable wooden statuette, known as the " Village Sheik," commands attention. This was found in a tomb near Sakkarah, by Mariette. It is one of the earliest specimens of the sculptor's art in existence, being attributed to the fourth dynasty. It owes its popular title to the fact that when it was brought to the surface the Arabs greeted it with shouts of " El-Sheik El-beled " (the Village Sheik). In this room also is the mummy of Aahmes I. (Amāsis), of the eighteenth dynasty. For some unknown reason — for the objects are usually arranged according to dynasties — it is placed here, and not with the other mummies of that period.

Of far greater artistic and antiquarian value than the " Village Sheik," is the green diorite statue (Room 5) of Chrephren, the builder of the second Pyramid. The modelling is wonderfully correct and lifelike, and the muscles would delight an anatomist. It was discovered by Mariette, in a well in the Temple of the Sphinx. Chrephren is represented seated on a throne which is decorated with the papyrus and lotus intertwined, which symbolises the union of

Upper and Lower Egypt. On the pedestal is inscribed: "The image of the golden Horus, Chrephren, beautiful god, lord of diadems." Dr. Wallis-Budge, who has written the most complete and most intelligible popular account of the Museum of any hitherto published, considers this statue "one of the most remarkable pieces of Egyptian sculpture extant."

In the first room on the ground floor is a remarkable painting, which is particularly interesting as the oldest specimen in existence known to antiquarians. It was discovered in a tomb-temple at Medoum. The picture, which is painted in water-colours, the pigments retaining their colouring in a remarkable manner, represents geese, and the execution shows considerable skill and knowledge of draughtsmanship. The picture dates from the fourth dynasty, so that we are looking at the work of an artist who lived from five to six thousand years ago.

The Hall of Jewels (No. 7) is of special interest to lady visitors. Formerly the finest collection of ancient Egyptian jewelry were those of Queen Aah-Hotep (mother of Aahmes I.), who flourished about 1600 B. C., which were found with the mummy of the Queen, in 1860, at Thebes. These, however, are quite eclipsed in beauty by those discovered by M. de Morgan (the successor as curator of the Museum of the great Egyptologist Mariette Pacha) in the Pyramid of Dashur, near Sakkarah, in 1894. These are, perhaps, the oldest jewels in the world, dating from the twelfth dynasty. The gold ornaments consist of bracelets, necklaces, pectorals, etc., of the Princess Hathor-Sat. The workmanship and design are very beautiful, and show the high pitch of artistic skill attained by the ancient Egyptian goldsmiths. Among the most beautiful objects of the earlier find is a model in gold of the sacred bark of the dead, with Amāsis I. seated in the stern. The rowers are of silver, the chariot of wood and bronze. A gold head-dress

THE NATIONAL MUSEUM. 161

inlaid with precious stones is another object of exquisitely beautiful workmanship.

Still making our way through the lower rooms, there is nothing of great attraction to the ordinary visitor till we reach Room 16, where is the famous Sphinx of the Shepherd Kings, cut from a block of black granite. This statue, with its features so different from the Egyptian type, is, no doubt, of special interest to the anthropologist and student of ethnology, but artistically it is disappointing. It was discovered by Mariette at Tanis (Zoan of the Old Testament), in 1863, and its origin and period are still a bone of contention with Egyptologists. Mariette considers it was made for one of the Hyksos sovereigns, popularly known as the Shepherd Kings. Dr. Wallis-Budge, however, attributes the statue to an earlier period.

In Room 40 is the famous Decree of Canopus, perhaps to the historian the most interesting object in the whole Museum. In all probability, had not the still more famous Rosetta stone — now one of the most valued treasures in the British Museum — been first found, this tablet, with its trheefold inscription, would have proved the key to the language and writings of the ancient Egyptians. Like the Rosetta stone, it is inscribed in hieroglyphics, with a popular translation in demotic (non-pictorial writing) characters, and Greek. The decree was made at Canopus, by an assembly of priests, in the reign of Ptolemy III. It ends with a resolution ordering a copy of this inscription to be placed in every large temple. Yet only two of these copies have ever been discovered; one is at this Museum (placed next the original), and the other at the Louvre Museum.

Of the recent acquisitions, the most interesting is the black granite stela which was discovered by Professor Petrie at Thebes, in 1896. It is a kind of palimpsest inscription, for there are signs of erasures of an earlier inscription by Amen-Hotep III. (B. C. 1500), under one by

Seti I. (Mer-en-Ptah). This stela is of the greatest importance to Biblical students, as on the back of the stone is a long description describing wars with the Libyans and Syrians, in which occurs the phrase, "The people of Israel is spoiled: it hath no Seed." This is the "*first allusion to the Israelites*" by name found as yet on any Egyptian monument, and is several centuries older than any allusion to them in Assyrian records." (Murray's "Handbook to Egypt.")

Perhaps the most popular features in the whole museum are the famous royal mummies of the Pharaohs. These are a recent acquisition, and the story of their find is rich in dramatic episodes, and is not without its humorous side, as will be seen from the amusing narrative of Mr. H. D. Traill, in "From Cairo to the Soudan Frontier," parts of which I quote below. The tombs and conjectural sites were not, at the time of the discovery of the royal mummies by the Arabs, as well guarded as now, and a large portion of the natives of the Theban plain for many years supplemented their earnings by the "harvest of the tombs," undetected by the native police. It seems that a certain Arab, called Ahmed, still known at Luxor as the "tomb-robber," — a sobriquet of which he is inordinately proud, — while digging with his companions in the "Tombs of the Kings" on the search for antiquities, struck upon a shaft, which Ahmed descended, and saw at once that he had hit upon a vast mortuary chamber, which meant untold riches to the discoverer. He cleverly prevented the necessity of sharing the booty with his fellows who had lowered him down the shaft, by calling upon them in an agitated voice to haul him up to the surface. On rejoining them, he declared that he had seen a ginn (evil spirit). Ahmed was as cautious as he was resourceful, and "thinking to give additional colour to his story of the tombs' being haunted by an evil spirit (which is supposed to manifest its presence by an intolerable stench)," he threw, one night, a donkey down the shaft.

A few days afterwards, every one in the neighbourhood was firmly convinced that an unclean spirit lived at the bottom of the shaft, and forthwith Ahmed had the monopoly in the lucrative find of antiquities, which he gradually disposed of to the foreign visitors at Luxor. This, of course, aroused suspicion in the minds of Egyptologists, and in 1881 Brugsch Bey and M. de Maspero made their celebrated expedition to Thebes in spite of the sweltering summer heat, and Ahmed, having been betrayed by his brother, conducted the two savants to the spot. The sensations of Brugsch Bey on the discovery of this most stupendous of all archæological finds is thus graphically described:

"My astonishment was so overpowering that I scarcely knew whether I was awake, or whether it was only a mocking dream. Resting on a coffin, in order to recover from my intense excitement, I mechanically cast my eyes over the coffin-lid, and distinctly saw the name of Seti I., father of Rameses II., both belonging to the nineteenth dynasty. A few steps farther on, in a simple wooden coffin, with his hands crossed on his breast, lay Rameses II., the great Sesostris himself. The farther I advanced, the greater the wealth displayed: thirty-six coffins, all belonging to kings, or queens, or princes, or princesses."

Even the least imaginative of travellers can hardly help being impressed at beholding the actual features of the Pharaoh of the Oppression, now brought to light after a lapse of thirty centuries; and yet there is another aspect of the case. After inspecting these disinterred monarchs, there comes an uneasy feeling that as representatives of a cultured race we are guilty of the grossest vandalism, and as Christians, of something approaching to sacrilege, as well as setting a bad example to the natives in rooting up the bones of the ancient kings and making them a kind of side-show to satisfy the curiosity of scientists, or to provide entertainment for the gaping tourist. Egyptologists and scholars may smile with contemptuous tolerance at this view as mere sentiment, but it is one that is held by a considerable number of intelligent visitors to Egypt.

Mr. Fraser Rae's vigorous protest is worth quoting: "To expose the remains of a man or woman to public view in the Gizeh Museum is a sickening and sad spectacle. Knowledge may be increased by rifling the sepulchres of the ancients and groping among the cerements of the dead, but I question if a single being is benefited by gazing at the leathern lineaments and limbs of ancient priests and kings." The legitimate curiosity of Egyptologists and scientists should be satisfied when the remains have been photographed, identified, and scientifically examined, and the remains should then be restored to their tomb. In no country are the remains of mortal men treated with greater indignity than in Egypt. Yet a parallel suggests itself irresistibly. Imagine the indignation of a highly cultured Bostonian if, at some remote future, Mount Auburn's beautiful cemetery should be treated as a mine in which shafts were sunk for the discovery of human remains, to be sold to foreigners as curios, or exposed in the chief museums of the country!

What, for instance, can be more opposed to all canons of good taste, to say nothing of art, than the exhibition of the gruesome relics of King Seqenen Ra (seventeenth dynasty), who was killed while fighting against one of the Hyksos kings, some thirty-five hundred years ago. The appearance of this mutilated mummy is graphically and forcibly described in the following sketch by Mr. Moberly Bell: "Look at him closely and read his history, told as graphically as if by Macaulay, and perhaps more truthfully. That wound there, inflicted by a mace or hatchet, which has cleft the left cheek, broken the lower jaw, and laid bare the side teeth, was probably the first, and must have felled him to the ground. See there, how his foes fell on him! That downward hatchet-blow split off an enormous splinter of the skull. That other blow, just above the right eye, must have been a lance wound, passing through his temple, and probably finished him. Look at the agony in the face, and the tongue bitten through in anguish. He gave his life dearly, did Seqenen Ra; and after the fight the body has been embalmed and had decent though hurried sepulture." There is a touch of unconscious irony in this reference to " decent sepulture," when we consider that this ill-fated monarch, after enjoying undisturbed burial for so many thousand years, has been at length exhumed to serve as a spectacle for nineteenth century tourists, and as a peg for their flippant cynicism.

It is usually supposed that embalming the dead and converting them into mummies was the earliest and universal mode of disposing of the dead among the ancient Egyptians. Recent researches have, however, tended to discredit this popular view.

Fresh light has been thrown on the methods of burial of the ancient Egyptians by a remarkably able and suggestive article in a recent number of the " Contemporary Review" (June, 1897), by Prof. Flinders Petrie. In this article, the well-known Egyptologist ventilates a very remarkable but highly plausible theory, which attempts to show that a kind of modified, or what can be better described as ceremonial, cannibalism obtained during the age of the pyramid-building kings (? circa 3500 B.C.) of the Ancient Empire.

While excavating among the tombs of that age at Deshasheh, some sixty miles south of Cairo, in the winter of 1896-7, Doctor Petrie was astonished to find, after a careful examination of the bodies, that a considerable number had been most carefully and elaborately " boned " after death. The bones of the skeletons had in fact been most carefully rearranged after removal of the flesh and tissues, and the skeleton carefully reconstructed and buried. This wholesale cutting up of the bodies could not have been due to plunder, injury, or the act of enemies towards the victims of war, — the most natural explanation, — as was first conclusively proved from the number of female skeletons thus treated, the careful method of burial, and the distribution of the tombs. The Professor's conclusion is that this unusual method of sepulture points to an adoption of a modified form of cannibalism, akin to that of the later Libyan invaders who overran Egypt about 3000 B. C. It is well known that these tribes practised a kind of cannibalism. Doctor Petrie considers that in all probability the actual consumption of the bodies of the dead — which, by the way, was often done from the idea of honouring the dead, or of benefiting the consumer, who would thus attract to himself the good qualities of the person eaten — was not at that time the essential part of the ceremony; but the flesh was carefully removed, bones separated, and so forth, as if actual cannibalism were to take place.

This mode of sepulture was later modified by the influence of a ruling race, who practised embalming and mummification, with all its attendant complex ceremonies. This, in short, is an outline of Professor Petrie's theory.

Though the Ghizeh Museum is unquestionably, taken as a whole, the finest Egyptological museum in the world, some of the departments are poorly represented, notably the collections of historical papyri, scarabs, and Græco-Roman antiquities. More valuable papyri are to be found in the British Museum, the Louvre, and in the Museum of Egyptian Antiquities in Turin. This latter museum contains many of the antiquities collected by Napoleon's commission of savants at the time of the French occupation of Egypt. The famous Prissé papyrus, in the Bibliothèque Nationale of Paris, is the oldest in the world, and was written about 2500 B. C.

The Turin papyrus, the most valuable of any yet discovered, was the principal source from which Brugsch and other historians drew their Egyptian chronologies. It contains a complete list of all the sovereigns, from the quasi-mythical god-kings down to those of the Hyksos dynasty (B. C. 4400 to B. C. 1700). Unfortunately, the papyrus is in parts almost undecipherable, so that the names of some of the kings in the usually accepted list are partly conjectural.

In former days, Dr. Wallis-Budge observes, the collection of scarabs was very large and complete; but the best have been disposed of at various times, and many private collectors, not to speak of the great museums of Europe, possess far more complete and more valuable collections.

As to Ptolemaic and other Graeco-Roman antiquities, the authorities of the Cairo Museum disclaim any desire to add to their collection, as the Museum at Alexandria, which was opened in 1895, was specially built to preserve the collection of all Greek and Roman antiquities discovered in Egypt, and many of the objects in the Ghizeh galleries have been transferred to the Alexandrian Museum.

Just as a visit to the monuments of Upper Egypt should be supplemented by a visit to the matchless collection of antiquities enshrined in the Ghizeh Palace, so it is essential for a right understanding and appreciation of mediæval Saracenic art to visit the Museum of Arabian Art in connection with the exploration of the mosques. The Museum is in a temporary building in the courtyard of the Mosque El-Hakim, and consists chiefly of objects of artistic or antiquarian interest, collected from ruined mosques or rescued from the hands of the dealers in antiquities, who for years, with the cognisance of the guardians, had been pillaging certain of these mosques. The Museum is mainly due to the zeal of the late Rogers Bey, and to Franz Pacha, formerly director under the Wakfs Administration. In its temporary home the collection is rather cramped, and the Government has recently voted a sum of £32,000 for a special building, the foundation-stone of which was laid in the spring of the present year (1897).

The most beautiful and characteristic objects will be found in Rooms 1, 3, and 5. In the first room is the incomparable collection of enamelled mosque-lamps. Most of these have been taken from the mosques, especially that of Sultan Hassan. The dates of these lamps are of the thirteenth, fourteenth, and fifteenth centuries, but their place of manufacture is unknown. The earlier of these lamps, which constitute the chief glory of the Museum, are in the purest style of Arabic decoration, though probably the fifteenth century ones are not indigenous, but imported from Murano. Scarcely a hundred of these lamps are extant, and most are to be found in this unique collection. In Rooms 5 and 7 is a large and representative collection of Mushrabiyeh (lattice-work) and mosaic woodwork. Other rooms contain specimens of metal-work, faience, stucco, pottery, etc.

In one essential respect this Museum, says Mr. Stanley Lane-Poole, differs from others. The objects here are relative, and were not designed as separate works of art. They are, in fact, dependent upon the monuments to which they once belonged. Most of the objects consist of portions of the decoration and furniture of mosques and private houses. This, of course, makes it the more regrettable that, owing to the neglected condition of the mosques, they cannot be seen *in situ*, where they would be more in harmony with their environment.

CHAPTER XIII.

THE ACROPOLIS OF CAIRO.

> Ambition, like a torrent, ne'er looks back;
> It is a swelling, and the last affection
> A great mind can put off. It is a rebel
> Both to the soul and reason, and enforces
> All laws, all conscience; tramples on Religion,
> And offers violence to Loyalty.
>
> BEN JONSON.

THE citadel which frowns over Cairo appears, at a distance, to overhang the city, and, no doubt, in the age of Saladin its position was as impregnable as Gibraltar or Malta. It is, however, completely commanded by the Mokattam Hills immediately behind it, and in 1805 Mehemet Ali was able to rake it completely with his cannon posted on these heights, and took it with little difficulty. Its walls are built of the stones which formed the casing of the Great Pyramid, and this waste of precious material seems especially wanton and inexcusable, considering the proximity of the Gebel Mokattam, which is one vast quarry of excellent building material.

The great adventurer who, with some reason, has been styled the Oriental Napoleon, is, indeed, the *genius loci* in this grim fortress. His is the one dominant figure in the later history of Egypt, and a slight sketch of his career may conveniently be given here, when describing the scene of his triumphs and his crimes.

Mehemet Ali's life is as romantic and remarkable, and as rich in eventful episodes, as that of his great namesake the founder of the Moslem faith, or as that of Saladin, or, to come to modern times, as that of Napoleon, or Bernadotte. It is a curious coincidence that Mehemet Ali, Napoleon I., and Wellington, each came into the world in the same year — 1769. Mehemet came of humble parentage, his father being a fisherman, and he does not appear to have received any education at all. In fact, even when Viceroy of Egypt, he scarcely knew how to write. His boyhood was adventurous, and when quite a lad he distinguished himself by leading an attack on some pirates who had been pillaging the coast, driving them off, and recovering the spoil. This early display of promise brought him to the notice of the governor of the province, and, helped, it is said, by the influence of the wife of this functionary, he succeeded him in office on his death, and married his widow. When Napoleon invaded Egypt, Mehemet saw his opportunity, and, being given the command of a troop of irregulars, sailed for his future kingdom. He distinguished himself conspicuously in this short campaign, and was promoted to the rank of colonel. After the evacuation of Egypt by the French troops, the Mameluke beys — who had, ever since Egypt became a Turkish pachalic, regarded the Turkish viceroy as a mere *roi fainéant*, and had practically obtained control of the country — attempted to set up a viceroy of their own, and rebelled against the Turkish governor, Khosref Pacha. Mehemet, foreseeing on whose side victory was likely to remain, took a prominent part in the agitation against Turkish rule, and threw in his lot with the beys. Summoned to a midnight conference by the Pacha, ostensibly to discuss the grievances of the soldiery, Mehemet, fully realising that the moment for overt action had arrived, sent a polite acceptance of the significant invitation. "Then, summoning his Albanian soldiery," — I quote Warburton's spirited description of this dramatic scene, — " gave them the Pacha's message. ' I am sent for by the Pacha, and you know what destiny awaits the advocate of your wrongs in a midnight audience,' he exclaimed. 'I will go, but shall I go alone?' Four thousand swords flashed back the Albanians' answer, and their shout of fierce defiance gave Khosref Pacha warning to escape to the Citadel; there, it is unnecessary to say, he declined to receive his dangerous guest. 'Now, then,' said Mehemet Ali, 'Cairo is for sale, and the strongest sword will buy it.' The Albanians applauded the pithy sentiment, and instantly proceeded to put it into execution by electing Mehemet Ali as their leader. He opened the gates of the city to the hostile Mamelukes, defeated Khosref Pacha, took him prisoner at Damietta, and was acknowledged as general of the army by the beys, in gratitude for his services."

After the defeat of Khosref, the common enemy of the Albanian and Mameluke soldiery, a great rivalry sprang up between the two chief Mameluke beys, Osman El-Bardesee and Elfee, who were virtually the rulers of the country,— the government, though nominally a tributary pachalic of the Porte, being really a military oligarchy. Mehemet, though backed by his Albanian troops, was not yet strong enough to attack the Mameluke leaders, and contented himself with stirring up dissensions between the two parties, and ingratiating himself with the Cairenes as well as with the army. His intrigues against El-Bardesee were crowned with success, and showed considerable powers of statesmanship and diplomacy. The Bey was both governor of the city and commander of the Albanian troops; so Mehemet, by his agents, incited the soldiers to demand their arrears of pay, — a perennial grievance with these mercenaries,— and at the same time he encouraged the citizens of Cairo to resist the heavy contributions levied by El-Bardesee in order to satisfy the demands of his mutinous troops. The Bey, unable to make headway against this simultaneous resistance, sought safety in flight. His rival, Elfee Bey, had already fled. Mehemet Ali, with his Albanians, then took possession of the Citadel, and while awaiting the firman for the appointment of a new pacha, assumed the reins of government. Khursheed Pacha, Mehemet's nominee, was duly invested with the viceroyalty; but he was regarded merely as a convenient figurehead by Mehemet, who, in a short time, having by intrigue got the support of the Mamelukes, was himself named viceroy in 1805. In the next year his powerful rivals El-Bardesee Bey and Elfee Bey, who had still a considerable following, died, and left Mehemet with only one serious enemy to fear,—the Sultan, who was jealous of his powerful vassal.

In 1811 he firmly established his power by crushing the turbulent element of the Mamelukes, who were "sacrificed as a hecatomb to the peace of the province." The only possible palliation for this great blot on Mehemet Ali's career, by which he " waded through slaughter to a throne," was that the extermination of these powerful mercenaries was necessary for the security of his throne, and he had, himself, some reason to suspect treachery at their hands. At all events, the massacre was not so wantonly cruel as that of the Janissaries, some ten years later, by his suzerain Mahmoud II., who was styled, with grim irony, Mahmoud the Reformer.

The history of Egypt for the next thirty years is simply the history of Mehemet's various campaigns of conquest. Up to 1831 his victorious career went on unchecked. In this year, after taking Acre and several other Syrian pachalics, he felt himself strong enough to declare war with the Porte, who had refused to recognise his Syrian conquests. After several successes over the Ottoman troops, the European Powers intervened on behalf of the Porte. Peace was made on the terms that Mehemet should evacuate Asia Minor beyond the Taurus, and be formally invested with the title of Pacha of Syria, for which he would pay tribute. Mehemet Ali's position was, no doubt, considerably strengthened by his new territories being nominally under the sway of Turkey. " His principal security consisted in his being ostensibly a dependent of the Porte; and he was fully aware that Europe would respect his territory only so long as it professedly belonged to the Sultan: that position once abandoned, any person had the same right, that ' of the strongest hand,' to Egypt, that Mehemet or any other could lay claim to."

The peace was, however, temporary. The success of one who was more his rival than his vassal did not dispose Sultan Mahmoud to look favourably upon Mehemet, and soon a pretext for attacking him afresh was found, and war broke out again. Ibrahim Pacha (Mehemet's eldest son), however, inflicted a crushing defeat on the Sultan's army at Nezib, and the fleet (which had just been refitted) surrendered. Even Constantinople itself was menaced by the victorious troops, and the Sultan was compelled to fall back upon the good offices of Great Britain and the European Powers, who compelled Mehemet to restore Syria to the Porte. Virtually, then, as early as 1841, the Ottoman Empire was placed under the protection of the Great Powers, and the one great formula of European politics — the " integrity of the Turkish Empire " — which has ever since been a cardinal postulate in the Eastern question, was first enunciated.

The Powers had the greatest difficulty in inducing Mehemet, who was encouraged in his refusal by France, to sign the convention. Finally, by the diplomatic pressure brought to bear upon him by Admiral (then Commodore) Napier, backed by the strong personal influence of the envoy, the Viceroy consented to sign it. Napier, with the convention in his pocket, went fifteen times to interview Mehemet before he succeeded in obtaining his signature. In the London Foreign Office the story was current at the time that a casual reference to the Queen of England as a "lucky woman," by Admiral Napier, did more than any arguments or threats to induce Mehemet to give way. The interpreter, who was also British vice-consul, was a Mohammedan. He was sent for by the Viceroy, when a conversation to this effect took place:

"You were, Effendi, in London, at the Queen's coronation. Were there any bad omens?"

"None; only good omens."

"Did you see her on that occasion?"

"I saw her twice."

"Were you near her?"

"No; but I was near her at the Lord Mayor's dinner that she went to."

"How did she strike you?"

"She was young, blooming, and innocent — very affable, and looked so happy."

"But did you think that luck was written on her forehead?"

"I did not think then on the matter; but now that you ask me, I do think that it was. Allah takes into consideration the prayers of the guileless. The young Queen's eyes, I heard, ran over, when at her coronation she prayed Him to protect and guide her, and to govern all her doings for the honour and happiness of England."

"And so you conclude that she is lucky?"

"Yes."

Next morning, the same agent went with the *ultimatum*. Mehemet was quite willing to sign. "What was the use," he remarked, "of withstanding the lucky Queen of a great nation?"

Had not the Great Powers come to the aid of Turkey, which, deprived of its fleet and troops, was absolutely at Egypt's mercy, Mehemet could have dictated his own terms before the walls of Constantinople, and might even have dispossessed the hapless Sultan of his throne, and instead of founding a new dynasty in Egypt, raised up a new one over the whole Ottoman Empire, to replace that of the House of Othman.

The dreams of foreign conquest, and of bringing Syria and the Levant under the rule of Egypt, were effectually dispelled by the determined attitude of the Great Powers; and for the rest of his reign, till his death in 1849, Mehemet had to confine his energies to developing the natural resources of Egypt, fostering native industries, encouraging trade, establishing schools, building canals and other public works. He also did his best to introduce Western manners and customs, and to create a Civil Service based on European methods. Though Mehemet did so much for the material progress of his country, he did not succeed — even if he could be said to have seriously attempted such a task — in infusing a sentiment of nationality, or in creating anything approaching to an expression of public opinion among the Egyptians; nor, for the matter of that, have his successors succeeded in inspiring a spirit of patriotism in their subjects. But, after all, to alter the national characteristics of a people is the work of centuries. How can one expect to inspire a feeling of loyalty in a race which, from the time of Cleopatra, has never had a ruler of Egyptian birth, or to arouse a sentiment of nationality among those who have never had a national cause, and whose lives for thousands of years have been passed in one long effort to satisfy the tax-collectors? This is what makes the plausible party cry, " Egypt for the Egyptians," little more than a mere sentiment almost impossible of realisation.

Such is a brief outline of the life of the greatest ruler Egypt has had since the Ptolemies. We will now proceed to explore the fortress which is so intimately associated with his name.

This fortress is the most striking landmark of Cairo, and is, perhaps, one of the most interesting of the historic buildings of the Egyptian capital. The name of its real founder, Saladin, is apt to be overshadowed in the minds of visitors by that of Mehemet Ali, who only partially restored it. This is not to be wondered at, for the name of "The Napoleon of Egypt" is closely associated with the chief historical events connected with the later history of the Citadel. The nomenclature, too, of the chief objects of interest partly accounts for this prominence given to the traditions of this great ruler. For instance, the famous Alabaster Mosque, one of the most striking in Cairo, and the great modern highway leading straight as the crow flies from the Ezbekiya to the Citadel, are both called after the great national hero; while the founder of the fortress is only commemorated by Joseph's Well, — Yusuf, the Arabic form of Joseph, being Saladin's other name, — and even this famous shaft is popularly ascribed by tourists to the Patriarch Joseph. The Acropolis of Cairo is, like the Kremlin and the Alhambra, a walled town within a city; and, besides, several mosques, hospitals, barracks, a palace, an arsenal, mint, and other Government buildings are, or were once, comprised within its precincts.

In the opinion of the Cairo guides and dragomans, the most interesting site within the walls is the one where Emin Bey made his historic, or rather legendary, leap over the battlements, to escape the slaughter of the Mameluke beys by Mehemet Ali, in 1811.

"The beys came, mounted on their finest horses, in magnificent uniforms, forming the most superb cavalry in the world. After a very flattering reception from the Pacha, they were requested to parade in the court of the Citadel. They entered the fortification unsuspectingly: the portcullis fell behind the last of the proud procession; a moment's glance revealed to them their doom. They dashed forwards — in vain! Before, behind, around them nothing was visible but blank, pitiless walls and barred windows; the only opening was towards the bright blue sky; even that was soon darkened by their funeral pile of smoke, as volley after volley flashed from a thousand muskets behind the ramparts upon this defenceless and devoted band. Startling and fearfully sudden as was their death, they met it as became their fearless character, — some with arms crossed upon their mailed bosoms, and turbaned heads devoutly bowed in prayer; some with flashing swords and fierce curses, alike unavailing against their dastard and ruthless foe. All that chivalrous and splendid throng, save one, sank rapidly beneath the deadly fire into a red and writhing mass; that one was Emin Bey. He spurred his charger over a heap of his slaughtered comrades, and sprang upon the battlements. It was a dizzy height, but the next moment he was in the air — another, and he was disengaging himself from his crushed and dying horse amid a shower of bullets. He escaped, and found safety in the sanctuary of a mosque, and ultimately in the deserts of the Thebaid."

Thus Warburton graphically describes the Bey's remarkable escape from this treacherous massacre. It is a pity to spoil such a thrilling and dramatic story, but there is little doubt that this remarkable feat of horsemanship is purely legendary. Emin Bey, as a matter of fact, never attended this grim levée of his Sultan. He had been warned at the last moment, and fled into Syria.

The Mosque of Mehemet Ali was built, it is said, in a spirit of cynicism, on the very threshold of this scene of carnage, by the grim old Sultan. It is true that some chroniclers attribute a more charitable motive to the choice of a site, and suggest that it was built by Mehemet as an expiation of this ruthless massacre. The following incident, however, does not give colour to this suggestion: More than thirty years after this terrible crime, a privileged Englishman, admitted to view the bedchamber of the aged Viceroy, was struck by the fact that the only picture in the room was a portrait of the Mameluke who had escaped his vengeance. "The sole memento of that ancient crime," aptly observes Mr. H. D. Traill, "which

Mehemet Ali cared to cherish, was one which would serve to remind him, for precaution's sake, of the features of his one surviving enemy."

This beautiful mosque is well worth a visit, though it takes a very low rank among the Cairene mosques in the estimation of archæologists. It is quite modern, the greater portion dating from 1857, when Said Pacha added a great portion to the original mosque of Mehemet, and it is said to be a poor copy of the Mosque of Nasr Osmaniya at Constantinople. The proportions are, however, imposing, and the interior is very richly decorated. The lofty and graceful minarets are justly admired. It is one of the show mosques of Cairo, despite its artistic demerits, and owes, no doubt, its popularity to its size, its noble situation, — from every point of Cairo this striking landmark dominates the city, — and as the burial-place of Mehemet Ali.

The Mosque of Mohammed Nasr, son of the Sultan Qalaun, is generally known as the Old Mosque, in contradistinction to that of Mehemet Ali. It was formerly considered the royal mosque of Cairo, — a position now held by Sultan Hassan Mosque, — but for many years it served as a military prison. Thanks to the exertions of the Ancient Monuments Preservation Committee, it has been restored, and can now be seen by visitors. The arcaded quibla is beautifully ornamented with rich arabesques. Of the other mosques in the Citadel, the only one worthy of inspection is the Mosque of Sulieman Pacha,[1] who is better known as Sultan Selim, the Ottoman conqueror of Egypt (1517). It is an exact replica in miniature of St. Sophia at Constantinople, and is one of the best examples of the Turkish type of mosque in Cairo.

Joseph's Well is a huge square shaft of vast proportions

---

[1] For some reasons the title of Sulieman Pacha was that chosen by the French renegade officer, Colonel Sève, to whom the late Khedive Ismail intrusted the organisation of his army.

THE ACROPOLIS OF CAIRO. 179

and great depth, cut through the solid rock. It need hardly be observed that, though of respectable antiquity, it has nothing to do with the Hebrew patriarch. It is named after Saladin, who either excavated it, or opened up an existing well hewn in the rock by the ancient Egyptians. This latter theory is now generally accepted by Egyptologists, and certainly the vast proportions of this well are in favour of its having been built in an age which produced the most stupendous architectural monuments in existence. The depth to the level of the water is nearly three hundred feet. It is quite worth exploration. The descent is by means of a kind of spiral roadway, formed of a gently inclined plane, so broad that a carriage might almost be driven down to the first platform. It is said that the bottom of the well is on the same level as the Nile. The water is now only used by the natives, as, since 1866, the Citadel has been supplied with water by the Cairo Water Company.

The view of Cairo, especially at sunset, from the southern ramparts is very fine, and is justly included among the world's most famous points of view. In natural beauty and varied interests, the prospect deserves to rank with the view from Europa Point at Gibraltar, or from the Alhambra over the golden plain of the Vega, or with the noble panorama of sea and land from the Hermitage at Capri, or from the Greek Theatre at Taormina, to name a few of the fairest prospects in the whole range of European scenery. Yet, grand though the view is from the Citadel, that from the summit of the Mokattam, which towers over Saladin's stronghold, is still more magnificent, being far more commanding and comprehensive. Here, not only Cairo, but the Egyptian Delta, lies below the spectator.

Very graphically and suggestively does Mr. Moberly Bell describe the innumerable historical associations this unique view summons up:

"The forty, or let us say seventy, centuries look across to us from the Pyramids; the Sphinx, from even a remoter period, stands still waiting the answer to its never-solved riddle; and down from long ages, with huge *lacunæ*, indeed, we trace the history of the world, marked by the ruined foot-prints of Time. There is Memphis, earliest of cities; there are the colossal tombs of the ancient empire, stretching from Sakkarah to Ghizeh. To the right lies Heliopolis, with its Sun-temple of the Middle Monarchy; and the Nile hurrying by to Tanis of the Hyksos, to Sais and Bubastis of the New Empire, to Naukratis of the Greeks, and to Alexandria of the Ptolemies. There is Babylon of the Romans, away to the left, — the Fostat of the Arabs; El Azhar of the Abbasides; El Katayeh of the Tooloonides; and Cairo itself of the Fatimites. At our feet lies the Citadel of the Great Salah-ed-Deen,— Saladin of our childhood,— the founder of the Ayyoubites. The minarets of Kalaun and Hassan, Kait Bey and El Ghuri, recall the Mameluke dynasties; and there, by the Mosque El Mowayud, is the Bab El Zuweilah, where the Turkish Sultan Selim hanged Toman, last of his race, assumed the title of Khaliph, and secured Egypt to the hated rule of the Turk."

This wealth of historical tradition, which serves to make the prospect a kind of mnemonic object-lesson in Egyptian history, is apt to distract one's attention from the æsthetic features of this glorious view:

> While far as sight can reach, beneath as clear
> And blue a heaven as ever blest this sphere,
> Gardens and minarets and glittering domes,
> And high-built temples fit to be the homes
> Of mighty gods, and pyramids whose hour
> Outlasts all time, above the waters tower.
>   MOORE.

CHAPTER XIV.

OLD CAIRO AND THE COPTIC CHURCHES.

THE principal facts in the early history of Old Cairo are familiar to every tourist; and there is scarcely a guide-book, or book of Egyptian travel, which omits to mention that Old Cairo, now fenced off from the modern capital by an extensive barrier of huge mounds of rubbish, was formerly called Fostat, in allusion to the tent (fostât) of the victorious Amru, who pitched his headquarters here when he invaded Egypt in 638 A. D. The Mohammedans, however, had only followed the example of the Romans, who, a few hundred years before, had utilised this commanding position as a military post. This garrison town, in turn, occupied the site of a city founded by Babylonian colonists, under Cambyses, in 525 B. C. Perhaps, as in the case with most of the buried cities of Egypt, Old Cairo can trace its history back to a Pharaonic period; but this is not thoroughly established, and in the Persian period we may consider we have got to the bed-rock as regards Old Cairo's history. Diodorus is responsible for the statement that it was founded by Assyrian captives in the time of Rameses II. Modern scientific historians are not often disposed to treat seriously this historian's statements as regards the early history of Egypt, as myth, legend, and unsupported tradition are inextricably commingled with historical facts. This assertion, however, is of indirect value as an argument in favour of the extreme antiquity of Old Cairo, as it clearly shows that in his time it was generally believed that Babylon of Egypt was of very ancient foundation. Some writers, indeed, have attempted to identify this city with Karkar, under which title there is a reference to it, according to these authorities, in a stela of Thotmes IV. (1700 B. C.) The site was of great strategic and political importance, as it commanded both the Nile and the Delta, and it was also on the direct route between the two most important cities of Lower Egypt, — Memphis and Heliopalis.

Some historians, tempted by the etymological coincidence, have brought forward an ingenious argument in favour of a close connection between this Egyptian Babylon and Heliopolis, and suggest that Babylon is a corruption of Bab-li-On; that is, Gate of On (Heliopolis).

These prefatory remarks will perhaps help the non-historical visitor to understand that Old Cairo is not, as might be supposed from the name, a mere suburb or native quarter of Cairo, but a distinct city, separated from Modern Cairo by half-ruined streets and mounds of rubbish. It is fully two miles beyond the walls, and though the chief sights are more interesting to those fond of historical and antiquarian studies, two or three days should be devoted to its exploration. In fact, if the visitor wishes something more than a cursory inspection of the ancient Coptic churches, a whole week should be devoted to these Greek and Coptic churches and monasteries which cluster round the ruins of the Roman Babylon, the Mosque of Amru, and the ruins of Old Babylon. The usual way of visiting Old Cairo is on donkey-back, but a quicker and less tiring method is to take the train to Madagh Station, which is within a few minutes' walk of the old Roman Fortress.

The interest of the Amru Mosque is rather historical than architectural. In a certain sense it may be called the oldest mosque in Egypt; but there are few traces of the original mosque. In fact, as we see it, it is one of the most recent in Cairo, dating from the fourteenth century. In the rebuilding, however, the original form — a copy of the Kaaba of Mecca — was preserved, and some of the old materials were incorporated in the walls. This mosque is still held in the greatest veneration by the Mohammedans of Cairo, who call it the "Crown of Mosques." Just as the Mosque of Sultan Hassan ranks as the great Mosque of the State or Royal Mosque, this ancient foundation of Amru is regarded by Cairenes as peculiarly the mother-church of Cairo; and a prophecy, implicitly believed by devout Moslems, predicts the downfall of Moslem power whenever this mosque shall fall to decay. It is here that the universal service of supplication, when a tardy or insufficient rising of the Nile threatens the prosperity of Egypt, takes place, — a service attended by the Khedive, the principal officers of state, and the ulemas, and officials of all the Cairo mosques.

The gloomy interior, with its forest of pillars (many being spoils from the temples of Memphis and Heliopolis) resembles the El-Azhar Mosque. The late Khedive contemplated the complete restoration of this mosque, but little has been done.

A curious architectural feature is the pointed arch, which, according to some authorities, is the earliest prototype of the Norman arch known. Fergusson, however, is of opinion that these pointed arches are of later date than the round ones adjoining them.

The much disputed question of the origin of the pointed arch mainly concerns architectural experts, and most visitors will consider the "Pillar of the Whip," concerning which various legends are told by the guides, as the most interesting object. As a preliminary to the story, the guide will point out certain veins in the marble which are said to be the marks of the Caliph's kourbash whip. The legend runs that when Amru built the mosque, he wished to place some kind of relic from the Mecca mosque within the new sanctuary, and therefore requested his master, the Caliph

Omar, to send him one of the columns from the Kaaba. The Caliph complied, and bade a certain column transport itself to Egypt. The request being unheeded, the enraged Caliph struck the offending column with his kourbash, whereupon the column obeyed. This story being received with a sufficient show of credulity, the guide will probably proceed to point out some curious formations in the veining of the marble, which he declares are the names of Mohammed and the Sultan Sulieman. As few visitors can read Arabic, this assertion is not likely to be disputed.

Next to the miraculous column, the chief objects of interest in the estimation of the guides are a pair of columns between which a man can barely squeeze. These are known as the "Needle's Eye," and the tradition is that this feat can only be performed by men of the highest integrity, the Arabs apparently attributing peculiar virtue to tenuity of build. These columns have, however, been recently walled up by the Khedive Ismail. In fact, — according to the story told by English residents, — the space was walled up by Ismail's orders, because he saw at a glance that his portly form could not stand the test! Consequently, he did not think it fitting that the salvation promised to his subjects should be denied to their sovereign.

Clustered within and around the ruined walls of the old Roman Castle are many Coptic churches and convents. With the exception of Abou Sergeh, generally called St. Mary's Church, they are little known to visitors, or, for the matter of that, to the European residents; yet their high architectural importance and the beautiful workmanship of the internal decoration invite careful inspection. The comparative neglect of these early Christian churches on the part of travellers is probably partly due to the ignorance of the dragomans and guides, whose knowledge of the ecclesiastical buildings of Old Cairo is, as a rule, confined to the Mosque of Amru, the Church of St. Mary, and the Greek convent. It is, therefore, the best plan to dispense with the ordinary Cairo guide and engage one on the spot. There are nearly a dozen Coptic churches in Old Cairo; but except to those who take a special interest in ecclesiastical architecture and art, a visit to those mentioned above, and the churches of Abou Sephin and El-Adra, both situated within the walls of the old Roman citadel, will probably suffice.

The one modern authority on the Coptic churches is Mr. A. J. Butler, whose monograph, "The Ancient Coptic Churches of Egypt," ranks as a classic, and should certainly be consulted by every person who wishes to obtain full and accurate information about these unique sanctuaries.

The exterior of a Coptic church is characterised by a marked simplicity and absence of decoration, and with the windows looking like loop-holes, it has more resemblance to a fort, and the Byzantine basilica influence is clearly traceable. The internal arrangements approximate more nearly to those of a Greek church than to a Roman Catholic or Protestant temple. The body of the church is divided into three compartments separated by wooden screens. The first is a kind of vestibule; the second compartment is set apart for women; and the third, next the choir, is reserved for men. East of the chancel or choir is the hekel, or sanctuary, and behind this again the apse, with the episcopal throne. The ritual in some respects resembles that of the Greek church. There is no organ, the only instruments being cymbals, and brass bells struck with a rod held in the hand. "The voices of the clergy, as they 'praise God with the loud cymbals' have a singularly wild and impressive effect. There are no images, but a great number of paintings in the stiff Byzantine style, but some of them are not wanting in a kind of rude grandeur. The principal painting is always that of our Lord in the act of benediction."

The Copts are supposed to be the direct descendants of the ancient Egyptians, and there is a less admixture with alien conquering races than is the case with other inhabitants of the Nile Valley. The early Egyptian, or Coptic, church dates probably a couple of centuries before the famous edict of Theodosius, A. D. 379, — that religious *coup d'état* which officially established Christianity as the state religion of Egypt. The earliest Christians were probably monks.

"To Egypt," observes Mr. Lane-Poole, "belongs the debatable honour of having invented monasticism." Though the early Egyptian church is to all intents and purposes the Coptic church, the historical origin of the church dates from 451 A. D., when, adopting the heresies of Eutychus, it seceded from the mother-church of Rome; and from that time its believers rank as a distinct sect. Their ritual, however, resembles in many respects that of the Greek church.

Their churches and convents are scattered throughout all Egypt, from the Mediterranean shore to the Theban plain. The most important settlement is, however, in Cairo, where there are two large Coptic colonies, — one in the neighbourhood of the uninteresting, miscalled Coptic cathedral, north of the Ezbekiya, which is seldom visited by tourists; and the other, scattered among the ruins of the old Roman Castle of Babylon.

"When we enter the stronghold, the strange character of the fortress grows upon us. Passing through narrow lanes, narrower and darker and dustier even than the back alleys of Cairo, we are struck by the deadly stillness of the place. The grated windows are small and few, and but for an occasional heavy door half-open, and here and there the sound of a voice in the recesses of the houses, we might question whether the fortress was inhabited at all. Nothing, certainly, indicates that these plain walls contain six sumptuous churches, with their dependent chapels, each of which is full of carvings, pictures, vestments, and furniture, which in their way cannot be matched. A Coptic church is like a Mohammedan harem: it must not be visible from the outside. High walls hide everything from view. The Copts are shy of visitors, and the plain exteriors are a sufficient proof of their desire to escape that notice which in bygone days aroused Mohammedan cupidity and fanaticism, and now too often excites the no less dangerous envy of the moneyed traveller.

"Of the six churches within the fortress of Babylon, three are of the highest interest; for though the Greek Church of St. George, perched on the top of the round Roman tower, is finely decorated with Damascus and Rhodean tiles and silver lamps, the tower itself, with its central well and great staircase, and curious radiating chambers, is more interesting than the church above it. Of the three principal Coptic churches, that of St. Sergius, or Abu Sarga, is the most often visited, on account of the tradition that it was in its crypt that the Holy Family rested when they journeyed to the land of Egypt."[1]

As if to give some colour to this tradition, the Copts exhibit a manger in which the Infant Christ was said to have been laid. Apart from this exceedingly doubtful testimony of the supposed manger, it is possible that this crypt does mark the alleged site. It is certainly many centuries older than the church. The screen here is particularly fine; and among other valuable specimens of wood-carving is a beautifully executed representation of the Nativity in high-relief.

The most striking, however, of all the Babylonian churches is that known as the Mn'allaka, or Hanging Church. It is so called because it is built in between two bastions of the Roman wall, so that it has the appearance of being suspended in mid-air. Apart from this factitious attraction, which naturally makes it the most popular with guides and tourists of all the churches contained in the castle precincts, the church is noteworthy in many respects. It is the oldest of the Coptic churches in Old Cairo, part of it dating probably from the third century. Then there are

[1] S. Lane-Poole.

no domes and no choir. In fact, this church approaches more nearly to the strict basilican pattern than any other church in this quarter. There is a curious hanging-garden attached to the church, where the bold experiment of planting palms in mid-air has succeeded in perpetuating the tradition that it was here that the Virgin first broke her fast with a meal of dates, on her arrival in Egypt. The cleft to be found in date-stones is, according to this Coptic legend, the mark made by the Virgin's teeth. This fact should interest students of sacred folk-lore.

A visit to Roda Island and the famous Nilometer, being generally combined with the excursion to Old Cairo, a short description of this beautiful island may be conveniently included in this chapter. The island is a pretty and shady retreat covered with groves and gardens. An Arabic tradition has chosen a certain part of the shore, opposite the Hospital of Qasr-el-Aini, as the site of the finding of Moses by Pharaoh's daughter. The spot is marked by a tall palm with an unusually smooth trunk, which is, of course, called Moses's Tree.

The Nilometer (the column used to mark the rise of the Nile) is the chief object of interest in the island; it is situated at the southern end, exactly opposite the site of the old Roman fortress of Babylon, and consists of an octagon column of red granite, about thirty feet high. This pillar has been frequently repaired, and probably very little remains of the original Nilometer, built by the Caliph Sulieman in 715 A. D. It is erected at the bo tom of a well-like chamber or cistern, crowned by a modern domed roof, which has, of course, direct communication with the Nile. Owing to the elevation of the river-bed, the traditional height of sixteen cubits (about twenty-eight feet) on the column, when the cutting of the banks of the irrigation canals is permitted, does not actually mean a rise of the Nile to this extent. At Cairo, a rise of twenty-six feet is thought to be a good average. This traditional number of cubits is symbolised in the famous Vatican statue of Father Nile, who is surrounded by sixteen genii, who are intended to represent those cubits.

In former times, the taxation of the fellah was arranged on a sliding scale, dependent on the rise of the Nile. It need scarcely be said, when we remember the fiscal methods of the Egyptian Government, even as recently as the time of the Khedive Ismail, that this custom gave rise to much dishonesty on the part of the officials who had the custody of the Nilometer, who invariably proclaimed the rise to be greater than it actually was.

The rise of the Nile, and the consequent ceremony of cutting the dam of the Khalig Canal, is celebrated by an important festival. It is not a poetical metaphor, but an actual fact, that the Nile is the one beneficent Providence of Egypt; and therefore it is not surprising that, as a period of universal rejoicing and holiday-making, the Khalig fête outshines many of the great religious festivals.

A graphic description of this fête is given in Murray's Handbook:

"The ceremony is performed in the morning by the Governor of Cairo or his deputy. The whole night before this the booths on the shore and the boats on the river are crowded with people, who enjoy themselves by witnessing or joining the numerous festive groups. The Governor of Cairo and other high officials have marquees pitched along the north bank of the Khalig, and ask their friends to witness the ceremony. Towards morning the greater part of the Cairenes either retire to some house to rest, or wrap themselves up in a cloak and sleep on board the boats, or upon the banks in the open air. About eight o'clock A. M., the Governor, accompanied by troops and his attendants, arrives; and on giving a signal, several peasants cut the dam with hoes, and the water rushes into the bed of the canal. In the middle of the dam is a pillar of earth, called Aru-seten-Nil, 'The Bride of the Nile,' which a tradition pretends to have been substituted by the humanity of Amru for the virgin previously sacrificed every year by the Christians to the river-god. While the water is rushing into the canal, the Governor throws some silver to the men who have been employed in cutting the dam, who swim about with great skill in the rushing water. It occasionally happens that some swimmer, less able to withstand the strength of the current, is carried away and drowned. As soon as sufficient water has entered it, boats full of people ascend the canal, and the crowds gradually disperse, as the Governor and the troops withdraw from the busy scene."

The ceremony is rarely witnessed by tourists, as it usually takes place in the beginning of August. If the improvements promised by the Egyptian Government are carried out, one of the most picturesque and characteristic of Cairene festivals will probably be abolished altogether, or degenerate into a meaningless ceremony, as by the drainage of the Khalig its *raison d'être* will be abolished. As mentioned in a previous chapter, the intention is to convert this ancient waterway — in the early summer virtually an open sewer — into an electric tramway.

Just beyond the Khalig is the ruined aqueduct, which is a very picturesque feature; and though the guide-books are inclined to ignore it, it is quite worth a visit. The local guides ascribe it to Saladin, but it was actually built by the Sultan Ghuri. It was intended to supply the Citadel with water from the Nile, and though now in a ruinous condition, traces of the grand workmanship of the Mameluke builders can still be recognised. The length is about two and a quarter miles, and the water was conducted by seven stages, being raised from one level to the other by means of sakyehs. The southern end terminates in a massive square tower over two hundred feet high. The summit can be conveniently reached by a gently inclined pathway, similar to the one at Joseph's Well in the Citadel. The view from the top is very striking. Those who intend visiting the Coptic churches will find it a convenient way of making acquaintance with the puzzling topography of this Coptic quarter.

CHAPTER XV.

SOME SIDE-SHOWS OF CAIRO.

THERE are certain well-known sights in Cairo, which are more popular in character than most of the antiquities and curiosities described in earlier chapters. Such are the performances of the Howling Dervishes, those of the Twirling Dervishes, the dances of the Ghawazee girls at the Arab cafés, the snake-charmers, street-conjurers, etc. These side-shows of Cairo, as they might well be called, constitute what Ruskin or Grant Allen would probably term "Vulgar Cairo." Though no doubt they appeal more to the taste of the ordinary sight-seer than to that of the intelligent tourist, yet such an intolerant attitude would be deprecated by the student of men and manners, who is capable of looking beneath the surface, and appreciating the substratum of Oriental life and atmosphere which underlies these somewhat vulgarised attractions of the casual tourist.

Cairo abounds in Egyptian cafés, where dances by the *soi-disant* members of the Ghawazee tribe are the sole attractions. They are, however, altogether lacking in local colour, and are, in fact, run by enterprising Greeks and Levantines for European visitors, and the performance is as banal and vulgar as at any *café chantant* in Antwerp or Amsterdam. The whole show consists of a few wailing musicians sitting on a raised platform at one end of the café, accompanying the endless gyrations of a stout young woman of unprepossessing features, who postures in particularly ungraceful and unedifying attitudes. Then her place is taken by another, equally ill-favoured and obese, who goes through the same interminable gyrations, to be relieved in her turn; and this goes on hour after hour. This strange " unvariety show " is, nevertheless, one of the established sights of Cairo, and is frequented in great numbers by tourists. Genuine performances of these dancing girls are seldom seen in Cairo, except occasionally at weddings among the rich Cairenes; and, in fact, the public dances of the Ghawazee are forbidden by the authorities. They can, however, be seen at most of the towns of the Upper Nile Valley, especially at Keneh and Esneh.

There is a strong family likeness between all these Oriental dances. The Ghawazee dance has many points of similarity with the Spanish gypsy dances, one of the stock sights of Seville and the Alhambra, which is said to have been introduced into Spain by the Phœnicians. These exhibitions of muscular contortion are practically the same as the repulsive *danse du ventre*, familiar to all Algerian tourists. The Indian nautch-dance, equally sensuous but more graceful, is also closely related to these terpsichorean performances. In short, all these sensuous and muscular, as distinct from locomotive, dances have doubtless a common origin.

These repulsive and stupid exhibitions would not probably be so much patronised by foreigners, were it not for the singular dearth of ordinary urban amusements and public recreations in Cairo. Probably no tourist-centre of equal importance affords so few opportunities to visitors of amusing themselves rationally in the evening, when ordinary sight-seeing is impracticable. An opera two or three times a week during the season, and one or two café concerts, sum up the resources of the city in the shape of evening entertainments.

This lack of evening recreation is the more noticeable from the fact that Cairo is popularly supposed to be one of the gayest and liveliest winter resorts in the world. In the limited society sense this reputation is well deserved, though the passing tourist will not probably be enabled to test its accuracy. The Cairo season is like that of Cannes or Nice,—one endless round of entertainments of all kinds. But these social gaieties are for the most part confined to the European winter-residents and the little world of Cairo officialdom. In the case of guests at the big hotels, there is, however, a certain amount of social intercourse among the residents and tourists; and the balls which are frequently given by the fashionable hotels, such as Shepheard's, Continental, and the Ghezireh Palace, serve a useful purpose in bringing about this amalgamation.

The al-fresco exhibitions of the snake-charmers, conjurers, story-tellers, etc., are a characteristic feature of Cairo street-scenes; but the most amusing of all these out-door entertainments are the performances of Kara Guz, the Egyptian Punch. This Arabic form of the friend of our childhood is perhaps the prototype of the English Punch-and-Judy show. The only essential difference between the English and Egyptian versions seems to be that the Egyptian Punch is polygamous, and it is one of his numerous wives, and not the baby, who is thrown out of the window. A Nemesis, however, awaits the murderer, as in the case of the English Punch, and his soul is conveyed to Hades by an Egyptian devil of appalling ugliness.

With strangers, however, the most popular of all the sights of Cairo are the performances of the two sects of dervishes, known as the Howling and the Twirling Dervishes. They take place every Friday afternoon in their respective *tekiyehs*, as the convents of this fanatical sect are termed. These quasi-religious services, technically known as *Zikrs*, though repulsive and brutalising enough to satisfy the most morbid tastes, are, however, tame and perfunctory compared with the performances which take place at the great religious festivals at the Mosques of the Hasaneen and Mehemet Ali.

The ordinary weekly *Zikrs* of the Twirling Dervishes cannot always be reckoned upon by the sight-seer, as they are often suspended. The Howling fraternity, however, perform with great regularity every Friday afternoon, between two and three, in the Tekiyeh-Kasr-el-Ain; and to enable their guests to witness the spectacle in comfort, the proprietors of the principal hotels advance the hour of the *table d'hôte* lunch on that day.

The dervishes stand in a circle, with their eyes fixed upon their sheik, who remains in the centre of the ring of worshippers, and directs the exercises and controls the pace of the movements with gestures, as a musical conductor directs a band or orchestra with his baton.

The beginning is comparatively sober and restrained, the dervishes slowly bending their heads to and fro, and perpetually ejaculating invocations to Allah with staccato grunts or groans. Soon the swaying becomes more violent, and the body is bent backwards and forwards till the forehead and the back of the head almost touch the ground alternately. The groaning and howling increases in force and volume, and is unpleasantly suggestive of the roar of wild beasts. By this time most of the fanatics have flung aside their turbans, and their long black manes sweep backwards and fowards like a punkah curtain, with the regularity of a pendulum. Some of the more excitable worshippers are at this point foaming at the mouth and yelling *hu! hu!* in an ecstasy of religious frenzy only partially simulated. Occasionally a dervish will fall on the floor in a paroxysm of ecstatic emotion which has all the appearance of an epileptic fit. In fact, there is a certain element of genuine fanaticism in the performance when at its height that might prove dangerous to the spectators. Ladies are not advised to remain to the end; or if the spectacle proves too engrossing, they should be especially careful not to sit too close to the dervishes, or to brush up against the performers. The dervishes maintain that the touch of a woman is contamination, and the half-maddened fanatics might possibly resent this contact in a very unpleasant fashion. Male visitors, too, will be well advised to avoid letting it be seen that they are affected by the ludicrous aspect of some phases of this performance.

To a spectator of an impressionable temperament there is something horribly fascinating in this performance. He may be told, and be quite prepared to believe at the time, that the groaning and howling of these fanatics is as much a mercenary show, in which the Christian dogs of tourists and other unbelievers, instead of the Egyptians, can be conveniently "spoilt," as a religious exercise. But there is no doubt that the frenzy of the dervishes is not wholly simulated, for towards the end of the service the howling, groaning, and swaying worshippers seem in a manner hypnotised by the wild strains of the excruciating music.

Besides being a less obnoxious spectacle, regarded from a secular point of view, the Twirling Dervishes' performance is a far more remarkable one, regarded as a gymnastic feat, than that of their confrères, the Howling Dervishes. After all, it does not require to be a Mohammedan counterpart of the Salvationists to groan, gasp, and sway the body by the hour together. Any of the European spectators could perform the feat, if necessary. The Twirling Dervish may be half impostor, half fanatic ; but at all events, like the sword-swallower or slack-wire dancer, he is doing something which none of the European spectators could do. To revolve at the rate of from sixty to one hundred times a minute for nearly half an hour is an accomplishment to which the feats of the record wielders of the Indian clubs alone can offer a parallel. Then, too, one must allow a certain amount of religious fervour and exaltation, which seems wanting to the ceremonies of the " Howlers." The Twirling Dervish has all the air of a genuine mystic.

"It is impossible to contemplate the countenance of the twirling fanatic, and the contrast of its strange quietude with the ceaseless motion of his body, without being powerfully impressed by it. As the endless gyrations continue, the position of the arms is repeatedly varied. Now both are extended at full length; now one is dropped by the side, while the other remains still stretched out; now one, now both, are bent till the tips of the fingers touch the shoulders. But all the time the eyes remain closed, and the face wears the same expression of perfect and imperturbable calm. To gaze intently upon him is to feel his condition gradually communicating itself to your own brain. That spinning figure with the unmoved countenance begins to exercise a disturbing effect upon you.

"The world of sight must have long disappeared from his view; the whizzing universe would be a mere blur upon his retina were he to open his eyes. But does he see nothing beyond it through their closed lids? Has he really twirled himself in imagination to the Gates of Paradise? Perhaps the incessant rotary movement acts on the human brain like hashish. This dervish, at any rate, has all the air of the wonder-seer. He is of the true race of the Visionaries; and even if he were not, the stupor of trance is, at any rate, a less unwholesome and distressing subject of contemplation than the spasms of epilepsy. The performance of the Twirling Dervishes leaves no sense of a degraded humanity behind it; but you quit the company of their grunting and gasping brothers with all the feeling of having assisted at a 'camp-meeting' of the lower apes."[1]

The best *Zikrs* are to be seen at the chief mosques on the night of the Middle of Shaban. This great festival takes place during the most solemn night in the whole Mohammedan year, when, according to immemorial custom, the Khedive pays his devotions in the Mosque of Mehemet Ali. The belief is, that, on this night of Sidr, the lotus-tree, which bears as many leaves as there are human beings, is shaken by an angel in Paradise, and on each leaf that falls is inscribed the name of some person

[1] H. D. Traill.

who will infallibly die before the end of the year. Naturally, a strong personal interest is behind the prayers and intercessions made to Allah and Mohammed on this night, and it is not surprising that all the mosques are thronged.

With the Egyptians themselves the numerous religious festivals are regarded more as excuses for holiday-making than as occasions for religious exercises. So the inclusion of these fête-days among the Cairo side-shows may be pardoned.

The public festivals (Molids) offer even a better field for the study of Cairene native life than continuous visits to the bazaars. The religious significance of these feasts is, as a rule, quite ignored by the pleasure-loving Cairenes, and they are more like fairs on a large scale than religious festivals.

Most of these fêtes take place out of the European season, but the Molid (birthday anniversary) of the Hasaneen, which is celebrated in the winter, should not be omitted from the tourist's programme.

"Nothing more picturesque and fairylike can be imagined than the scenes in the streets and bazaars of Cairo on the great night of the Hasaneen. The curious thing was, that, in the winter after Tel-el-Kebir, when I stood — for riding was impossible — in the midst of the dense throng in the Mooski, and struggled into the by-street that leads to the Mosque of the Hasaseen, there was not a sign of ill-humour or fanaticism, in spite of the presence of many Europeans. It might have been expected that at least some slight demonstration would have been made against the Europeans who wandered about the gaily illuminated streets; but English ladies walked through the bazaars, English officers and tourists mingled in the throng, and even reached the doors of the sacred mosque itself, without the slightest molestation or even remark.

"The scene, as I turned into one of the narrow lanes of the great khan which fronts the mosque, was like a picture in the Arabian Nights. The long bazaar was lighted by innumerable chandeliers and coloured lamps and candles, and covered by awnings of rich shawls and stuffs. The shops had quite changed their character, and each was turned into a tastefully furnished reception-room. Seated in the richly hung recess, you can see the throng pushing by, — the whole population, it seems, of Cairo, in their best array and merriest temper. All at once the sound of drums and pipes is heard, and a band of dervishes, chanting benedictions on the Prophet and Hoseyn, pass through the delighted crowd. On your left is a shop — nay, a throne-room in miniature — where a story-teller is holding an audience spellbound, as he relates, with dramatic gestures, some favourite tale. Hard by, a holy man is revolving his head solemnly and unceasingly, as he repeats the name of God, or some potent text from the Koran. In another place, a party of dervishes are performing a *Zikr*. The whole scene is certainly unreal and fairylike." [1]

It seems, perhaps, strange to include what to Western minds is a purely private and domestic function in this chapter; but a native wedding seems to be considered, at all events by lady travellers, one of the recognised sights of Cairo. Strangers who wish to be present at one of these characteristic entertainments will have little difficulty in effecting this. In fact it is cynically said by residents that no self-respecting dragoman would allow his patron to be balked of his desire by the fact that no Cairene wedding was at that time to take place. He would probably, by means of baksheesh, arrange one on purpose!

There is not, indeed, much difference in the ceremonial between a wedding in Cairo and one in Constantinople, Algiers, or other Mohammedan cities; and male visitors, at all events, will probably consider the interminable ceremonies of the marriage festival tedious and puerile.

The preliminary negotiations are usually arranged by professional intermediaries or match-makers, and the bridegroom, as a rule, never sees his bride unveiled till the actual day of the wedding. The legal preliminaries being satisfactorily arranged, the formal festivities begin with the procession of the bride to the bridegroom's house. In the

---

[1] S. Lane-Poole.

case of rich people, the bridal procession is conducted on a very elaborate scale. The train is usually headed by buffoons, musicians, and jugglers. Then comes the bride, walking under a canopy borne by four attendants, and surrounded and followed by a crowd of female relatives and friends. Sometimes, however, the bride and her train of relatives are mounted on asses; but among the richer classes an incongruous note of modernity is sometimes given to the spectacle, by the bride being driven to the house in an ordinary European brougham, which is preceded by a band of music, and the picturesque procession of troops of dancers and singers is altogether dispensed with, thus robbing the pageant of the most characteristic feature of Cairene wedding processions.

Formerly, in the case of weddings among the Cairene traders, the most striking part of the procession was a cavalcade of decorated cars, each containing members of a particular trade or craft engaged in their special callings: " in one, for instance, a kaivejy, with his assistants, and pots and cups and fire, making coffee for the spectators; in a second, makers of sweetmeats ; in a third, makers of pancakes; in a fourth, silk-lace manufacturers ; in a fifth, a silk-weaver with his loom ; in a sixth, tinners of copper vessels at their work. In short, almost every manufacture and trade had its representatives in a separate wagon." This vehicular Arts and Crafts Exhibition is copied now-a-days in many Continental carnival processions.

The bride and her party having arrived at the house, the wedding banquet takes place. The bridegroom, however, is not present, and in fact does not see his future wife until the end of the day. The repast is followed by what would in modern parlance be called a reception; and the long-suffering bride, for all the rest of the day, is literally on show to the throng of invited guests, which usually number many European ladies. It would, of course, be contrary to the etiquette of the Mohammedans for the chief personage to respond in any way to the felicitations of her friends, and for the whole of the day she remains silent and motionless, on a kind of throne at one end of the room.

Meanwhile, etiquette requires that the bridegroom should in the mean time visit the bath and the mosque, attended by his friends and acquaintances.

" Returned to his house, he leaves his friends and attendants in a lower apartment, and goes up to the bride, whom he finds seated with a shawl thrown over her head, so as to conceal her face completely, and attended by one or two females. The latter he induces to retire by means of a small present. He then gives a present of money to the bride, as 'the price of uncovering her face;' and having removed the covering (saying, as he does so, 'In the name of God, the Compassionate, the Merciful'), he beholds her, generally for the first time. On the occasion of his first visit, he is recommended to perfume himself, and to sprinkle some sugar almonds on the head of the bride and on that of each woman with her. Also, when he approaches her, he should perform the prayer of the *rekas*, and she should do the same, if able."

Among the upper classes of the Cairenes and the official Turkish families the spectacular portion of the bridal procession is shorn of much of its glory, though the rites and ceremonies in the house are carried out in the orthodox manner. The bride and her friends are in carriages, and are escorted to the husband's house by troops of soldiers and officials of all ranks; for Western manners and customs are outwardly, at least, being steadily assimilated by the upper classes in Egypt as in Turkey. It is only the lower classes in Cairo who are consistently conservative in all their modes of life.

The notoriously inferior and degraded position which women occupy in countries under the yoke of Islam, which is the chief blot on the Mohammedan social system, is even symbolised in some of the apparently meaningless forms and ceremonies of an Egyptian wedding. Though universal equality and fraternity are the cardinal principles of the Moslem cult, women are altogether excluded from the benefits of these liberal tenets. The essential inferiority of the gentler sex is, indeed, a part of the Mohammedan religion. Innumerable passages in the Koran testify to the view taken by the founder of the Moslem faith of the ineradicable iniquity of womankind. " I stood at the gate of Paradise," wrote the Prophet, " and, lo! most of its inhabitants were the poor; and I stood at the gates of hell, and, lo! most of its inhabitants were women."

In fact, no Mohammedan takes a woman seriously. He regards her as merely an ornamental appendage of his household, and is not quite satisfied that she has a soul, though the more tolerant are inclined to give her the benefit of the doubt. All over the East, women are the rich man's toys and the poor man's slaves. " The worst of this deplorable state of things," writes Mr. Stanley Lane-Poole, " is that there seems no reasonable prospect of improvement. The Mohammedan social system is so thoroughly bound up with the religion that it appears an almost hopeless task to separate the two. . . . As long as the Mohammedan religion exists, the social life with which it has unfortunately become identified will probably survive; and whilst the latter prevails in Egypt, we cannot expect the higher results of civilisation."

CHAPTER XVI.

THE PYRAMIDS OF GHIZEH.

PERHAPS there is no single ancient monument in existence which has been so much written about as the Pyramid of Cheops, usually known as the Great Pyramid. The number of volumes devoted to this mausoleum would, in fact, fill a respectable library. The wildest theories have been ventilated in an attempt to solve the meaning and account for the object of the Pyramid.

To quote only a few. Some have supposed, with a sublime indifference to the adaptation of ways and means, that they were intended merely to act as an indestructible metrical standard. Pliny thought that they were built mainly to give the people employment; in fact, to serve the same purpose as public works subsidised by modern governments in time of famine, plague, or great national distress. Others held, and this theory long maintained its ground, that the perfect orientation of the Pyramids indicated that they were built for astronomical purposes. By mediæval chroniclers, when Egyptian chronology was at a discount, they were said to have been built by Joseph for granaries.

Many writers, however, contented themselves with attributing a merely symbolical motive to the Pyramids. Perhaps the most original idea was that of a French savant, who held that the Pyramids were built as a barrier to protect the cities on the banks of the Nile from sandstorms. Now, happily, the fables, speculations, and misconceptions to which these structures have given rise are, for

the most part, exploded. The overwhelming weight of evidence, the fruit of the exhaustive researches of trained observers and scientists, is in favour of their having simply been used as royal tombs.

The stupendous size of these cairns, the incalculable amount of labour their building entailed, is not, however, so extraordinary as the astonishing architectural skill shown in the construction. As Fergusson observes in his "History of Architecture," notwithstanding the immense superincumbent weight, no settlement in any part can be detected to an appreciable fraction of an inch. In short, what probably first strikes the spectator is its matter, and then its manner of construction.

An architect cannot help being amazed at the wonderful skill and elaboration of the workmanship; "the flatness and squareness of the joints is extraordinary, equal to opticians' work of the present day, but on a scale of acres instead of feet of material. The squareness and level of the base is brilliantly true, the average error being less than a ten thousandth of the side in equality, in squareness, and in level."[1]

The real meaning and true inwardness of the Pyramids is admirably suggested in the following passage in Prof. Flinders-Petrie's "History of Egypt," now in preparation:

"The essential feeling of all the earliest works of the ancient Egyptians is a rivalry with Nature. In other times buildings have been placed either before a background of hills, so as to provide a natural setting for them, or crowning some natural height. But the Egyptian consented to no such tame coöperation with natural features. He selected a range of desert-hills over a hundred feet high, and then subdued it entirely, making of it a mere pedestal for Pyramids, which were more than thrice as high as the native hill on which they stood. There was no shrinking from a comparison with the work of Nature; but, on the contrary, an artificial hill was

[1] W. M. Flinders-Petrie.

formed which shrunk its natural basis by comparison, until it seemed a mere platform for the work of man. This same grandeur of idea is seen in the vast masses used in construction. Man did not then regard his work as a piling together of stones, but as the erection of masses that rivalled those of Nature."

It is scarcely necessary to recapitulate here the popular information about the Pyramids, which is to be found described at length in all guide-books. Every Egyptian traveller is aware that these buildings are royal tombs, built by the first three sovereigns of the fourth dynasty,— Khufu, Khafra, and Menkaura (or, popularly, Cheops, Chephren, and Mycerinus); that they are probably the oldest monuments in tolerable preservation in Egypt, dating from a period so remote that almost as many centuries separate them from the famous temples of Abydos, Thebes, and Abou Simbel as separate these famous ruins from the great buildings of the Ptolemies. We all know that the Pyramids were built of limestone from the Turra quarries on the other side of the Nile, and cased with polished granite, which was laid under contribution, after the Arab's conquest, to build the walls and mosques of Cairo.

At the risk of boring my readers, I will venture to quote a few statistics. According to the latest measurements (Petrie), the height of the Pyramid of Cheops is 451 feet. It may be interesting to compare it with other great buildings, ancient and modern. The Washington monument at Washington, D. C., is 555 feet high, and the Eiffel Tower 984, while the dome of St. Peter's, Rome, is but 429 feet high. Each side is 755 feet at the base, so that a walk round the Great Pyramid would be a little over half a mile in length. Perhaps this will convey a better notion of its size than the often-quoted statement that the area is thirteen acres, exactly that of Lincoln's Inn Fields, London, and about four times the area of the Capitol at Washington. The weight of this truly royal sepulchre is computed at seven million tons. Perhaps the fact that St. Peter's of Rome could be erected in this Pyramid, supposing it were hollow, and the curious computation of a French savant that the stones of the three Pyramids (Cheops, Chephren, and Mycerinus) would be sufficient to make a wall six feet high and one foot wide all round France, brings home to the spectators a clearer idea of the size of the Great Pyramid than whole pages of dry figures.

Considerable doubt has been thrown by commentators on Herodotus's famous account of the building of the Pyramids, especially in regard to the passage in which he declares that the Pyramid of Cheops was the result of the labours of 100,000 men, who worked three months a year, for twenty years, at the task.

Prof. Flinders-Petrie, however, makes out a convincing and excellently reasoned case in favour of the accuracy of Herodotus's statement. The actual work was probably organised as follows: Each year, towards the end of July, when the Nile had fairly risen, the men would assemble. The blocks of stone average about two and a half tons, and each would require not less than eight men. Supposing, then, each gang brought over and placed in position ten or a dozen blocks during the three months' corvée, and reckoning that some 2,300,000 stones — the calculation of the best authorities — would be required for the Great Pyramid, it will at once be seen that the total number could easily be brought over and the Pyramid built in rather less time than the twenty years mentioned by the Greek historian. In fact, there seems no reason to discredit the traditional account of the methods employed in carrying out what seems at first sight an almost superhuman enterprise. Then it must be remembered that the transport of these colossal blocks to the site of the Pyramids would be much facilitated, owing to the inundation. They could be transported in boats or barges right up to the edge of the plateau.

The ascent of the Great Pyramid, as usually undertaken, is not only absolutely free from danger, but requires no climbing abilities at all; in fact, a child of six would have no difficulty in reaching the summit. The only objection is that it is rather trying to the wind and temper, owing to the heat of the sun. Two or three Arabs practically haul the visitor up to the top, and, unless the tourist is strong-minded enough to take the initiative, only a couple of halts are as a rule allowed the breathless climber; and at these resting-places he will be pestered with unattached Arabs offering him water and clamouring for baksheesh.

We are supposing, of course, that the traveller is "doing" the Pyramids in the conventional way, with one of a band of tourists marshalled by the satellites of one of the great tourist-agencies, who arrive every morning from Cairo during the season. The main object of the conductor being to get his party back to the hotel by lunch-time, the examination of the Sphinx, the Temple of the Sphinx, and other sights is, of course, perfunctory in the extreme. The Arabs cannot, at any rate, reasonably be blamed for the hurried manner in which the ascent is performed. Naturally, their aim is to conduct as many tourists to the top as possible in the day.

The summit reached, a magnificent view may be enjoyed during the regulation half-hour's rest. The Delta of the Nile, interspersed with countless channels and rivulets winding about like silver threads, seems to resemble the silver filigree ornaments of Greece. Looking down at Cairo, from which the silver threads radiate, one is reminded of the fanciful Oriental comparison of the Delta with "a fan fastened with a diamond stud." The spectator's poetical fancies, however, are soon put to flight by clamorous demands for baksheesh.

While resting on the summit, the Arab version of the Cumberland guides' race may be witnessed, as any of the

Arab guides for a few piastres (at first the Arab will magnanimously offer to do the feat for five shillings) is quite willing to race up and down the Great and Second Pyramids in ten minutes. The feat of climbing the Second Pyramid (Chephren's) might better not be emulated by the ordinary tourist, as the smooth granite casing still remains for some hundred and fifty feet from the top. To a mountaineer or cragsman, however, the climb is mere child's play; but even an experienced climber would better not attempt it in ordinary boots. Furnished with ordinary tennis-shoes there would be little difficulty. Mark Twain, as is well known, thought little of the feat. The above description will serve as an illustration of how *not* to do the Pyramids. The best plan, and one which can be recommended even to the hurried tourist, is to stay the preceding night at the Mena House hotel, and make the ascent early in the morning, before the daily incursion of the tourists from Cairo.

But in order to realise the stupendous bulk and the immensity of the Great Pyramid, it is, perhaps, better to forego the ascent altogether. To persons of an æsthetic or imaginative temperament, this somewhat banal and commonplace expedition is decidedly disillusionising. Hauled like a bale of goods up this gigantic staircase of something like two hundred steps,— to be accurate, 206, for everything pertaining to the structure of the Pyramid has been exhaustively examined, noted, measured, and tabulated,— by grinning and chattering Arabs, the visitor is scarcely in a position to appreciate properly the grandeur or the solemnity of this vast monument. If, instead of following the hordes of tourists to the summit, we stand a few hundred yards away and quietly examine this wonderful result of a civilisation of nearly five thousand years ago, gradually an overwhelming sense of their stupendous bulk and immensity will be experienced.

It is not easy to reproduce in imagination these magnificent sepulchres as they appeared in their full glory some five thousand years ago. In this connection it is worth quoting Dean Stanley's graphic description, in his "Sinai and Palestine," although a hypercritical reader may perhaps feel disposed to pick holes in the author's archæology, — for instance, it is now well known that the ancient Egyptians never inscribed the exteriors of the Pyramids; but the Dean, though a man of wide culture, never laid claim to a profound knowledge of Egyptology:

"The smooth casing of part of the top of the Second Pyramid, and the magnificent granite blocks which form the lower stairs of the Third, serve to show what they must have been all from top to bottom. The First and Second, brilliant white or yellow limestone, smooth from top to bottom, instead of those rude, disjointed masses which their stripped sides now present; the Third, all glowing with the red granite from the First Cataract. As it is, they have the barbarous look of Stonehenge; but then they must have shone with the polish of an age already rich in civilisation, — and that the more remarkable, when it is remembered that these granite blocks which furnish the outside of the Third, and the inside of the First, must have come all the way from the First Cataract. It also seems, from Herodotus and others, that these smooth outsides were covered with sculptures. Then you must build up or uncover the massive tombs, now broken or covered with sand, so as to restore the aspect of vast streets of tombs, like those on the Appian Way, out of which the Great Pyramid would arise, like a cathedral above smaller churches. Lastly, you must enclose the two other Pyramids with stone precincts and gigantic gateways; and, above all, you must restore the Sphinx, as he was in the days of his glory."

After the ascent, the exploration of the interior will probably be undertaken. This trip, though far more tiring than the climb to the summit, is particularly interesting, and should not be omitted. Ladies, however, unless accustomed to scrambling, are not recommended to visit the interior. As in all the Pyramids, the entrance is on the northern side. After descending a gallery some sixty feet, the passage which leads to the Great Gallery is reached. The inclined passage continues to a subterranean (or rather sub-pyramidal, for, of course, all the galleries and chambers in the interior are, in a sense, subterranean) chamber, known as the Queen's Chamber, which is rarely visited by ordinary tourists. The origin of the names of the two chambers is curious and fortuitous. These names were given first by the Arabs, in conformity with their custom of making men's tombs flat-topped, and those for women with a concave roof. As these names happened to accord with the facts, they have been adopted by Egyptologists, as well as by the public. The Great Gallery, still mounting upwards, leads to the King's Chamber,— a room some seventy-four feet long, seventeen broad, and nineteen high. The roof is flat, and formed of simple blocks of granite, resting on the side walls, which are built of the same materials; " and so truly and beautifully are these blocks fitted together, that the edge of a penknife could not be inserted between them." (Murray's Guide.)

Here is the famous sarcophagus — the *raison d'être*, indeed, of the Great Pyramid — in which the remains of King Cheops, no doubt, once rested. The discovery of this red-gradite coffin did not, it is needless to say, upset the preconceived fantastic theory of Piazzi Smyth. Though obviously a sarcophagus, the professor did not allow himself to be disconcerted, but declared that it was a coffer intended as an indestructible measure of capacity to all time!

Many traditions and myths have centred round the Pyramid of Mycerinus (Third Pyramid), which is still said to be haunted. A Coptic legend, which recalls the myth of the sirens in the Odyssey, tells the story of a beautiful woman enthroned on this pyramid, who allures desert wayfarers from the South and West, embraces them in her arms, and deprives them of reason.

"Fair Rhodopè, as story tells,
The bright unearthly nymph, who dwells
'Mid sunless gold and jewels hid,
The lady of the Pyramid."

Students of folk-lore are well aware that the germ of most of our nursery tales can be traced back to the legendary stories of the remotest ages of antiquity; and a story of this same Rhodope, told by the "Father of History," Herodotus, suggests the source of the nursery legend of Cinderella. While bathing in the Nile, an eagle flew off with one of her sandals, and, carrying it to Memphis, dropped it at the feet of the King Mycerinus (Menkaura). Struck by its beauty, he sent out his messengers in all directions to find the owner of this little sandal; and when they had found her, he made her his queen. Thus, too, in many of the pictorial sculptures in the temples of Thebes can be traced prototypes of the characters in the Arabian Nights' Stories.

Campbell's Tomb is the best known of the royal sepulchres of this great cemetery of ancient Egyptian sovereigns. It is so called, in accordance with the popular and illogical method of nomenclature which formerly obtained, of naming tombs after some modern notability instead of the tenant, — in this case after the British consul-general at the time of the discovery of the tomb by Colonel Howard Vyse. It is comparatively modern, being attributed by scholars to the twenty-sixth dynasty, when that of Sais, with the help of Greek mercenaries, over-ran Egypt. The tomb is really a pit about fifty-five feet deep; at the bottom is a small chamber, in which were found four sarcophagi, one of which was given to the British Museum. It is a usual feat of the Arab guides to climb down the almost perpendicular sides of the shaft; but if strangers wish to explore the tomb chamber, they will have to be let down by a rope, — a feat which, considering the little there is to see at the bottom, is rarely performed. There are numerous other

THE PYRAMIDS OF GHIZEH.

tombs in the extensive necropolis which surrounds the Pyramids, but they are not of popular interest. The sight-seeing of most visitors to the Pyramid field will, in short, be confined to the ascent of the Great Pyramid, possibly a visit to the interior, a hasty glimpse of the Sphinx, Campbell's Tomb, and the Sphinx Temple.

The Sphinx, for thousands of years the greatest enigma in Egypt, has not succeeded in baffling the investigations of modern antiquarians, who have stripped it of much of the mystery which constituted its great charm. Its builder, however, is still a matter of conjecture with students of Egyptology. It is now conclusively proved that it is nothing but a colossal image of the Egyptian deity, Harmachis, the "god of the morning," and, therefore, of his human representative, the king (unknown) who had it hewn. A stela found by Mariette, near the Great Pyramid, shows that the Sphinx was probably repaired by Cheops and Chephren, the builders of the Great and Second Pyramids respectively.

The Sphinx is not an independent structure, like the Pyramids, but is for the most part hewn out of the rocky cliff, or promontory, which juts out here from the desert plateau. The body and head are actually hewn out of this living rock, but sandstone masonry has been built up to connect the natural outline. The measurements given in many of the books of reference are of little value, as they vary according to the amount of sand which had drifted round the statue; but the latest measurements of Professor Petrie give the length of the body as 140 feet, while the head measures thirty feet from the top of the forehead to the bottom of the chin. The height of the Sphinx, from the forehead to the base of the monument, is seventy feet.

Some successful excavations at the foot of the Sphinx have recently been undertaken by an American Egyptologist, Colonel Ram. In 1896 he discovered the klaft, or stone cap, with the sacred asp on the forehead, which was known to have once been the head-covering of the Sphinx. Dean Stanley, for instance, in his "Sinai and Palestine," wonders, apropos of the colossal head, "what the sight must have been when on its head there was the royal helmet of Egypt."

A thorough and systematic excavation of this colossal figure, and the removal of the steadily encroaching desert sands which have buried the greater portion of the body, is much to be desired. The cost, however, would be enormous, amounting at least to that of a whole year's excavation carried out by the joint efforts of the National Museum and the Egyptian Exploration Society. Such a work should be undertaken by private enterprise. If another public-spirited man like Sir Erasmus Wilson would provide the funds for the work, it is believed that discoveries of the greatest importance would repay the work of excavating. The late Miss A. B. Edwards, indeed, was of opinion that the greatest find in the whole field of Egyptian antiquities is likely to be round the base of the Sphinx, "which probably marks the site of a necropolis, buried a hundred feet in the sand, of the kings of the first and second dynasties!"

The first view of the Sphinx is, undoubtedly, striking and impressive in the highest degree, but it must be admitted that the conventional rhapsodies of modern writers who enlarge on the beauty of its features are overstrained. Before the figure had been mutilated by Mussulman fanatics, it is possible that the mediæval critics were justified in speaking of the Sphinx as a model of human symmetry, wearing "an expression of the softest beauty and the most winning peace." Now, however, the traveller is confronted by a much disfigured stone giant, with a painfully distorted mouth, broken nostrils, and the grimace of a hideous negro.

But though there is little concrete beauty in this

colossal figure, there is an undeniable fascination about the Sphinx, due to its impressive surroundings, its mysterious traditions, and its solemn immobility of expression. To realise the charm of this monument, we must read the classic and oft-quoted description of Kinglake, who, in a passage of incomparable prose, has succeeded where so many writers have failed:

"And near the Pyramids, more wondrous and more awful than all else in the land of Egypt, there sits the lonely Sphinx. Comely the creature is, but the comeliness is not of this world: the once worshipped beast is a deformity and a monster to this generation; and yet you can see that those lips, so thick and heavy, were fashioned according to some ancient mould of beauty, — some mould of beauty now forgotten, — forgotten because that Greece drew forth Cytherea from the flashing foam of the Ægean, and in her image created new forms of beauty, and made it a law among men that the short and proudly wreathed lips should stand for the sign and the main condition of loveliness through all generations to come. Yet still there lives on the race of those who were beautiful in the fashion of the elder world; and Christian girls of Coptic blood will look on you with the sad, serious gaze, and kiss your charitable hand with the big pouting lips of the very Sphinx.

"Laugh and mock, if you will, at the worship of stone idols; but mark ye this, ye breakers of images: that, in one regard, the stone idol bears awful semblance of Deity, — unchangefulness in the midst of change, — the same seeming will and intent for ever and ever inexorable! Upon ancient dynasties of Ethiopian and Egyptian kings, upon Greek and Roman, upon Arab and Ottoman conqueror, upon Napoleon, dreaming of an Eastern empire, upon battle and pestilence, upon the ceaseless misery of the Egyptian race, upon keen-eyed travellers, — Herodotus yesterday and Warburton to-day, — upon all and more this unworldly Sphinx has watched, and watched like a Providence, with the same earnest eyes, and the same sad, tranquil mien. And we, — we shall die, and Islam will wither away; and the Englishman, straining forever to hold his loved India, will plant a firm foot on the banks of the Nile, and sit in the seats of the faithful, and still that sleepless rock will lie watching and watching the works of the new busy race, with those same sad, earnest eyes, and the same tranquil mien everlasting. You dare not mock at the Sphinx!"

A short distance south of the Sphinx is the so-called Temple of the Sphinx, a structure, probably, of the fourth dynasty. The sand drift of thousands of years has so covered it that the non-observant traveller would suppose the Temple to be a subterranean building. The Temple is a worthy pendant of the mighty mausoleum, to which it seems to serve as a kind of mortuary chapel, for the discovery here of the famous green basalt statue of Khafra (Chephren), which we have seen in the Ghizeh Museum, is held by most authorities to prove that this sovereign was the builder of this temple, as well as the Second Pyramid. In short, it is probably the mastaba of this sepulchre. The building is a fine specimen of the architecture of the Ancient Empire. It is lined in some parts with huge blocks of alabaster.

CHAPTER XVII.

THE CITY OF THE SACRED BULLS.

THE ruins of Memphis and the necropolis of Sakkarah are most conveniently reached by steamer or train from Cairo to Bedrashen, a small village on the banks of the Nile, about fifteen miles from the city. Most Egyptian antiquarians and historians agree in assigning the date of its foundation to Menes, the first historical, as opposed to the quasi-mythical god-kings, king of Egypt. At all events, this ancient capital is certainly of a very remote antiquity.

It is not difficult to understand why the kings of the Ancient Empire established their capital here. Its situation was of distinct political, commercial, and strategic value. From the comparatively feeble tribes on the western bank of the Nile there was no danger of attack, while a city on the eastern bank would invite attacks from the inhabitants of Mesopotamia, Syria, and Arabia. Then, in addition to its natural advantages of a fertile and well-wooded soil, the city was not far from the seacoast, and occupying a fairly central position in Egypt, and having command of the Nile, it would control the country from Philæ, on the south, to the Mediterranean, on the north. Under the fourth and sixth dynasties, whose kings sprang from Memphis, the city reached a height of splendour which was probably never excelled; but the rise of Thebes, in the eighteenth dynasty, considerably diminished the glories of Memphis, and though it was still an important city, Thebes was the metropolis of all Egypt. After the New Empire, Memphis declined in importance, and from that period its history is very similar to that of Heliopolis, — another historic city, of which scarcely any ruins remain. Both cities were taken and retaken in turn by Assyrian, Ethiopian, Persian, and Greek invaders. It was gradually shorn of most of its glories, and the founding of Alexandria was the final blow, fulfilling the gloomy prophecy of Jeremiah: "O daughter of Egypt, make ready that which can serve thee in thy captivity, because Memphis shall become a desert; she shall be forsaken, and become uninhabited." Such, in brief, is the outline of the history of this once famous city.

Those who have visited Thebes, with its rich treasure-trove of magnificent temples and monuments, are, perhaps, a little puzzled to account for the total disappearance of a city which, though some two thousand years older than the City of the Thousand Gates, possessed many buildings of the age of the nineteenth and twentieth dynasties, of later date than many of Thebes's famous buildings. It is, however, necessary to remember the very different conditions. In the first place, Memphis lay in the path of all the invading nations who overthrew Egypt in turn. Then Thebes had no Fostat or Cairo at its threshold, — a city which was literally built out of the ruins of Memphis and Heliopolis. Then, too, the devastating character of the Nile inundation, to which low-lying Memphis was peculiarly subject, must not be forgotten. As Miss Brodrick, in Murray's admirable Handbook, aptly observes, the waters of the inundation, long ago unrestrained by the protecting dykes, covered the plain with a gradually increasing layer of mud deposit, beneath which every trace of such ruins as were left completely disappeared.

The only antiquities which remain to us of Memphis itself — for the pyramids, tombs, etc., are quite distinct, and form part of the Memphian cemetery at Sakkarah — are the two colossal statues of Rameses II. This vainglorious monarch seems indeed to have been as fond of erecting

these portraits in stone of himself as modern sovereigns are of being photographed. At Thebes, Tanis, Abou Simbel, and other sites, have been discovered other monolithic counterfeit presentments of this much-portrayed ruler. These two statues, in all probability, stood at the entrance of the famous Temple of Ptah, the tutelary god of Memphis. One is recumbent; the other was raised in 1887, by Major Bagnold and his engineers. The monarch is now concealed under a hideous, roofless shed. The statue is about forty-two feet high; that is, not quite half as tall as the colossal broken portrait-statue of the same monarch, recently discovered on the site of Tanis by Prof. Flinders-Petrie. This is the largest colossus ever sculptured by the hand of man, and when complete was ninety-two feet high. The Memphian colossus was presented to the British Museum in 1840. In view, however, of the almost insuperable difficulty of conveying it across the desert sands to the Nile, and the enormous cost, the offer had to be declined. For though this statue is much exceeded in bulk and weight by Cleopatra's Needle, yet, owing to the position of this obelisk, situated within a short distance of the Alexandrian coast, the task of its removal was comparatively easy.

The Memphian necropolis at Sakkarah may, however, be considered sacred ground to the Egyptologist and historian. It was here that the earliest work of Egyptian mural sculpture was discovered. This is the famous funerary tablet, which may now be seen at the Ashmoleum Museum in Oxford. Its period is the second dynasty, which means that the stela was carved about 4000 B. C. Then, among the tombs of the New Empire (the conventional term given by modern historians to denote the golden age of the eighteenth to the twenty-fifth dynasties), was found the famous, and still more valuable historically, stela, known as the Tablet of Sakkarah. This, with the Abydos tablet, certain fragments of Manetho's history, and the Turin papyrus are the chief authentic sources from which we derive our knowledge of the earliest period of Egyptian history.

A very valuable collection of Greek papyri (B. C. 168) was found on this site early in the present century, which is now in the British Museum. Apart from its antiquarian value, its intrinsic and literary interest is considerable. The papyri consist for the most part of letters, reports, petitions, and other documents chronicling the efforts of a certain Macedonian monk, called Ptolemy, in behalf of two female employés in the Serapeum, who were being defrauded by the officials of their modest allowance. In short, the record is a veritable human document, palpitating with actuality, to adopt the expressive slang of the day.

The chief object of interest in the Memphian cemetery of Sakkarah is the Mausoleum of the Divine Bulls, usually known as the Serapeum, which is the term popularly but incorrectly applied to the series of underground mortuary chambers in which were buried these sacred bulls, from 650 B. C. to 56 B. C. It is, no doubt, the most popular feature of this great necropolis, and probably, to nine out of ten persons who have visited Sakkarah, it is the chief attraction.

This remarkable mausoleum was discovered as recently as 1850, by Mariette. He had noticed, in the course of excavations in various parts of Egypt, sphinxes upon which were inscribed dedications to Osiris-Apis (Greek, Serapis), and conjectured that they must have some reference to the long-lost Temple of Serapis, near Memphis, spoken of by Strabo. He was fortunate in his preliminary excavations on the site of this buried city, and soon lit upon the vaults in which the bulls were buried. Over sixty vaults were discovered. Only one part of this bovine necropolis is now shown to visitors. It contains twenty-four granite sarcophagi, and they measure on an average thirteen feet long, seven feet broad, and eleven feet high.

By one enormous niche, leaning against a sarcophagus rifled by Christian plunderers in the time of Theodosius, and desecrated by fanatics of other creeds, stands a ladder, up which we may climb, and cast a glance at the interior of the tomb, which was destined to preserve to all time the coal-black body of the sacred bull. The lid of the coffin has been moved aside; a heap of stones is piled up on one side of it. The mummy of the animal has disappeared. The treasures which gathered here, brought as pious offerings, have long been carried off by unknown treasure-seekers. The strange surroundings seem quite legendary. The giants who were their creators seem beings from another and an unknown world.

The weight of these sarcophagi was so great that all the efforts of Mariette's engineers to remove them, for transport to Ghizeh, were absolutely ineffectual. This is indirectly a striking testimony to the wonderful resources of the ancient Egyptians, to whom such a task would have been child's play in comparison with the undertaking of removing the obelisks from Assouan to Lower Egypt. No remains of the sacred animals were found in any of the sarcophagi, all of which had evidently been rifled, probably at the time of the Arabian conquest of Egypt.

The history of the animal worship of the ancient Egyptians offers innumerable subjects of interest to the theologian, as well as to the anthropologist and historian.

One of the most characteristic features of the ancient Egyptian faith was the reverence paid to certain animals. In some places the people worshipped the crocodile; in others, the cat; in others, again, certain mythical birds and beasts; but especially it was the bull that was adored. At Heliopolis this animal was called Mnevis. At Memphis it was Apis who was reverenced.

According to common belief, either the lightning or a moonbeam fecundated a cow, and the divinity then appeared upon earth in the shape of a bull. Special distinguishing marks guided the search for the sacred bull among the local herds. It sometimes happened that for years the priests were unable to discover the particular animal which, by certain complex external marks, corresponded to the ideal Apis. The discoverer of the incarnation of the god Apis was rewarded with an immense fortune.

The elect animal was next tamed, as far as possible; and then at the first new moon it was taken in a sacred boat of gold to Memphis, where it was placed in the sanctuary of Ptah. A special court was assigned for its exercise, and when it was in its stall the faithful strove to peep in at it through the window.

Extraordinary were the divine honours paid to this quadruped. The Pharaohs spared no money in making its worship as splendid as possible. Alexander the Great and the Roman Emperor Titus found it expedient to offer up sacrifices to Apis, who was believed to be endowed with prophetic powers, and who foretold the future in a peculiar manner. When the sacred bull licked the garments of a noted Greek astronomer, it signified that the latter was to die soon, and this really came to pass. A similar meaning the priests saw in its refusal to take food from the hands of Germanicus. Its bellowing foretold a foreign conquest. Those who consulted Apis used to guess into which of his stalls he would next enter. If the guess was correct, then the answer to the question was affirmative, and *vice versa*. People slept in his temple, hoping for prophetic dreams. Sometimes questions were addressed directly to the bull, and the inquirers then listened to the voices of the children playing without the wall of the temple; and a saying having some bearing on the matter was then constructed out of the disconnected expressions which reached the ear. When Apis was led out among the people, the accompanying youths, in a state of extreme ecstasy, sang and prophesied.

At home Apis dwelt behind purple curtains, slept on a soft bed, ate and drank out of vessels of gold and silver.

But though the sacred bull was adored in this extraordinary fashion, if he lived too long (above the age of twenty-eight, at which age Osiris died), then the priests, attired in mourning garments, led the horned embodiment of the god in state to the Nile, and solemnly drowned him there. Those of the sacred bulls which died a natural death were embalmed and buried with indescribable pomp, no expense being spared for this purpose. Priests remarkable for their moral influence were, on rare occasions, honoured by burial near the sacred bulls.

Whole rows of tombs, in vaults of corresponding size, arose in this subterranean cemetery. The faithful came hither to worship, and inscribed their names on special tablets of stone, which still remain here, with the precise date of each visit. These votive tablets are of the greatest historical value, as they mention the length of the reign of the king in which each Apis bull was born and buried.

The story of the slaughter of the sacred bull by Cambyses is familiar to all students of history. The Persian conqueror had, in the earlier period of his rule in Egypt, attempted to gain favour with the priests by patronising the native cult, and getting initiated into the mysteries and ceremonies of its worship. After the utter collapse of the ill-advised expedition to Ethiopia (B. C. 535) Cambyses's tolerance of the Egyptian religion was turned into the most bitter hostility. Hurrying back to Memphis from Nubia, after the loss of a great portion of his army, he found that the population were holding festival because the god Apis had just manifested himself in a new steer, which had been duly consecrated by the priests. In a paroxysm of rage, Cambyses ordered the priests to be beaten with rods, the worshippers of Apis to be massacred, and the sacred animal to be brought to his presence. Raising his sword, the enraged king killed the innocent animal with his own hand, to the horror of the whole native population. The actual epitaph written on this bovine martyr was found by Mariette, and is now to be read in the Musée Egyptien, in the Louvre.

A dramatic element is given to the discovery of the sepulchral chambers of the bulls, in the fact that when Mariette effected an entrance he found on the layer of sand that covered the floor the *actual footprints of the workmen* who, 3700 years before, had laid the sacred mummy in its tomb, and closed the door upon it, as they believed, forever.[1]

Owing to most travellers visiting Sakkarah and Memphis after Ghizeh, the Pyramids here usually come in for only very perfunctory notice. Yet the one known as the Step Pyramid — platform or terrace pyramid would perhaps convey a more accurate idea — is even in point of dimensions a noble monument. It is about 197 feet high. Unlike most pyramids, the sides are of unequal length, — the north and south faces being 351 feet, while the other sides are each 394 feet.

If Mariette is correct in attributing it to a king of the third dynasty, this pyramid or the Sphinx must be the oldest historic building in the world. It must have been in existence some five centuries before a single stone was laid of the Pyramids of Cheops, and over two thousand years before Abraham was born.

A small pyramid next the Step Pyramid, known as the Pyramid of Unas (fifth dynasty), is worth visiting. It has been opened up at the expense of Messrs. Thos. Cook and Sons, the well-known tourist agents. This was the sepulchre of the monarch a portion of whose mummified remains are to be seen in the Ghizeh Museum. It constitutes,

[1] For some portions of this description of the Serapeum, I am indebted to an admirable account in the volume which chronicles the Eastern travels of the present Czar of Russia in 1891-92.

indeed, the oldest historical mummy in any collection in the world. The official responsible for the descriptive labels attached to the various objects in this museum is presumably lacking in a sense of the ridiculous. The label affixed to the case containing the mummified débris of this sovereign bears the following humiliating, if justly descriptive, title : " Fragments of King Unas "!

The small pyramids of Teta, Pepi, and other kings show the marked degeneration in workmanship compared with the Ghizeh pyramids. For instance, the masonry, instead of hewn stone, is a kind of rubble formed of stone flakes filled in with loose chips.

Besides the valuable discoveries by Mariette in recent excavations in this pyramid field, already alluded to, were some tomb-paintings which throw fresh light on the disputed question of the origin of chess. Hitherto, it was assumed that the ancient Indians had invented the game; that it was introduced from India to Persia in the sixth century ; and that, in consequence of the Crusades, it spread from East to West. This theory was substantiated by the fact that an Indian, Persian, and Arabic influence is traceable in the character of the figures at present used, and in some of the words connected with the game, such as " shah " (check), and "matt" (mate). Now, north of the Pyramid of King Teta, two grave-chambers have been discovered which were erected for two high officials of that ruler, called Kaben and Mera. The grave-chamber (mastaba) of the former consisted of five rooms, built up with limestone. Its walls are covered with exceedingly well-preserved bas-reliefs and pictures representing various scenes. Mera's mastaba is, however, the most valuable. At present no fewer than thirty-two halls and corridors have been uncovered. Among the many wall-paintings in this and other rooms, hunting and fishing scenes, a group of female mourners, the three seasons, Mera and his sons holding each other by the hand, and *Mera playing chess* are to be seen. King Teta belonged to the sixth dynasty, and his reign was assigned by Professor Lepsius to about the year 2700 B. C. Professor Brugsch, correcting this chronology, puts it back to still greater antiquity; namely, to the year 3300 B. C., — so that chess would appear to have been known in the once mysterious land of Mizraim something like 5200 years ago.

The mastaba of Ti, a priest of the fifth dynasty, is one of the most elaborately decorated tombs in Egypt, and deserves more attention than the hurried visitor, or the ordinary sight-seer who attempts to " do " Sakkarah in one day, is able to devote to it.

Ti, it appears, held a post analogous to that of Chief Commissioner of Works for Upper and Lower Egypt, and he was also Secretary of State, Head of the Priests, etc.; in short, if the parallel be not profane, this many-sided functionary was a kind of Egyptian Pooh-Bah. He married a royal princess, who shared his tomb. This, perhaps, accounts for its magnificence. The chambers are a series of picture galleries; and these tinted sculptures give more illustrations of every phase of life in Egypt, five thousand years ago, than are to be found in any tomb or temple yet discovered. " These paintings," writes Mr. Joseph Pollard in his recently published " Land of the Monuments," " depict, in a most vivid and natural manner, the habits and customs of the dwellers on the Nile when Ti was Secretary of State, etc. The work is excellent throughout, and all the details are most carefully executed and finished ; every design was sculptured in low-relief and then painted. The colours are wonderfully bright and good; but when the tints have faded or peeled off, the carved design remains, and we see the whole of the artist's subject."

The Arabic word *mastaba*, which means a "bench," — so called because its length in proportion to its height is

THE CITY OF THE SACRED BULLS. 225

great, and reminded them of the long low seat common in Oriental dwellings,—is constantly occurring in descriptions of ancient Egyptian tombs. These tombs are the chief features in the Sakkarah necropolis, and a brief description of this kind of sepulchre may conveniently be added here. The mastaba is a heavy, massive building, of rectangular shape, the four sides of which are four walls symmetrically inclined towards their common centre. They vary much in size. The largest measures 170 feet long by 86 feet wide, and the smallest about 26 feet by 20 feet. In height, they vary from 13 to 30 feet. The ground on which the mastabas at Sakkarah are built is composed of rock covered with sand to the depth of a few feet; their foundations are always on the rock. Though they have at first sight the appearance of truncated pyramids, they have nothing in common with these buildings except their orientation, which is invariably towards the true north. Mastabas are of two kinds, of stone or of brick, and are usually entered on the eastern side. A mastaba is a more complex kind of tomb than might be supposed from its exterior. Its interior is divided into one or more mortuary chambers, a kind of anteroom for friends and relatives of the dead, a place of retreat (sirdab), and the pit which was the actual tomb. The walls of the interior are sometimes sculptured, and in the lower part of the chamber is an inscribed stone tablet, or stela. At the foot of this stela a small table of offerings is often found. A little distance from the chamber, built into the thickness of the wall at some distance from the floor, was a secret place of retreat. This niche was walled up, and the only means of communication between it and the chamber was by means of a narrow hole just large enough to admit the hand. This passage was supposed to carry off the fumes of incense which used to be burnt in the chamber. The sepulchral pit was a square shaft sunk from the floor of the mastaba, through the solid rock, to a depth varying from forty to sixty feet. There was no communication from the chamber to the bottom of the pit; so that the mummy and its sarcophagus, when once there, were inaccessible. The mummy was not, however, simply placed at the bottom of the pit. There was an opening from the bottom, excavated through the side of the shaft, which led obliquely towards the southeast. The passage, as it proceeded, was made larger until it became the sarcophagus chamber. This sarcophagus, rectangular in shape, was usually of limestone, and rested in a corner of the chamber. When the mummy had been laid in the sarcophagus, and the other arrangements completed, the entrance to the passage leading to the sarcophagus chamber was walled up, and the pit filled with stones, earth, and sand, so that the friends of the deceased might reasonably hope that he would rest there undisturbed forever. Alas! man proposes, and the Egyptian Exploration Society disposes!

The age of the mastabas discovered by Mariette is, of course, of the greatest importance to historians and antiquarians. He found three belonging to one or other of the three first dynasties, 43 of the fourth, 61 of the fifth, and 23 of the sixth dynasties; while in the case of nine he was unable to assign a date.[1]

---

[1] For most of this information on mastabas, I am indebted to an admirable series of articles contributed by Mariette to the "Révue Archéologique."

CHAPTER XVIII.

THE CITY OF THE SUN.

THE exact date of the foundation of Heliopolis, in spite of the great advance the science of Egyptology has made within the last few years, is still conjectural. It is probable, however, that the City of the Sun is almost as old as Memphis, though its period of greatest splendour dates from the decline of the latter city. According to the Turin papyrus, the worship of the Sacred Bulls, both at An (Heliopolis) and at Memphis, was established by Ka-Kau, of the second dynasty, in the year 4100 B. C. It may even be older, for some historians consider that the wording in the papyrus implies rather a revival than a primary inauguration of the cult of Apis.

The work of the sight-seer at Heliopolis is easy. There is only one curiosity,—the famous obelisk, the sole relic of the ancient capital which once ranked only second to Memphis in importance. This monument, being the sole object of attraction here for tourists, is naturally less perfunctorily examined than are those at most other goals of travellers in Egypt, where there is an embarrassing wealth of antiquities of all kinds. It is the oldest obelisk in Egypt yet remaining erect and *in situ*. The material is the usual rose-coloured granite of Assouan, the source of nearly all the Eygptian obelisks. Owing to a considerable part — some ten or a dozen feet — being buried in the soil, and to its somewhat commonplace surroundings, it lacks the dignity and impressiveness of the Theban obelisks. The annual inundation raises the soil of the Delta about six inches in a century, so that the amount of deposit covering a monument is an approximate indication of its age. The monolith is covered with hieroglyphics, which, as is the case with all well-known monuments in Egypt, have been carefully deciphered by Egyptologists, though they are now almost illegible, owing to bees having utilised the deeply incised hieroglyphics for their cells.

"Though Heliopolis is the least monumental of all the sites of Egypt, without temple or tomb, nor any record but the obelisk, it is yet eloquent of greater things than the solemn Pyramids of Memphis, or the storied temples of Thebes. What these tell is rather of Egypt's history than the world's; the idea that Heliopolis suggests is the true progress of the whole human race. For here was the oldest link in the chain of the schools of learning. The conqueror has demolished the temple; the city, with the houses of the wise men, has fallen into hopeless ruin, downtrodden by the thoughtless peasant, as he drives his plough across the site. Yet the name and the fame of the City of the Sun charms the stranger as of old while, standing beside the obelisk, he looks back through the long and stately avenue of the ages that are past, and measures the gain in knowledge that patient scholars have won." [1]

The erection of this obelisk probably synchronises with the building of the famous Temple of the Sun, of which it was doubtless one of the chief ornaments. Recent discoveries have enabled Egyptologists to assign the date of the foundation of the temple to the third year of the reign of Usertsen I., a king of the twelfth dynasty. This fact was established by Doctor Brugsch, in 1858, who discovered at Thebes a leather roll (now in the Berlin Museum) which gives an account of the founding of the temple.

But one need not be an antiquarian or student of ancient history to appreciate the extraordinary interest of this grand relic of an ancient civilisation. The least imagina-

[1] S. Lane-Poole, "Cities of Egypt."

tive of visitors can scarcely help being impressed at the sight of a monument which there is every reason to suppose Moses must often have looked upon, when a student at this ancient seat of learning. Then this obelisk must have been standing for over seven hundred years when Pharaoh gave Asenath, the daughter of Potiphar, the high-priest of the Temple of the Sun, to the Patriarch Joseph.

The sun is the most ancient object of Egyptian worship found upon the monuments. His birth each day, when he springs from the bosom of the nocturnal heavens, is the natural emblem of the eternal generation of the divinity. The rays of the sun, as they awaken all nature, seemed to the ancients to give life to animated beings. Hence that which doubtless was originally a symbol became the foundation of the religion. It is the Sun (Ra) himself whom we find habitually invoked as the Supreme being.

According to many scholars who have given special attention to that branch of Egyptology which concerns itself with the religion and mythology of the ancient Egyptians, notably Doctor Brugsch, the worship of Apis was not crude idolatry like the totem-worship of the North American Indians, but mere symbolism. According to these exponents of the Egyptian pantheon, the ancient Egyptians were virtually monotheists, who recognised in Ra the supreme solar deity, while the minor deities were mere personifications of his divine attributes. Kuum, for instance, represented his creative properties; Thoth, his wisdom; Anubis, his swiftness; while the bull, Apis, typified his strength. This view is certainly the most popular one, though many authorities are not prepared to admit that the Egyptians, though avowedly the most wonderful people of antiquity, had, at all events so early as the first dynasty, reached such a high spiritual standard as monotheism implies.

Perhaps, however, we shall find the true solution of the

problem in a modified monotheism, as Miss A. B. Edwards suggests in the following instructive passage:

"Their monotheism was not exactly our monotheism: it was a monotheism based upon, and evolved from, the polytheism of earlier ages. Could we question a high-priest of the nineteenth or twentieth dynasties on the subject of his faith, we should be startled by the breadth and grandeur of his views touching the Godhead. He would tell us that the god Ra was the Great All; that by his word alone he called all things into existence; that all things are therefore but reflections of himself and his will; that he is the creator of day and night, of the heavenly spheres, of infinite space; that he is, in short, the eternal essence, invisible, omnipresent, and omniscient. If, after this, we could put the same questions to a high-priest of Memphis, we should receive a very similar answer, only we should now be told this great divinity was Ptah; and if we could make the tour of Egypt, questioning the priests of every great temple in turn, we should find that each claimed these attributes of unity and universality for his own local god. All, nevertheless, would admit the identity of these various deities. They would admit that he whom they worshipped at Heliopolis as Ra was the same as the god worshipped at Memphis as Ptah, and at Thebes as Amen."

Heliopolis, during the middle empire, was the chief seat of learning in Egypt; and the sacred college, attached to the Temple of the Sun, was the forerunner of all European universities. Thales, Solon, Pythagoras, and even Plato are among the famous scholars who are said to have studied at this ancient university. Then, to go back to a remoter period, it was at Heliopolis that Moses was instructed "in all the wisdom of the Egyptians."

Its fame was, however, dimmed by the rise of Alexandria, and the transfer of its library to the new metropolis of Egypt, by Ptolemy I., proved its death-blow.

Manetho (who might be called the Gibbon of Ancient Egypt), whose records are the chief source from which all modern historians and Egyptologists derive their chronology, was the keeper of the archives of the Great Temple in the reign of Ptolemy Philadelphus. His actual history has never been found, and all we know of this invaluable work of reference is from a few quotations in Josephus and other chroniclers. Still, as Miss Edwards observes, there is no reason why some fortunate explorer should not yet find a copy of the lost history of Manetho in the tomb of some long-forgotten scribe, just as many transcripts of Homer have been found.

Heliopolis may be considered the mother-city of Baalbec, as, according to some historians, the Assyrian " City of the Sun" was founded by a colony of priests who migrated from Heliopolis. The magnificent ruins of this second Heliopolis, whose outer walls were composed of huge blocks hardly excelled in size by those used for building the temples of Rameses the Great, will give some indication of the architectural splendour of the Egyptian capital, as the latter was not likely to be exceeded in magnificence by the daughter-city. According to recent measurements, the largest of these blocks is sixty-four feet long, fourteen feet wide, and fourteen feet thick.

It is an interesting fact, but one which seems to have escaped the notice of the writers of popular text-books on Egyptian history, that the famous Rosetta stone was originally one of the inscriptions which covered the walls of the Temple of the Sun. An account of its discovery will be found in another chapter.

The legendary phœnix is familiar to every one in its proverbial application, and it was from Heliopolis that the myth of this fabled bird, sacred to Osiris, originated. It was said to visit the Temple of the Sun every five hundred years, and set fire to itself, fanning the flames with its wings, from whose ashes sprang a new phœnix.

Many of the early Fathers — Cyril, Clement, Tertullian, among others — so firmly believed in the story of the phœnix, that they did not hesitate to bring it forward seriously as a proof of the resurrection. Even in the present day, believers in the truth of this fable are to be found; and, as recently as 1840, a certain fellow of Exeter College, Oxford, published a long pamphlet in favour of the existence of this legendary bird. The most plausible theory of the origin of the myth is that it was a symbolic representation of the ancient astronomers to denote the recurrence of an astronomical period marked by the heliacal rising of some prominent constellation.

The village of Matarieh is usually included in the excursion to Heliopolis. It is little more than a mile distant, and those going by road will pass it on their way to the City of the Sun. According to the etymology of the village ("place belonging to the Sun"), it must originally have been an outlying portion of Heliopolis, and the famous well was in fact the "Fountain of the Sun." The excursion from Cairo is particularly pleasant, the road being bordered with tamarisks, palms, and sycamores. The village of Matarieh is charmingly situated, and from the number of palaces in its environs belonging to various members of the Khedivial family, it might well be termed a village of palaces.

The chief interest to visitors lies in the famous Virgin's Tree and Virgin's Well. Under this holy tree the Virgin and Child are said to have rested after their flight into Egypt. The tree is a magnificent old sycamore, — not, however, the kind of sycamore with which we are familiar, which belongs to the maple family, but a kind of fig. It need scarcely be said that the tree now seen is not the veritable tree of the legend; in fact, even the guides do not dare to assert this. The tree is probably not more than three hundred years old. There is, however, little doubt but that it is planted on the site of an older tree, to which the same tradition attaches; and, indeed, there is nothing to prevent the present tree having been produced from a sapling of a tree which, in its turn, sprang from the original tree. Many curious Coptic legends cluster round this venerable tree. According to some chroniclers, the Virgin Mary hid herself from the soldiers of Herod among the branches, and a spider, by spinning a web, effectually screened her hiding-place. These legends are a curious illustration of the proverbial repetition of history, or rather historical tradition, and recall to us the stories of Charles II. and the Boscobel oak, and Robert Bruce and the spider. The tree has been much hacked about by relic-hunting travellers; and the present proprietor, a Copt, with a sarcastic appreciation of the instincts of vandalism which seems to prompt latter-day tourists, has considerately planted another sycamore close by, from which pieces can be cut instead of from the original, a knife being chained to the tree for the purpose!

The late Khedive Ismail made a present of this tree to his guest, the ex-Empress Eugénie, in 1869. The gift was graciously accepted, but the empress's good taste prevented her taking any steps for the removal of this precious relic. Possibly, too, she was aware of Ismail's practice of making presents of antiquities — obelisks for instance — which were quite opposed to the wishes of the natives, or regarded the offer as an Oriental form of politeness never intended to be taken seriously, just as a modern Spanish grandee will not fail to tell a guest who incautiously admires any possession of his host, "Esta muy a la disposicion de Usted" ("It is yours"). This fictitious kind of hospitality is, perhaps, a traditionary habit bequeathed to Spaniards by their Saracenic conquerors.

The Virgin's Well is close by; and round this spot, also, have centred many early Christian legends. It has earned peculiar sanctity as the well in which the Holy Child was bathed. The fact that the water is fresh, being fed from springs, while that of most wells in the Delta is either salt or brackish, has naturally given colour to this tradition. According to the Coptic legend, the water was salt until the Virgin bathed her child in it.

The balsam shrub, the Balm of Gilead of the Bible, formerly grew here in profusion. The Coptic tradition is that the shrubs sprang from the drops of water which fell from the swaddling-clothes of the infant Jesus, which had been washed in the well. They were brought from Judæa to this spot by Cleopatra; who, trusting to the influence of Mark Antony, removed them, in spite of the opposition of Herod, as they had been hitherto confined to Judæa. Josephus tells us that the land where the balsam-tree grew belonged to Cleopatra, and that "Herod farmed of her what she possessed in Arabia, and those revenues that came to her from the regions about Jericho, bearing the balsam, the most precious of drugs, which grows there alone." The plants were in later times taken from Matarieh to Arabia, and grown near Mecca, whence the balsam is now brought to Egypt and Europe, under the name of Balsam of Mecca; and the gardens of Heliopolis no longer produce this valuable plant. A still more profitable article of commerce, one of the most lucrative in Egypt, — namely, the cotton-plant, — is due to some experiments in the culture of this plant at Matarieh in 1820.

CHAPTER XIX.

MINOR EXCURSIONS.

IT is not altogether surprising that the list of minor excursions in the neighbourhood of Cairo recommended in the standard guide-books, and known to the local dragomans and guides, should be such a meagre one. The ancient monuments of Ghizeh, Memphis, Heliopolis, etc., to say nothing of the important specimens of Saracenic architecture with which Cairo abounds, are so numerous and engrossing that few tourists can spare time for ordinary drives and expeditions, and consequently Murray and Baedeker are content with a brief notice of only a few excursions in the neighbourhood. Those, however, who are making Cairo their headquarters for the winter would find many objects of interest to occupy their time after exhausting the regulation sights, and, indeed, to know Cairo properly means more than a winter's study. To the artist Cairo offers an illimitable field, and one which is, to a great extent, a virgin one. Outside certain hackneyed points of view in the favourite bazaar quarter, and in the neighbourhood of the tombs of the Caliphs and Mamelukes, where one is constantly meeting artists of all kinds and degrees attempting to assimilate local colour and atmosphere, the artistic side of Cairo seems a good deal neglected. Those familiar with picture exhibitions know only too well the mosque interiors and scenes of Cairo street-life which, in the opinion of most amateurs, sum up the artistic possibilities of the City of the Caliphs. It is painful to see the absence of originality or freshness of invention, or any aptitude for the selection of a really striking or novel point of view among these innumerable artists of the "tea-tray school," who have eyes only for the conventional picturesque.

It is curious, too, that Cairo, with its undeniable wealth of subjects, does not seem ever to have been made a field of study by an artist of renown, as is the case with Florence, Venice, Rome, Granada, Athens, Constantinople, and other famous cities of Europe. Yet what a magnificent opportunity, for instance, the port of Boulag, as little known to the artist as to the ordinary tourist, offers to a "colourist" like Clara Montalba or Henrietta Rae, with its pictures of native life, its variety of form and colour!

Strangers probably do not realise that Cairo has an important trading-port at its threshold, and no dragoman would dream of suggesting that the quays of Boulag might be included in the traveller's daily round of sight-seeing.

It is a particularly lively scene, this emporium of all the commerce of Upper Egypt and Nubia. An endless succession of all kinds of vessels line the shore,— trading dahabiyehs, canges, steamers, rafts, transports, yachts, and, since the enterprise of Messrs. Tagg & Co., the famous Thames boat-builders, even steam-launches and rowing-boats. The most curious of all the crafts are the rafts composed of jars from Keneh, which may be seen here discharging their cargo. Montbard's lively description gives a good idea of what the traveller may see, though, of course, since the closing of the Soudan to traders, the trading-vessels with cargoes from Khartoum and from Southern Nubia are no longer to be seen:

"From the South come the vessels from Assouan loaded with senna, gathered in the desert by the warlike Abadiehs; elephants' tusks, rhinoceros' horns, and antelopes' horns from Darfour; skins of jaguars, zebras, and giraffes from Khartoum. Dahabiyehs with elevated poops advance; they hail from Esneh, with ivory, ostrich feathers, gum, nitre, etc., transported across the desert from Abyssinia; coffee and incense from Arabia; spice, pearls, precious stones, cashmeres, and silk from India, arriving by the deserts of Kosheir. Edfu sends its pipes, its charming vases in red and black clay, elegant in form, with gracefully modelled ornaments; and there are heavy barges from Fayoum, the land of roses, filled to the top with rye, barley, cotton, indigo; dahabiyehs full of carpets, woollen stuffs, flagons of rose-water, mats made with the reeds of Birket-el-Keroun."

An additional picturesque touch is given by the netting with which the precious freights are usually covered, instead of the commonplace and ugly tarpaulin which we are familiar with in Western ports. This netting is, however, more for the purpose of keeping the cargo together than to protect it from the elements.

We will now describe the more conventional excursions in the environs of Cairo. Helouan and the ancient quarries of Turra make a pleasant morning's or afternoon's expedition. The modern town of Helouan, on the strength of a few palm-trees surrounding the modern bathing-establishment, has been grandiloquently termed an oasis in the desert. It is about two miles from the dirty native village of the same name situated on the Nile. There is not much to see here except the bathing establishment and the Khedivial palace.

Of all his numerous palaces, — and the Khedive of Egypt seems to possess as many royal residences as King Humbert of Italy, — Helouan was the favourite one of the late Khedive Tewfik. It was here that this sovereign died, and, in consequence, it has long remained empty; for a foolish superstition — prevalent in all Mohammedan countries — makes even the present Khedive, in spite of his European training, disinclined to live in a palace where one of his relatives has died. This prejudice, no doubt, accounts for the palace of Ghizeh being turned into a national museum, and Ghezireh Palace into a fashionable hotel. Probably this is the destiny which awaits the palace of Helouan; for Helouan, now that its bathing establishment has been controlled by a German syndicate, and run on the lines of a Continental kursal, is beginning to be frequented a good deal by Europeans.

A great variety of waters are to be found here, — sulphur, saline, and iron; but the principal springs, and those which give Helouan its chief *raison d'etre*, are the sulphur springs, which are similar to those of Aix-les-Bains. The claims made for Helouan, as the most ancient health-resort and medicinal baths in the whole world, are probably justified. There can be little doubt that these are the sulphur baths near the quarries on the eastern side of the Nile, to which, on the authority of Manetho, the Ptolemaic historian, King Amen-hetep, sent "the leprous and other cureless persons, in order to separate them from the rest of the Egyptians."

Though Helouan contains little of interest, it is a convenient starting-point for a trip to the ancient quarries of Turra. These quarries supplied much of the stone for the Pyramids. Fortunately, the modern quarrying is of the surface rock for the most part, so that visitors can see the vast caverns excavated by the Pharaohs, in order to get the fresh stone, almost as they were when the Pharaouic labourers excavated them. Mediæval historians, misled by the similarity of the ancient name Ta-ro-fu, did not hesitate to call it Troja, and as a plausible pretext declared that it was so called because the captive Trojans, who were said to have followed King Menelaus to Egypt, had a settlement here. It is curious how many myths, gravely set down as authentic history by Diodorus, Strabo, Herodotus, and other great writers, are due to errors in etymology. Some stelæ found here, of the sixteenth dynasty, conclusively prove that the Turra hills were used as quarries by several kings of that early period. A local guide might better be taken, for the Cairo guides are not likely to know the way among the ancient galleries and cuttings.

These quarries are probably the oldest in the world, older even than those of Assouan. Many are still in use, and it is curious to think that the streets of the modern city of Cairo are paved with flags of the same magnesium limestone that the Egyptian masons used for building the temples of Memphis over four thousand years ago.

The ancient method of quarrying is so well described in Murray's Handbook, that it is worth quoting in full:

"They first began by cutting a trench or groove round a square space on the smooth perpendicular face of the rock; and having pierced a horizontal tunnel a certain distance, by cutting away the centre of the square, they made a succession of similar tunnels on the same level; after which they extended the work downwards in the form of steps, removing each tier of stone as they went on, till they reached the lowest part or intended floor of the quarry. Sometimes they began by an oblong tunnel, which they cut downwards to the depth of one stone's length; and they then continued horizontally in steps, each of these forming as usual a standing-place, while they cut away the row above it. A similar process was adopted on the opposite side of the quarry, till at length two perpendicular walls were left, which constituted its extent; and here again new openings were made, and another chamber connected with the first one was formed in the same manner, pillars of rock being left here and there to support the roof. These communications of one quarry or chamber of a quarry with the other are frequently observable in the mountains of Masara, where they follow in uninterrupted succession for a considerable distance; and in no part of Egypt is the method of quarrying more clearly shown. The lines traced on the roof, marking the size and division of each set of blocks, were probably intended to show the number hewn by particular workmen."

The quarries also served as a field of labour for prisoners of war and criminals, and were, in short, the Portland or Dartmoor of the ancient Egyptians. This is thought to be indicated by certain marks on the walls of the galleries, which are supposed to mark the progress of the work of the prisoners.

These quarries offer an admirable field of study for the geologist, as fossils of all kind are plentiful. The ethnographical student will also be interested in the remarkable specimens of flint implements — relics of the Stone Age — which are occasionally found in the desert, between Helouan and the Gebel Mokattam. These so-called prehistoric relics do not, however, point to such an extreme antiquity as is usually attributed to implements of the Stone Age; for it is well known to scholars that the Egyptians used these kinds of implements as recently as the twentieth dynasty.

The Petrified Forest, *pace* Baedeker, who declares that it is one of the sights of Egypt which every traveller makes a point of visiting, is of slight interest to most tourists, unless they are geologists. It is, however, an expedition which should not be omitted by strangers; for though there is little to see at the forest itself but a few fossilised trunks, the ride on donkey-back makes a pleasant little desert expedition, and the route across a spur of the Mokattam mountains affords magnificent views of Cairo, better even than those obtained from the Citadel, and at sunset the atmospheric effects of the desert are superb. It is possible to drive, for the rough track, which the guide-book diguifies by the name of road, is practicable for wheeled vehicles; but this mode of locomotion will not be found at all satisfactory, and it is far preferable, even for ladies, to make the trip in the orthodox way, on donkeys. A guide is quite unnecessary, as every donkey-boy knows the way. Donkeyboys, it may be observed, is a conventional term, the boys being often married men of thirty or forty years of age, just as the post-boys of the old coaching-days.

The journey there and back can be comfortably managed in a morning or afternoon, though the guides will naturally insist that it is a whole day's excursion. For the Great Petrified Forest, some half-dozen miles farther, a whole day should be allowed; but the ride is tedious, and a little too tiring for all but the most robust. If ladies attempt it, they should be careful to see that their mount has a well-fitting saddle.

To resume our itinerary of the Small Forest excursion, a halt is usually made at the so-called Moses's Well. It need scarcely be said that this spring has not even the slightest legendary association with Moses, but the Arabs are fond of naming geographical features after famous biblical characters. This spring is in a gorge of one of the Mokattam hills, and the Petrified Forest can be soon reached by active pedestrians, by climbing the crest of the mountain. The mounted members of the party must, however, return to the mouth of the ravine, and follow the path which winds round the spur of the hill, when the Forest will be reached in about half an hour. The remains of the fossil trees strew the plateau for several miles. It is a moot point with geologists whether the trees are indigenous, or whether they were floated by water and became embedded in the ground, being converted in the course of many thousands of years into stone. Professor Fraas, a German geologist of note, considers that these trees are of a totally different family to that of the palm, to which they are usually attributed by the guides, who are, of course, as ignorant of the elements of geology as the ordinary Nile dragoman is of archæology. In his opinion, the trees are a kind of balsam, and he offers the following theory of their origin: when the sandstone became disintegrated, and in course of time was converted into the sand of the desert, then the silicised trunks were gradually disengaged from their sandstone bed, and they now cover the surface of the Little Khashab for a distance of ten to fifteen miles. Travellers who are not familiar with the appearance of a vein of coal will be greatly struck by the appearance of this formation, regarding which all kinds of fanciful theories have been set up. The geologist, however, will simply regard it as akin to the coal-measures of the Meiocene period, with this difference,—that while the waters of Europe favoured the preservation of the carbon and the fibre of the wood, the silicious sandstone of the Mokattam converted the tissue of the wood into silicic acid. Specimens of similar fossilised trees are also seen in the desert beyond the Pyramids of Ghizeh, but these are rarely visited.

A charming excursion is the one to the Ostrich Farm, near Matarieh. The route is past Shubra, the suburb of palaces, and round by Heliopolis and Matarieh. The farm is run by an enterprising Frenchman. Though the dry and warm climate of Egypt is particularly well adapted for the breeding of ostriches, the experiment here does not seem to have proved a great commercial success. Eggs can be bought as mementoes of the visit. They are not pitted like those of the South African ostriches, but are quite smooth.

Perhaps the most interesting of all the excursions near Cairo is the one to the Barrage. This huge structure, which is so striking a feature in the landscape in the railway journey from Alexandria to Cairo, requires to be noticed at some length.

The Barrage, as it now stands—remodelled, restored, and thoroughly serviceable—is an excellent illustration of the excellent work carried out within recent years by the Public Works Department in the irrigation of Egypt. All efforts to ameliorate the condition of life among the fellaheen are summed up in a thorough system of irrigation. In Egypt, indeed, so far as practical benefit to the community is concerned, irrigation and drainage are of equal importance with improvements in means of locomotion in other countries,—railways, bridges, roads, and other renumerative public works.

Egypt is destined by nature to be the granary of Europe,

and its natural riches consist in agricultural products. One can hardly thus exaggerate the importance of developing the resources of its soil. In Egypt, indeed, the saying that the true benefactor is one who makes two blades of grass grow where formerly only one grew, seems especially applicable. We may even say that the one great apology for the English occupation of the country is the way in which Egypt's natural resources have been developed by the Public Works Department, the creation of the English.

That " Egypt is the gift of the Nile " — a maxim which has been repeated with " damnable reiteration " by almost every writer on Egypt since Herodotus — is no mere phrase, and its truth seems to have been recognised in the earliest age of Egyptian mythology, when the Nile was worshipped as the Creative Principle. Yet Mehemet Ali failed to appreciate properly the fact that the Nile is all in all to the Egyptian, and that the genius of the country is embodied in agriculture and not in manufactures; and that by concentrating his energies to fostering manufactures, for which the fellahs are naturally unfitted, he did as much to exhaust the national vitality as in attempting to realise his dreams of foreign conquest and his romantic ambition of regenerating the decaying Ottoman Empire. Under Mehemet, the peasants were torn away from their fields to serve in the Pacha's armies, or to work in his sugar and cotton factories; and Egypt was both a vast camp and a great factory, and its energies were strained almost to the breaking point. Even the climatic conditions of Egypt are opposed to the successful conduct of textile manufactures. The excessive heat is said to be injurious to the material, and the fine sand which is blown about by every breeze is destructive to the machinery. Notwithstanding, then, the low cost of labour, the Egyptians can be undersold by foreigners in cotton and linen stuffs. Besides, the cultivable soil of Egypt, which, by every canon of political economy, should first be attended to, requires as much native labour as the population can afford. At present it has been calculated that there is only one able-bodied fellah to every three acres of arable land. These observations may perhaps help the visitor to realise the significance of this magnificent monument of engineering enterprise known as the Barrage, which, by most travellers, is merely looked upon as a pleasant goal for a picnic, or, at best, as an *objectif* for an off-day's excursion.

The object of this huge dam — the largest weir outside India and the United States in the world — is to serve as a reservoir at low Nile, to maintain the river at the level of the banks and supply Lower Egypt with the same amount of water as at the period of high Nile. In theory the conception was a grand one, and some credit should be given to Mehemet Ali, who first saw the possibility of bringing an enormous area of the Delta under cultivation, which hitherto, for want of any means of irrigation, was absolutely unproductive. Unfortunately, the original engineers seem to have bungled, and did not make the foundations strong enough. The faulty foundations were due to haste, and to lack of efficient supervision over the thousands of ignorant fellahs impressed for the service. The engineers, under pressure from Mehemet, insisted on the foundations of the piers being completed during one low Nile period. The materials were not properly mixed, so that instead of a solid and cohesive base of concrete, the piers were built on a mass of loose rubble of sand and lime. This is scarcely to be wondered at, as over four thousand tons of concrete had to be mixed every day. Thus an admirably conceived undertaking was wrecked at the outset by puerile haste and deficient control over the army of labourers, amounting to over eighty thousand. In consequence of this "scamped" workmanship, from its completion in 1867 till 1885, when Sir Colin Scott-Moncrieff, the head of the Public Works Department, undertook the task of restoring it, this huge double dam, with its elaborate system of lock gates, sluices, etc., was regarded as a kind of white elephant by the Egyptian Government.

The Barrage consists of a double bridge or lock, each spanning one of the two branches of the Nile, the Rosetta and Damietta, at the point where they unite. The dam is on an enormous scale, and is strongly fortified. In fact, the Barrage was not merely a dam, but a bridge, a fort, and a barracks. At a distance it bears a striking resemblance to a couple of railway viaducts connected by a fort.

Abbas Pacha attempted to carry on this gigantic work, which had already swallowed up so many million piastres. A highly characteristic story of this worthless ruler, in connection with the Barrage, was told by one of the French engineers. It had struck the Pacha as a peculiarly happy thought to use the stones of the Pyramids for rebuilding it. "You see the Pyramids standing there useless: why not take the stones from them to do the work? They have already helped to build Cairo." The engineer, who was aghast at the suggestion, but careful to conceal his sentiments, retired from the presence, feeling that he was very awkwardly situated. To refuse to obey the Pacha was impossible, while if he consented to the destruction of these great historic monuments, his name would go down to posterity stamped with infamy as the destroyer of the Pyramids. However, a bright idea struck him. He would appeal to the well-known avarice of the Pacha. He therefore filled several sheets of paper with long columns of figures and imaginary calculations, which he brought to the Viceroy at his next audience as a rough estimate of the cost. Abbas, who, of course, could make nothing of the figures, though evidently impressed by them, insisted on having a verbal estimate. The engineer took care to make it a high one, and the Viceroy finally abandoned the project.

The Barrage, like the Suez Canal, was an undertaking which, doubtless, Napoleon would have carried out, had his scheme of conquering Egypt succeeded. Then Mehemet began it, and it was abandoned by Said Pacha. Abbas spent considerable sums in futile tinkering of the work. In 1885, Sir Colin Scott-Moncrieff, and his staff of engineers, found that the arches of the Damietta branch were badly cracked, and that the whole structure was faultily built; and though an English board of engineers had declared that to rebuild the Barrage and make it of any practical use £1,200,000 would be required, Sir Colin, after six years' continuous labour, succeeded in making the weir thoroughly serviceable at an expenditure of little more than a third of the estimate of the English experts. The ultimate gain to Egypt is almost incalculable. Already the export of cotton from the Delta, since the completion of the Barrage, has averaged in one year more than twice the cost of the six-years work of rebuilding it.

The Barrage is, however, only one of the great works in connection with the elaborate system of irrigation on which as much as eighty thousand pounds was spent in 1896. A project closely connected with the Barrage of the Delta is a huge dam, which is to be constructed at Assouan, and which will do for Upper Egypt what the former has done for the Delta.

Drainage is another public work of almost equal importance to that of regulating and utilising the flood-waters of the Nile. One of the most important drainage-works recently accomplished was the pumping out of Lake Mareotis, near Alexandria, in 1896. It is particularly fitting that the reclamation of this submerged land should be undertaken by English engineers, since the English troops, when occupying Alexandria in the early part of the century, wantonly cut through the narrow ridge which separated the sea from the lake, — at that time dry land.

Over half a million has been spent on drainage in Egypt; but, as Lord Cromer writes, in his last Annual Report (1896), "it may safely be asserted that funds could hardly be applied to a more necessary work, or to one which would bring in a quicker return on the capital expended. In Egypt, exhausted soil recovers its productive power very rapidly. Whenever a drain is dug, the benefit caused is quickly apparent in the shape of increased produce."

The prevailing impression among visitors is that the irrigation is effected solely by the natural submersion of the land by the inundation. This is only adhered to in Nubia and Upper Egypt. In the Delta, the flood is diverted into a network of canals, which intersect the Delta in all directions, giving it the striking appearance of a vast chessboard.

Lower Egypt produces three crops. The winter crop consists of cereals of all kinds. It is sown in November, and harvested in May or June. Cotton, sugar, and rice are the principal summer crops. They are sown in March, and gathered in October and November. Finally, there are the autumn crops, rice, maize, and vegetables, sown in July, and gathered in September and October. In Upper Egypt, where at present the inhabitants have to depend on the annual flood alone, there are only two harvests in the year; and the principal crop is the winter one of wheat, beans, or clover, gathered in May or June.

In order to complete our survey of the minor sights and excursions, some mention must be made of the various palaces belonging to members of the Khedivial family, which abound both in Cairo itself and the beautiful suburb of Ghezireh and Shubra. As is only natural in a city which is on the threshold of the grandest monuments of antiquity, royal palaces and other modern buildings — for the oldest of these are the work of Mehemet Ali's architects — receive but scant attention at the hands of tourists;

but to those sated with the magnificent relics of the oldest civilisation in the world, a morning devoted to visiting some of these royal residences and their beautiful gardens would afford a pleasing contrast. It must be remembered, however, that only a few can be seen by visitors, without special permission. Among these Mehemet Ali's palace at Shubra (now the residence of Prince Hasan, the uncle of the present Khedive) and the Ghezireh Palace are most interesting. The chief attraction of Prince Hasan's palace is the magnificent fountain and artificial lake, surrounded by kiosque, terraces, and hanging gardens, which are quite a triumph of landscape gardening. From a kiosque which crowns this series of terraces there is a charming view of the Nile.

The Ghezireh Palace is the largest of all the Cairo palaces. It was here that Ismail lodged his illustrious guest, the Empress Eugénie, in 1869. Though now converted into a fashionable hotel, the Oriental character of the building and its decoration have been scrupulously retained, and perhaps no Oriental city west of India can show such a superb specimen of modern domestic architecture as this admirably restored palace. Ghezireh, for though this is a generic term meaning island, — the official designation Ghezireh Boulag being seldom used, — is *the* island, and serves also as the Hyde Park and Hurlingham of Cairo, as well as the great focus and rallying-point of the European world of fashion. It has quite replaced the Shubra Avenue, once the fashionable drive; and the Ezbekiya Gardens, given up now-a-days mainly to Cairene tradespeople, nursery-maids of the European community, and English privates, might be called the Kensington Gardens of Cairo.

The palaces above mentioned, together with the Citadel, the Tombs of the Caliphs, and the Gebel Mokattam, constitute the finest points of view in Cairo.

CHAPTER XX.

THE NILE AS A HEALTH-RESORT.[1]

> It flows through old hushed Egypt and its sands
> Like some grave, mighty thought threading a dream;
> And time and things, as in that vision, seem
> Keeping along it their eternal stands, —
> Cavos, pillars, pyramids, the shepherd bands
> That roamed through the young world; the glory extreme
> Of high Sesostris, and that Southern beam,
> The laughing queen, that caught the world's great hands.
> Then comes a mightier silence, stern and strong,
> As of a world left empty of its throng,
> And the void weighs on us; and then we wake,
> And hear the fruitful stream lapsing along
> 'Twixt villages, and think how we shall take
> Our own calm journey on for human sake.
>
> LEIGH HUNT.

MANY English people, who are accustomed to spend the winter in one of the relatively cheap towns of the two Rivièras, are often deterred from wintering in the undeniably superior climate of Egypt by the expense of the journey and the high cost of living in Cairo. The City of the Caliphs is, no doubt, one of the most expensive health-resorts in the world, not only owing to the high charges of its splendidly equipped hotels, but to its great vogue as a fashionable cosmopolitan winter city. People are, however, beginning to realise that Cairo is not necessarily Egypt; and, indeed, as a health-resort pure and simple, it is, as we have shown in a previous chapter, by no means to be unreservedly recommended.

[1] From an article contributed to the **Westminster Review**, 1897.

Egypt, however, offers a choice of some four or five health-resorts besides Cairo; namely, Helouan, Mena House (Pyramids), Luxor, Assouan, and the Nile. As for Assouan, it should, perhaps, be regarded, in spite of its resident doctor and chaplain and good hotel accommodation, as a potential, rather than an actual, climatic health-station. Helouan is dull and depressing, and, in spite of its golf links, lacking in resources and attractions. Then the Teutonic element is rather too much in evidence at this sanatorium. Mena House, at the Pyramids, is undeniably expensive, and the fashionable society element too obtrusive to make it a desirable winter quarters for the invalid.

The Nile as a health-resort suffers from none of these drawbacks, and the climate of the Upper Nile and Nubia is undeniably superior to that of Lower Egypt.

The fullest benefit from the Egyptian climate is gained from a prolonged Nile voyage, while the asepticity — word beloved by the faculty — of the atmosphere is greater than at Luxor, where the hotels are terribly overcrowded in the height of the season. Then the Nile itself is more equable in temperature than its banks. On the other hand, invalid passengers on these miniature pleasure-barges — for one is bound to admit that the lines of the dahabiyeh approximate more nearly to those of a Thames house-boat than to a yacht — are not well protected from cold winds, which makes some physicians look askance on dahabiyeh trips for persons with delicate lungs. Besides, though the actual extremes of temperature are actually less on the rivers than in the desert, the difference is felt more by patients than when protected by the thick walls of a hotel. It is curious, too, that the cold at night seems to increase the farther one goes south. These constitute the only real drawbacks to dahabiyehs for delicate persons.

Formerly, the only orthodox way of doing the Nile voyage was by means of these native sailing-boats, universally known as dahabiyehs, and the costliness of this means of locomotion practically confined it to the English milord. Of late years, however, the wholesome competition of the great tourist-agencies has brought about a general reduction in the rents of these pleasure-craft. With a party of four or five, the inclusive cost of the two months' voyage to Assouan and back need not exceed £110 to £120 per head, — granting, of course, that the organiser of the trip knows the river, has had some experience of Nile travel, has a nodding acquaintance with Arabic, and is able to hold his own with his dragoman.

For the health-seeker as well as the mere holiday-maker, the dahabiyeh voyage is certainly the ideal method of spending a winter in Egypt. In short, this form of the new yachting is to the invalid what the pleasure yachting cruise — the latest development of coöperative travel — is to the ordinary tourist. Though independent, the traveller is not isolated, and can always get in touch with civilisation as represented by the tourist steamers and mail-boats, which virtually patrol the Nile from Cairo to Wady Halfa. Then he is never more than a few hours' sail from a railway station, — the line for the greater part of its length running along the Nile banks, and almost every station is a telegraph office as well. English doctors and chaplains are to be found throughout the season at the chief goals of the voyage, Luxor and Assouan; while, in cases of emergency, the services of the medical men attached to the tourist steamers are available. The voyage is eminently restful, without being dull or monotonous. In fact, the Nile being the great highway of traffic for Nubia and Upper Egypt to Cairo and Alexandria, there is constant variety, and the river traffic affords plenty of life and movement. One constantly passes the picturesque trading-dahabiyehs gliding along with their enormous lateen sails, the artistic effect being heightened by contrast with a trim, modern steam-dahabiyeh, as incongruous a craft as a gondola turned into a steam-launch, and utterly opposed to the traditions of Nile travel, — too reminiscent, perhaps, of Cookham Reach or Henley. The banks of the river, quite apart from the temples and monuments of antiquity, are also full of interest for the observant voyager, who may congratulate himself on the superiority of his lot to his less fortunate invalid brethren wintering on the Rivièra, "killing time till time kills them," — chained for the greater part of the day, perhaps, to the hotel balcony or Villa Garden at Mentone, Monte Carlo, or San Remo.

Delightful "bits" for the sketch-book are constantly to be met with. At almost every village, — and many are passed in a day's sail, — native women may be seen filling their earthen jars with water, and carrying them on their heads with all the grace and poetry of motion of a Capriote girl. Jabbering gamins are driving down the banks the curious little buffaloes to water. Every now and then we pass a shadoof tended by a fellah with skin shining like bronze, relieving his toil with that peculiar wailing chant which seems to the imaginative listener like the echo of the Israelites' cry under their taskmasters wafted across the centuries. The shrill note of a steamer-whistle puts to flight these poetical fancies, and one of the Messrs. Cook's tourist steamers, looking for all the world like a Hudson or Mississippi River steamer, dashes past at twelve knots an hour, filled with tourists more or less noisily appreciative of the Nile scenery. However, this incongruous and insistent note of modernity is fleeting enough. Has not the appointed goal — some fifty miles or so higher up — to be reached by dusk, else the arrangements of the whole Nile itinerary, and the plans of hundreds of tourists would be utterly upset?

Animal life, to say nothing of bird life, is far more

abundant than in Italy or France. Flocks of pelicans stud the sand-banks, and the white paddy-birds may be seen busily engaged in fishing, while brilliantly decked kingfishers, graceful hoopoes, sun-birds, and crested larks, to say nothing of our familiar friends the swifts, swallows, and water wag-tails, are flitting about over the water. Occasionally, a keen-sighted traveller will get a glimpse of an eagle or vulture.

Reptiles are represented by various kinds of lizards and chameleons. Crocodiles, of course, are never seen below the Second Cataract; though the monitor lizard, often mistaken for this reptile, is occasionally seen, and the unwary tourist occasionally has stuffed specimens palmed off upon him, by the wily Egyptian, as young crocodiles.

Hypercritical travellers occasionally complain that the scenery of the Nile, especially of that long two hundred miles' reach of desolate country which lies between the First and Second Cataracts, is monotonous. It is true that there is not as much variety in the landscape as there is south of Luxor, for instance, and human interest is certainly almost non-existent; but though the conventional picturesqueness may be lacking for the young lady artist who has only eyes for little bits that "compose" easily, the grand and impressive aspect of the Nubian landscape has a certain charm and attractiveness of its own to the imaginative traveller.

The monotony is, perhaps, more subjective than objective, and belongs to the spectator, and not to the things seen. To some a great London highway like the Strand would be monotonous, while another would find the same fault with the Alps, because each peak seems to him very like another. At all events, even if we grant a certain scenic monotony to the Upper Nile, who can complain when the traveller has daily presented to him the unique beauties of the Nile sunset, with its attendant glories of the zodiacal light?

Perhaps of all the wonderful scenic effects of the Nile, the almost miraculous afterglow which follows the sunset is the most impressive. Only those with a true "feeling for colour" can properly appreciate it, and to attempt to portray it either with pen or pencil would be futile. These startling effects may be called miraculous because inexplicable. In the tropics, as every one knows, there is no afterglow.

> "The sun's rim dips; the stars rush out;
> At one stride comes the dark,"

sings Coleridge's "Ancient Mariner." Only a scientist can explain why, in Egypt, on the very threshold of the Tropic of Cancer, the sunset's afterglow lasts thrice as long as it does elsewhere in the temperate zone.

Innumerable travellers have attempted to give an impressionist picture of the mysterious light-effect produced by the flood of liquid gold which suffuses the whole horizon after the sun's disc has disappeared. Mr. H. D. Traill, perhaps, is as happy as any observer in the following charming word-picture:

"Brighter and brighter grows the afterglow, and more and more golden as it brightens, — the red rays of the prism, which assume such prominence in most European sunsets, seeming here to be far surpassed in intensity by the yellow. . . . During this reillumining of the landscape, the deep orange of the western horizon has glowed steadily and undimmed; but, meanwhile, the quarter of the heavens lying immediately above it has undergone an astonishing change. For slowly, during all the time, there has been ascending, from the skyline of the desert as its base, and to an altitude of full thirty degrees above it, a glorious arc of the softest rose colour, which melts as it draws nearer to the blue of the zenith into a gradually paling lilac, through the very midst of which looks forth the silver of the evening star. The chastened magnificence, the sober splendour of this atmospheric effect, surpasses imagination. It is the very classicism of colour, just as the gorgeous hues of the actual sunset — its splashes of fierce crimson and blazing gold — might stand as typical of the rich exuberance of romance. But the time and space of this aerial marvel, the sphere of its radiance, and the spell of its duration are, perhaps, most wonderful of all. Laterally measured, this arc of glory spans a full quarter of the horizon. Vertically, as has already been said, it climbs at least one-third of the dome of sky between the horizon and the zenith; and it lasts in flawless and unimpaired beauty for a full half-hour. The sunset orange, against which yon passing string of camels and their turbanned leaders are silhouettes black as jet, will have faded into purple haze, the evening star will have changed from a rayless speck of silver into a flashing jewel, and the lake of lilac in which it swims will have become blanched and colourless ere that great rose-window through which we have been gazing, as into the lighted cathedral of the heavens, is itself at last swallowed up in night."

Life on a dahabiyeh has many of the advantages of a luxuriously appointed yacht, without its inseparable and obvious drawbacks. There are no storms, and, indeed, no calms, for a northern wind blows as regularly as a trade wind, almost continuously during the winter and spring months. You stop where you please, and as long as you please, without a thought of harbour dues, or anxiety as to the holding capacity of the anchorage. You can spend your time sketching, reading, or dozing, with a little shooting to give a fillip to the perpetual *dolce far niente*. You can explore ruined temples and ancient monuments at your leisure, without the disquieting reflections that the Theban ruins or the Ptolemaic temples of Philæ must be "done" in a certain time, else the tourist steamer will proceed on its unalterable itinerary without you. Finally, when tired of this perpetual picnic, you can enjoy for a few days the banal delights of a first-class modern hotel at Luxor or Assouan.

Such is life on a dahabiyeh; but, alas! this Epicurean existence is not for the ordinary sun-worshipper. As I have shown, it is a particularly costly form of holiday-making, though the expense has been much exaggerated.

The valuable advice given in Murray's "Handbook for

Egypt," on the hiring of dahabiyehs, may be supplemented by the following hints. If the hirer is a novice in Nile travel, or is not prepared to take a considerable amount of trouble, it will be better to hire the vessel through the Messrs. Cook or Gaze, direct. But in this case the hirer will not be so likely to feel himself "captain on his own quarter-deck" as he would if he hired direct from the owner. In the latter case it is decidedly an advantage to make a separate contract with the dragoman for the catering of the passengers, and another contract with the owner direct for the hire of the dahabiyeh, with fittings (which should be specifically set out), and for the wages of the reis (sailing-master) and crew. If, however, the contract is made with the dragoman solely, then take pains to ascertain that the boat is not the dragoman's property, else the temporary owner may find it difficult to maintain his authority; and, besides, the dragoman will naturally be inclined to be too careful of his craft, and will raise difficulties about shooting the cataracts or sailing at night. In short, the hirer will possibly find himself at as great a disadvantage as a yacht-owner in a foreign cruise who has neglected to have himself registered in the yacht's papers as master.

As to the time occupied in the voyage from Cairo to Assouan and back, with favourable winds, it can be managed in seven or eight weeks. But this would only allow three or four days at Luxor and Assouan. Besides, anything like hurry is utterly foreign to the traditions of Nile voyaging, and three months would not be found too long for this trip. It may be remembered, too, that if the contract is for three months, the cost would be considerably less relatively than for two months.

The rates for dahabiyehs vary considerably according to their size, age, and amount and nature of equipment and decorations. But as some indication of the prevailing price, it may be mentioned that the Messrs. Cook would charge a party of seven, for three months on one of the oldest type of dahabiyehs, £850 to £900, this price to include everything; while the charge for a modern dahabiyeh, luxuriously fitted up with bath-room, pantry, lavatories, etc., for the same period and the same number of passengers, might be anything from £1,100 upwards.

Life on a dahabiyeh is, no doubt, a lotus-eating existence, and it is not easy to resist the spell of the climate and the restful *genius loci* of this enchanted land.

> " To glide adown old Nilus, where he threads
> Egypt and Æthiopia, from the steep
> Of utmost Axumé, until he spreads,
> Like a calm flock of silver-fleecèd sheep,
> His waters on the plain; and crested heads
> Of cities and proud temples gleam amid,
> And many a vapour-belted pyramid."

But even the most hardened loafer and lover of the *dolce far niente* cannot help taking some interest in the grand monuments of an extinct civilisation, as well as in the archæological treasures, which so plentifully strew the river banks. Probably no great tourist-highway in the world offers so many *easily accessible* objects of historic and antiquarian interest as the Nile. Then, on a Nile voyage, sight-seeing is carried on under ideal conditions. It is a delightful relief to one accustomed to the hard labour of systematic sight-seeing at Rome, Florence, or Venice, for instance, to wander leisurely and uninterruptedly through the sun-steeped courts and shady colonnades of the ancient temples of Karnak or Philæ. Another advantage is that here the visitors need not be continually disbursing petty cash for entrance fees, gratuities to attendants, guides, catalogues, etc. In Egypt, the single payment of £1, 6*d*, the Government tax, franks the tourist not only to these Theban treasure-houses of ancient art, but to all the monuments and temples of Upper Egypt.

A series of voyages in the well-found and well-equipped tourist steamers of Messrs. Cook and Gaze will be found, however, a tolerable substitute for the invalid. In fact, the Messrs. Cook specially cater for this class of tourists by offering special terms to passengers making three consecutive trips on the basis of three voyages at the price of two. By this plan passengers can make three voyages from Cairo to Assouan and back for £100, the fare including board on the steamer during the few days' stay at Cairo between the voyages. Thus nine weeks may be spent on the Nile at a less cost than a stay for the same period at a fashionable Cairo hotel. Considering that the mileage covered by these voyages amounts to about 3,500 miles, — equal to the distance from London to Alexandria by sea, — it is not surprising that this remarkably economical method of undertaking what is supposed to be one of the most expensive of river trips in the globe-trotter's itinerary is becoming popular.

The cuisine on board these steamers, as will be seen from the annexed specimen menu, is varied and plentiful, if not actually luxurious, and should satisfy the most exigent traveller.

MENU ON NILE TOURIST STEAMER.
December 1st, 1896.
LUNCHEON.
Hors d'Œuvres.
Rougets au Vin Blanc.   Poulets au Sauté au Madère.
Roast Beef — Pommes de Terre.
Salade.   Fromage.
Dessert.
Café

DINNER.
Consommé Pâté d'Italie.
Poisson à la Orly.
Noix de Veau à la Livernaise.
Epinards aux Œufs.   Bécassines Roties.
Salade.   Baba au Pêches.
Dessert.
Café.

Many who take the Nile trip for the sake of health could scarcely be considered sick persons, and for the benefit of these sturdy invalids I add the following hints on the sport to be obtained during a Nile voyage.

Of course all the best shooting is in the Delta, but a certain amount of sport is obtainable by dahabiyeh travellers, especially in the Theban plain. Above Luxor, owing to the scarcity of vegetation, there is less cover, and hares and partridges are not so plentiful. Of late years, too, the English officers stationed at the different posts on the Upper Nile have thinned the game a good deal. In Lower Egypt fair bags of snipe can be obtained. In fact, snipe is the principal winter game in Egypt, just as quail is during the spring months. The former, however, are rarely seen on the Upper Nile, though quail are plentiful. Duck and teal, everywhere on the Upper Nile, afford the best sport for dahabiyeh passengers, and the dinghy (*filuka*, whence *felucca*) attached to every dahabiyeh will sometimes serve to capture the shot birds in wild-fowl shooting.

Big game is very scarce, even in the desert near Wady Halfa, and sporting tourists fired by the accounts of earlier generations of travellers, of hyenas, wolves, and jackals haunting the Theban temples, will be disappointed. Hyenas, like crocodiles, are rarely met with below the Second Cataract. In fact, even to get a remote chance of bagging these beasts, coöperation with the natives and a large outlay of baksheesh would be necessary. The sportsman would have to be prepared to camp out at night at their supposed haunts, which would have to be baited with the carcass of a donkey or some other domestic animal. Gazelles are occasionally shot, but they require a considerable amount of stalking. It must be remembered that, though permission to bring a sporting rifle or gun is readily granted to English tourists by the military authorities at Cairo, the import of powder or loaded cartridges has, since 1894, for obvious reasons, been strictly prohibited, and all ammunition must be bought at Cairo.

Sportsmen should be careful about shooting pigeons in the vicinity of a village, otherwise they may get into difficulties with the natives through shooting pigeons which are alleged to be domestic. As in France, no game license is necessary.

CHAPTER XXI.

THE NILE FROM CAIRO TO THEBES.

THE very mention of a Nile voyage recalls to most travellers the splendid monuments of Thebes, Philæ, and Abou Simbel, while the ruins south of Luxor, some of which (those of Abydos in particular) historically perhaps of equal importance, are forgotten. No doubt the wealth of architectural treasures collected in one spot in the Theban plain obscures in popular imagination the isolated temples of Abydos or Denderah, or the ancient rock-shrines of Beni-Hassan. In short, nine out of ten travellers hurry on to the ruins of the Theban plain, and leave the ancient temples or tombs which bestrew the Nile Valley between Cairo and Luxor for a hurried and somewhat perfunctory inspection on the return voyage, when, sated with the architectural splendours of ancient Thebes, the less striking monuments north of Luxor come as an anti-climax.

We are all apt to forget, as Miss A. B. Edwards is careful to remind her readers, that the ancient history of Egypt goes against the stream. If we omit the conjectural, perhaps mythical, site of This, which is almost prehistoric, — and indeed the claims of Abydos and Girgeh are still wrangled over by Egyptologists, — it is in the Delta and on the banks of the Lower Nile that relics of the most ancient cities are to be found (at Tanis, Memphis, and Heliopolis, for instance), while the latest temples and tombs are found in the Upper Nile Valley, and in Nubia.

Those whose study of Egyptian antiquities is confined to the standard guide-books forget, too, that only the more important monuments, or those in tolerable preservation, are ever mentioned. First-hand study of the chief authorities shows that a complete Egyptological itinerary of the Nile Valley would include antiquities of which only a very small portion are visited by the ordinary Nile voyager.

Beni-Hassan, one hundred and seventy miles from Cairo, is remarkable for the famous rock-tombs excavated in terraces on the precipitous bank of the Nile. The cliff has been cut through by the river, which formerly reached to its foot, but has since retired, so that a considerable expanse of plain lies between the tombs and the Nile. These tombs belong to the twelfth dynasty, which dates from about 3000 to 2500 years B. C. Though nearly a thousand years more recent than the Sakkarah mastabas, they have preserved the chief features of them, and have a deep shaft leading to a corridor which ends in a sarcophagus chamber. There are about fifteen of these tombs, most of which are carefully described in Murray's Handbook, but only two of them, those of Ameni or Amen-Em-Hat ahd Khnem-Hetep II., are likely to interest the average sight-seer.

"As in the tombs of Assouan, a suitable layer of stone was sought for in the hill, and, when found, the tombs were hewn out. The walls were partly smoothed, and then covered with a thin layer of plaster, upon which the scenes in the lives of the people buried there might be painted. The columns and the lower parts of some of the tombs are coloured red, to resemble granite. The northern tomb is remarkable for columns somewhat resembling those subsequently termed Doric. Each of the four columns in the tomb is about seventeen feet high, and has sixteen sides. The ceiling between each connecting beam, which runs from column to column, is vaulted. The columns in the southern tombs have lotus decorations, and are exceedingly graceful."[1]

To the artist these famous grottoes are of enormous interest as the birthplace of Greek decorative art. The influence of the most ancient school of design in the world of

[1] E. A. Wallis-Budge: "The Nile."

Greek art is most ingeniously traced by Miss A. B. Edwards in her "Pharaohs, Fellahs, and Explorers," a work which, though rather handicapped by its somewhat *ad captandum* title, is of the highest value as a thoroughly well-informed introduction to the science of Egyptology, treated in a popular manner. The Pelasgic decoration and paintings, of which excellent specimens have been found at Mycenæ, are thought by many scholars of the highest repute to be the originals of those of the Aryan Hellenes. The dark interval of four or five hundred years between the prehistoric ruins of Mycenæ and the oldest remains of the historic school cannot, however, be bridged over with any certainty. It is, nevertheless, conclusively proved that the "Pelasgians went to Egypt for their surface decoration, and the Hellenes for their architectural models."

The principal sculptural ornaments, such as the spiral, the key pattern, and the so-called honeysuckle pattern, — the latter, according to Mr. Petrie, a florid imitation of the Egyptian lotus pattern, — which are often regarded as purely Greek in origin, are undoubtedly Egyptian. "They were all painted on the ceilings of the Beni-Hassan tombs, full twelve hundred years before a stone of the treasures of Mycenæ or Orchomonos was cut from the quarry." The spiral is continually found, either in its simplest form or combined with the lotus, in the decorations of these tombs.

The earliest monument of Greek architecture is identified with the ruins of a Doric temple at Corinth of about 650 B. C.; and any one of the columns of this — the oldest ruin in Greece — might have been taken bodily from one of the pillared porches of Beni-Hassan. In fact, Fergusson, one of the highest authorities, does not hesitate to say that it is an indubitable copy of the Beni-Hassan column. This type of column, technically known as the protodoric, is, as the name implies, the prototype of the famous Doric columns, — loftier, more graceful, and with a decorated, not a plain, entablature. There are, of course, other examples of this style in Egypt, and those who have visited Thebes will remember the famous Corinthian columus of the Temple of Thotmes III. at Karnak.

An early origin may be allowed to the Ionic column. The lotus-leaf design — a characteristic, decorative feature of this class of column — "furnished the architects of the Ancient Empire with a noble and simple model for decorative purposes. Very slightly conventionalised, it enriches the severe façades of tombs of the fourth, fifth, and sixth dynasties, which thus preserve for us one of the earliest motives of symmetrical design in the history of ornament."

The evolution of the elaborate rock-sculptures of Beni-Hassan and Abou Simbel from the almost prehistoric rock grotto makes an interesting subject for those who are attracted by the study of necrology, and of the sepulchral monuments of the ancient Egyptians.

A very able and lucid summary of the development of rock-tombs is to be found in a chapter on the art of the ancient Egyptians in Baedeker's Handbook. It is, no doubt, customary among high-minded travellers to despise guide-book information, but in few technical works on this subject will so clever and readable a summary be found as in the above-mentioned indispensable work of reference.

"The original motive of the rock-tomb or sepulchral grotto was merely to find a tomb sufficiently removed from all risk of flooding by the Nile, with a sufficiently dry and aseptic atmosphere to arrest the decay of the corpse. Soon a kind of mortuary chamber for mourners and friends was also excavated in the rock. This was followed by a more pretentious mausoleum with several chambers. This large area of wall surface seemed to demand some kind of ornamentation. Hence the sculptures in low-relief and distemper paintings. Where there were several chambers, it was natural that openings should be made in the walls to admit the light. The next step was to convert the remaining portions of walls into polygonal pillars for the support of the roof. In the next place, the octagonal pillar was sometimes turned into one of sixteen sides, and sometimes it was fluted. Thus the pillars were converted into columns, — a distinction with a considerable difference, — those columns which were, no doubt, the direct originals of the better known Doric columns, and were called Protodoric or Egypto-Doric by Champollion and Falkener, from the resemblance to the Doric columns of Greece. Polygonal columns of this character occur in the first tomb of Beni-Hassan.

"The architects of these tombs, however, were not unacquainted with a light and elegant mode of building above ground, which cannot have originated in the grotto architecture. This is proved by their use of the lotus column, the prototype of which is a group of four lotus-stalks, bound together and secured at the top by rings or ligatures, the capital being formed by the blossom.

"While the architecture of the eleventh and twelfth dynasties bears some slight resemblance to the earlier style, the sculpture of the same period presents an almost total deviation from the ancient traditions. The primitive lifelike realism, to which we have already alluded, is displaced by the rigorous sway of the canon, by which all proportions are determined by fixed rules, and all forms are necessarily stereotyped. There seems, however, to have been no retrogression in point of technical skill, for, as in the time of Khafra, the hardest materials still became compliant, and the difficulties of the minutest detail were still successfully overcome by the sculptor of the Pharaohs."

The mural decorations consist mostly of pictures, painted on a specially prepared surface of fine-grained plaster; and there are few relief sculptures. These paintings represent scenes in the life of the deceased, and form a kind of pictorial biography, which are not, as in the case of the paintings of later tombs, intermingled with the conventional mystic representations of divinities. "In the grouping of the various scenes, the artists seem to have been guided by a natural principle, which led them to place the Nile in the lowest register, the agricultural scenes in the middle, and desert scenes at the top. But little technical skill is shown in the drawing. The birds are always better drawn than the human figures; but the natural features of the country are represented in the most conventional way, a series of zigzag lines standing for water, and a wavy outlined pink space, dotted with red and black, being the desert."[1]

The tomb of Khnem-Hetep II. is in the northern group of tombs. Remains of a dromos or avenue leading to the portico can still be traced. The principal chamber or shrine contains a large figure of the deceased, who was one of the feudal lords of Egypt in the time of the twelfth dynasty. This tomb is usually known as No. 1, for all the tombs here are numbered. In this shrine is a curious kind of dado, painted to represent rose-granite, and the scheme of colour of the ceiling consists of red and yellow squares, with black and blue quatrefoils. This sepulchre is best known for the painting, which is supposed, but on doubtful authority, to represent Joseph, and his brethren arriving in Egypt to buy corn. At all events, it represents the arrival in Egypt of a band of foreigners, thirty in number, who, from the features, seem to belong to the Semitic race. Heading the procession, and apparently acting as the introducer or conductor, is the Egyptian royal scribe, Nefer-hetep, and the main procession consists of the Aamn chief, Abesha, "the prince of the foreign country," and his fellow countrymen. They wear beards, and carry bows and arrows. Some have supposed that the Aman were shepherds or hyksos.

Equally interesting is the tomb of Ameni, of which the general structural arrangement is similar to that of the former tomb. Ameni, or Amen-Em-Hat, as he is sometimes called, was a high functionary of the court of Usertsen I., of the twelfth dynasty. One painting in the picture gallery of this tomb describes pictorially his expedition into Ethiopia, and his triumphant return, laden with spoil and trophies. In the inscription on the wall, couched in

[1] Murray's "Handbook for Egypt."

the usual vainglorious tone which was customary at that time, he sums up his achievements in peace and war, as follows:

"I have done all that I have said. I am a gracious and a compassionate man, and a ruler who loves his town. I have passed the course of years as the ruler of Meh, and all the labours of the palace have been carried out by my hands. I have given to the overseers of the temples of the gods of Meh three thousand bulls with their cows, and no contribution to the king's storehouses have been greater than mine. I have never made a child grieve; I have never robbed the widow; I have never repulsed the labourer; I have never shut up a herdsman; I have never impressed for forced labour the labourer of a man who only employed five men. There was never a person miserable in my time; no one went hungry during my rule, for if there were years of scarcity I ploughed up all the arable land in the nome of Meh, up to its very frontiers on the north and south. By this means I made its people live, and procured for them provision, so that there was not a hungry person among them. And, behold, when the inundation was great, and the owners of the land became rich thereby, I laid no additional tax upon the fields."

In addition to the tombs there is a kind of rock-temple dedicated to the lion-headed goddess Sechet or Pasht, called Artemis (Diana) by the Greeks, which is known as the Speos Artemidos (the cave of Artemis). It is excavated in a rock at the entrance of a gorge about ten miles from the tombs. The place is known by the guides as Stabl Antar. This shrine, or temple, was begun by Thotmes III. and the famous Queen Hatasu, and was embellished with a few sculptures by Seti I., but was never completed. The only finished reliefs are on the inner wall of the portico; and as they are of a good period of Egyptian art, it is to be regretted that the other sculptures are in an unfinished state. In the plain to the south, not far from this valley, the vast cemetery of cats was discovered, in 1887. These mummified relics were found to possess fertilising properties, and were transported to Europe by the ton for manure.

Between Beni-Hassan and the Theban plain, ruins of temples and tombs, Roman forts, eyrie-like convents, grottoes, etc., abound, and the Nile voyager is rarely out of sight of some ancient monument. To visit all would, however, require the antiquarian zeal of a Flinders-Petrie or a Mariette; and even a mere digest of all the antiquities in the four hundred and fifty miles of the Nile Valley, through which the traveller bound for Luxor, the great goal of all Nile voyages, passes, would require several volumes.

Some twenty miles beyond Beni-Hassan are the recently discovered rock-tombs of Tel-El-Amarna, hardly inferior in interest to the more famous ones we have just described. They were unearthed and scientifically examined by Prof. Flinders-Petrie, during excavations undertaken in 1892. This excursion is especially attractive to artists on account of the exquisite design and colouring in the painted pavements, — the relics of the palace of Khu-en-Aten (1400 B. C.), about two miles from the tombs. One floor is in an excellent state of preservation, and the colours are remarkably fresh. A new artistic influence is seen in the treatment of the figures represented in this beautiful series of frescoes; and animals, birds, insect life, plants, etc., are drawn with a remarkable fidelity to nature, offering a strong contrast to the stiff and conventional treatment in other animal paintings of the Middle Empire. This new art was introduced by the highly cultured King Khu-en-Aten, who seems to have introduced reform in art along with reform in religion, for Khu-en-Aten had calmly adopted the cult of Amen, the God of Thebes, to that of Aten, an Asiatic deity symbolised by the solar disk.

Near this palace was discovered, in 1887, the Record Office, as it may be called, of this enlightened monarch. A large number of bricks were found with the inscription, "The House of the Rolls," which clearly showed the object of the building. Here Professor Petrie came across a valuable find of the greatest importance to historians and archæologists. It consisted of several hundred clay tablets inscribed with cuneiform characters, comprising despatches to the king from his brother sovereigns of Babylonia and Assyria. "The tablets cast a vivid and unexpected light on Egypt and Western Asia in the fifteenth century before Christ, and show that Babylonian was at that time the language of education and diplomacy. They also show that education must have been widely extended from the Euphrates to the Nile, and that schools must have existed for teaching the foreign language and script. Canaan was governed at the time by the Egyptians, much as India is governed to-day by the English; but the officials and courtiers of the Pharaoh were for the most part Asiatics, the larger number being Canaanites."

Soon after passing the village of Beni-Hassan we come to one of the most picturesque series of reaches in the whole Nile voyage, and here the beautiful dom-palm is first seen. A few miles beyond Tel-El-Amarna the magnificent precipices of Gebel Abu Faydah are a striking feature of the scenery. They extend, a precipitous rampart, along the eastern bank of the Nile for nearly a dozen miles, and to American visitors will, perhaps, recall memories of the famous Palisades on the Hudson. Half concealed in the topmost clefts and fissures of these stupendons precipices may be seen the caves where dwelt the celebrated monks and ascetics of Upper Egypt; and in one of these caverns, according to a monastic tradition, Athanasius sought shelter for a time.

Innumerable tombs, as yet not systematically explored, and rarely visited by tourists, line the terraces of these cliffs. At the top is the famous cemetery of mummified crocodiles. These pits and caverns which comprise this saurian necropolis are not well known even to the local guides, and to visit them alone would be exceedingly hazardous. Within recent years a party of tourists lost their lives in exploring the suffocating labyrinth, and, if the guides are to be believed, their bodies were never recovered.

Abydos lies on the west bank of the Nile, some three hundred and fifty miles from Cairo, and was thought by many Egyptologists to occupy the site of This, the earliest historical city of Egypt, and the home of Menes, the first king of the first dynasty; but the systematic excavations of Mariette scarcely support this view. It was, however, one of the most renowned cities in ancient Egypt, attaining its greatest splendour in the eleventh and twelfth dynasties, and ranked second to Thebes as a centre of learning and religious thought.

The temples are, of course, the chief curiosities here; but to scholars and antiquarians the necropolis is of the greatest importance, as here can be seen specimens of the three types of tombs which were used at various periods by the Egyptians. The earlier tombs belong to the sixth dynasty, and are of the mastaba class. Those of the eleventh and twelfth dynasties are in the forms of small, brick pyramids, while those of the eighteenth dynasty show a revival of the early rectangular sepulchre.

It is curious that the usual practice of burying the dead in grottoes or caves excavated in the sides of cliffs or inland hills was not followed at Abydos. Instead of choosing the limestone hills, which lay ready to hand, the citizens of Abydos preferred for sepulchral purposes the sandy plains interspersed with rocks.

The principal monuments here are the temples of Rameses the Great and Seti. The former is said to be dedicated to Osiris, the tutelary deity of Abydos, whose head was supposed to be buried here. In fact, one of the chief titles of this god is "Lord of Abydos," as may be seen in the famous funerary tablet (now in the Haworth collection) of the Theban priest Napu, who lived nearly twenty-five centuries ago. Some doubt has, however, been thrown by the newer school of Egyptologists on the claim put forward for this temple as the original sanctuary of Osiris, since the failure of Mariette, in the course of his researches in 1864, to find any trace of the shrine of this god. "During the French occupation of Egypt," writes Dr. Wallis-Budge, "in the early part of this century, this temple stood almost intact; since that time, however, so much damage has been wrought upon it, that the portions of wall which now remain are only about eight or nine feet high." It was here that a fragment of the famous Tablet of Abydos, a duplicate of the one still *in situ* on the wall of the adjacent temple of Seti, was discovered by Mariette, in 1864. It is now in the British Museum. The tablet is of the greatest historical importance, as it gives the names of seventy-five kings, beginning with Menes and ending with Seti I. It is not, however, a complete list, and gaps have to be supplied from the Tablet of Karnak, now in the Museum of the Louvre.

The temple of Seti, often called the Memnonium, is the Palace of Memnon described in some detail by Strabo, who states that it was constructed in a singular manner, entirely of stone, and after the plan of the Labyrinth. The greater portion of the temple was built by Seti, but his son, Rameses II., is responsible for most of the relief and other mural decorations. Here we find another copy of the famous poem of Pentaur. This is the well-known illustrated historical epic of the Khita campaign of Rameses II. It is familiar to all Nile travellers, as the numerous episodes of this war, quaint pictures in bas-relief, confront the visitor, not only at Abydos, but at Abou Simbel, Luxor, Karnak, and Thebes. This poem, so evidently written to order by the poet laureate of the time, is published, as Miss Edwards forcibly puts it, in a truly regal manner, in an edition (necessarily limited) issued on stone, illustrated with bas-reliefs, while, to continue the metaphor, the temple walls form an imperial binding to this sumptuous epic.

The temple of Seti is unique as being the only ancient Egyptian roofed temple yet remaining, for of course the Denderah, Edfu, and other temples of the Ptolemaic era are modern in comparison. The construction of this roof was peculiar. Huge blocks, extending from the architraves on each side of the temple, were placed on their sides, not on their faces. Through this mass of stone an arch was cut which was decorated with hieroglyphics and sculptures.

There are three places in the Upper Nile Valley where the architecture of the Ptolemaic age can be studied, — Denderah, Philæ, and Edfu, where the finest monuments of the Ptolemies replace the ordinary architectural relics of the Pharaohs.

Denderah lies on the west bank of the Nile, only three or four miles from Keneh, so that it is very easy of access. The present temple is evidently built on the ruins of a temple dedicated to the goddess Hathor, the Greek Aphrodite, which, according to the results of Mariette's discoveries, was founded by Cheops. This temple, however, never held very high rank among the fanes of the Ancient Empire, perhaps owing to its proximity to the famous shrines of Abydos and Thebes. The wonderfully preserved building which we see is the work of the later Ptolemies, while it was completed as recently as the first century.

Egyptian sculpture had long been on the decline before the erection of the present temple of Denderah; and the Egyptian antiquary looks with little satisfaction on the graceless style of the figures and the crowded profusion of ill-adjusted hieroglyphs that cover the walls of this as of other Ptolemaic or Roman monuments. But the architecture still retained the grandeur of an earlier period, and though the capitals were frequently overcharged with ornament, the general effect of the porticoes erected under the Ptolemies and Cæsars is grand and imposing, and frequently not destitute of elegance and taste.

These remarks apply very particularly to the temple of Denderah; and from its superior state of preservation it deserves a distinguished rank among the most interesting monuments of Egypt. For though its columns, considered singly, may be said to have a heavy, perhaps a barbarous appearance, the portico is doubtless a noble specimen of architecture; nor is the succeeding hall devoid of beauty and symmetry of proportion. The preservation of the roof also adds greatly to the beauty as well as to the interest of the portico; for many of those in the Egyptian temples lose their effect by being destitute of roofs. Generally speaking, Egyptian temples are more picturesque when in ruins than when entire; being, if seen from without, merely a large, dead wall, scarcely relieved by a slight increase in the height of the portico. But this cannot be said of the portico itself; nor did a temple present the same monotonous appearance when the painted sculptures were in their original state; and it was the necessity of relieving the large expanse of flat wall which led to this rich mode of decoration.

The temple of Denderah is probably best remembered on account of the famous portraits in relief of Cleopatra and her son Cæsarion on the exterior of the end wall. The queen is conventionally drawn as an Egyptian type, according to the canons of Egyptian portraiture which had determined the portraits of gods and kings for over fifteen hundred years. For some reason Cleopatra's portrait has been accepted by modern writers as an excellent likeness of the " serpent of old Nile;" yet, as Professor Mahaffy observes in his " Empire of the Ptolemies," it is no more a likeness than the well-known granite statues in the Vatican are true portraits of Philadelphus and Arsinoe. The artist, in fact, had probably never seen the queen. "This Egyptian portrait is likely to confirm in the spectator's mind the impression derived from Shakespeare's play, that Cleopatra was a swarthy Egyptian, in strong contrast to the fair Roman ladies, and suggesting a wide difference of race. She was no more an Egyptian than she was an Indian, but a pure Macedonian, of a race akin to, and perhaps fairer than, the Greeks.

Another object of peculiar interest in this temple is the famous zodiac painted on the ceiling of the portico, which was erroneously supposed by Egyptologists of the last generation to be a relic of the Pharaonic ages. Mariette's researches have, however, established the fact that, like its fellow in the temple of Ezra, this zodiac must be attributed to the Roman period. Another zodiac was, till 1821, to be seen in the curious little upper chapel, or subsidiary temple, dedicated to Osiris, the tutelary deity of Denderah. This is usually known to the local guides as "The Temple of the Roof." Owing to the disgraceful vandalism so prevalent in the time of Mehemet Ali, who, although an enlightened monarch in many respects, does not seem to have possessed the slightest appreciation of Egyptian antiquities (of which he should have been the national guardian), the zodiac was actually cut out bodily from its wall, and presented to France, where it may be seen in the Louvre Museum. One is bound to admit, however, that the recollection of that shameful spoliation of the friezes of the Parthenon, by Lord Elgin, makes this natural indignation on the part of English visitors rather inconsistent. The only palliation in the case of the Elgin marbles was that there was some risk of their being spoilt by wind and weather if they remained *in situ*. In Egypt, however, this excuse cannot be urged. The preservative effects of the dry and rainless climate of the Upper Nile are well known.

The structural arrangement of the Denderah temple, or rather congeries of temples, is very interesting. Though this monument is for the most part the work of Greek and Roman architects, the main features of the Pharaonic temple have been retained. Owing to its well-preserved condition, this temple, albeit modernised, will, perhaps, give the spectator a better idea of what the ancient Egyptian temples were in their pristine splendour than even the magnificent ruins of the roofless temples at Karnak or Luxor.

Owing to the continuous work of excavation recently undertaken for several seasons by Mariette, this beautiful temple is now completely accessible, even to the last of its numerous chambers. It is difficult to speak too highly of the energy and enterprise which, by clearing away the accumulated rubbish of centuries, — for a whole village of mud-huts had actually sprung up on the roof, — has effected this.

One finds here the usual features of all Egyptian temples, — the crude brick wall enclosure, dromos, pylons, porticoes, regular series of halls corresponding to the nave, chancel, and choir of Christian cathedrals, etc. In some of the columns and internal decorations the influence of Greek art is, however, clearly traceable, and the same thing strikes the eye at once in some of the ancient temples of India.

We enter through a magnificent portico, or vestibule, supported by twenty-four columns. This leads into another hall, called the "Hall of the Appearance," and then we reach the "Sanctuary of the Golden Hathor." Around the great temple are several subsidiary shrines, of which the most interesting is the temple dedicated to Isis. It is here that the sacred cow is sculptured, and, according to Murray's Handbook, the Sepoys, who formed part of the English army of occupation in the beginning of the century, prostrated themselves before the figure of this sacred animal.

Edfu, which is only seventy miles north of the First Cataract, ought strictly to be left for the chapter on Assouan, as our order is mainly topographical. It is, however, best to include in one chapter a survey of the famous triad of Ptolemaic temples, — Denderah, Esneh, and Edfu, — all of which have much in common. The temples of the Ptolemies have, perhaps, gained a fictitious importance in the minds of tourists owing to their strikingly picturesque background, but architecturally they are inferior, and can more conveniently be described separately.

It is only within the last few years that credit for these magnificent architectural achievements has been allowed to the Ptolemies by modern historians. Owing to the adoption of the ancient Egyptian religious symbols in the sculptures of these Greek temples, and the grafting of the Egyptian faith by fusing their gods with those in the Greek mythology, — Serapis is a well-known instance, — modern scholars have long been at fault as to the origin of these temples, which were usually attributed to the Pharaohs; and it was imagined that the Ptolemaic sovereigns had left no permanent mark in Egypt. Letronne was the first to convince Egyptologists of their error, by showing that the Greek inscription agreed with those in hieroglyphics.

The Temple of Edfu was not, indeed, the work of any one sovereign. It took over one hundred and eighty years in building; and every Ptolemy, from its founder Ptolemy III., down to Ptolemy XIII. (Auletes), who completed it, seems to have had a hand in restoring or enlarging this splendid temple.

CHAPTER XXII.

"THE CITY OF A HUNDRED GATES."

"A rose-red city — half as old as time."

THE spot on which ancient Thebes stood is so admirably adapted for the site of a great city, that it would have been impossible for the Egyptians to overlook it. The mountains on the east and west side of the river sweep away from it, and leave a broad plain on each bank of several square miles in extent. It has been calculated that modern Paris would scarcely cover the vast area of ancient Thebes.

Luxor itself lies on the east bank of the Nile, some four hundred and fifty miles from Cairo, in the midst of this verdant and fertile plain. It is a considerable village, — in fact, a modest town, — and its inhabitants (some two thousand in number) apparently divide their time in agricultural pursuits, the exploitation of the tourist, and the manufacture of spurious antiquities.

The first view from the dahabiyeh or Nile steamer of the smiling expanse of verdant plain — so different from the tourist's preconceived idea of desert landscape — upon which are Karnak, Luxor, and the other scattered villages which lie on the site of ancient Thebes, whose ruins show it to have been one of the largest cities in the world, is singularly impressive from the striking contrast. At once one realises the felicitousness of Homer's epithet, —

"Not all proud Thebes' unrivalled walls contain,
The world's great Empress on the Egyptian plain

That spreads her conquests o'er a thousand states,
And pours her heroes through a *hundred gates*,
Two hundred horsemen, and two hundred cars,
From each wide portal issuing to the wars."

The stupendous masses of masonry, the propylons and pylons of the ancient temples, — *hecatompylons*, no doubt, refer to these gateways, and not to those of the city, which was never walled, — are seen towering above the palms. The valley is surrounded by a ridge of hills, broken into cone-shaped peaks nearly two thousand feet high. In January the plain is already verdant with barley, with flowering lentils and vetches, and interspersed with patches of golden sugar-cane.

Most of the Theban ruins are on the west branch of the Nile; but the grandest monument of all, the Great Temple of Karnak, the largest and most magnificent architectural ruin in the whole world, is on the east bank, about one and a half miles from Luxor. Its enormous size and Titanic proportions are the predominant impressions on the part of the tourist, and its architectural and artistic beauties are at first lost sight of in a bewildering sense of bulk and immensity. That the visitor should be almost stupefied by the vastness of scale is scarcely surprising, when we consider that four Notre Dame Cathedrals could be built within the area included by the outer walls of this temple, and that the propylon (entrance gateway) equals in breadth alone the length of the nave of many English cathedrals, and in height equals that of the nave of Milan Cathedral. Ten men would be required to span the colossal pillars in the great hall; yet there is no suggestion of unwieldiness in their cyclopean proportions, and the beautiful calyx-capitals " open out against the blue sky as lightly as the finest stone tracery above an English cathedral nave."

Thebes appears to have been for over two thousand years not only the capital of Egypt and the seat of govern-

"THE CITY OF A HUNDRED GATES." 279

ment, but also her ecclesiastical metropolis, a kind of Egyptian Rome or Canterbury. Almost every sovereign, from Usertsen I. (B. C. 2433) to the Ptolemies, seems to have regarded the embellishment of this famous shrine, or the addition of subsidiary temples, as a sacred duty. A glance at Mariette's plans of the original building, and that of the temple, or rather group of temples, in the time of the Ptolemies, shows very clearly the gradual development of the building. To those who take an interest in architecture, the mingling of the various styles during this long period is very instructive.

" For splendour and magnitude, the group of temples at Karnak forms the most magnificent ruin in the world. The temple area is surrounded by a wall of crude brick, in some places still 50 feet in height, along the top of which you may ride for half an hour. The great hall of the Great Temple measures 170 feet by 329 feet, and the roof, single stones of which weigh 100 tons, is supported by 134 massive columns, 60 feet in height. The forest of columns stands so thick that from no one spot is it possible to see the whole area of this stupendous hall; and weeks may easily be spent in following the detail of the pictures with which the walls are covered, — battles, sieges, sea-fights, processions of captives, offerings to the gods, massacres of prisoners, embassies from foreign lands bearing gifts and tribute, voyages of exploration and their results; the whole history of Egypt during the most splendid period of her greatness is recorded on the walls and pylons of the Theban temples." [1]

One of the most striking features of the Great Temple is the splendid obelisk in front of the fourth pylon, erected by Queen Hatasu, who may almost rank with Rameses the Great as one of the most famous royal builders of Egypt. This magnificent column stands preëminent as the loftiest, best proportioned, and most elaborately engraved of any obelisk in existence. It is one hundred and nine feet high in the shaft, and is cut from a single flawless block of red granite.

[1] Isaac Taylor.

The dates in the inscription engraved on the plinth show that this magnificent monolith was dug out from the granite quarries of Assouan, conveyed to Thebes, a hundred and thirty miles distant, dressed and engraved, and erected in its present position *within seven months*. The only erect obelisk which at all approaches Queen Hatasu's monolith in size is the one which stands in front of the Church of St. John Lateran, the mother-church of Rome, which was brought from Egypt in the reign of Constantine the Great. The famous twin " Needles of Cleopatra," now in the Central Park, New York, and on the Thames Embankment, are pigmies in comparison.

Though the Luxor Temple is of inferior interest, and in the matter of dimensions alone the stupendous fane of Karnak bears the same relation to it that a European cathedral does to one of its side-chapels, yet anywhere but here it would command respectful attention from the traveller. So great is the wealth of antiquities which strew the site of the ancient Egyptian capital that visitors there are, indeed, spoilt for all other ruins which are not of surpassing interest. As the Luxor Temple lies at the threshold of the hotels, it can be visited frequently by the conscientious sight-seer without much loss of time. To avoid the feeling of an anti-climax it is advisable that the first visit to this temple should be made before that to the Great Temple of Karnak. Its most noteworthy feature is a fine obelisk of red granite, covered with admirably carved hieroglyphics. Its fellow is familiar to most visitors, perhaps without knowing it, inasmuch as it adorns the Place de la Concorde, Paris.

It is interesting to trace the history of the Egyptian obelisks. Fifty-five, without reckoning the uncompleted ones at Assouan, are recorded in history. Twenty-seven of these historic monoliths were quarried at Assouan. A larger number than is usually supposed have been transported to Europe, the trophies for the most part of Greek and Roman emperors, and are scattered among the great Continental capitals. Nearly a dozen are in Rome, one is in Constantinople, another towers over the Place de la Concorde in Paris, while the most famous of all in popular estimation, the twin "Needles of Cleopatra," have found a home, as every schoolboy knows, in New York and London respectively.

It may be remarked that many modern writers on these characteristic monuments of Egypt — for a whole literature has grown up round these monolithic columns — have inveighed against the vandalism of the Romans in stripping Egypt of these memorials of her former greatness. From English and American authors, however, this scarcely comes with a good grace, considering the eagerness displayed in appropriating Cleopatra's famous obelisks. This, however, is but a venial error of taste compared with the exhibition of the mummified remains of the Pharaohs in the Ghizeh Museum.

Many are the theories ventilated by antiquarians to account for the characteristic shape of the obelisk. That it was symbolical is now generally admitted. According to some authorities, its peculiar form symbolises the rays of the sun, while some anthropologists are inclined to attribute a deeper and less obvious origin, and consider that, like the pyramids, obelisks are intended as an emblem of the vital principle for esoteric reasons, which need not be discussed in a non-technical work.

The temples of Luxor and Karnak, however, comprise only a small portion of the ruins which have made Thebes one of the most frequented shrines of tourist culture in Egypt. On the other bank of the Nile are the Ramasseum, the temples of Rameses II. and III., the Vocal Memnon, the rock-tombs of the kings, — the most impressive in point of situation of any collection of mausolea in the world, — and other ruins concerning which innumerable guide-books and Egyptian works of travels are eloquent.

The whole of ancient Thebes is, indeed, one vast buried museum of antiquities. In short, the saying that in the Nile Valley you have only to scratch the surface to come upon a crop of antiquities applies with especial force to the City of the Hundred Gates. Though the directors of the Ghizeh Museum have been particularly active in this region of late years, and have made considerable progress in the work of excavation, a great portion of the Valley of the Dead, in Western Thebes, is virgin soil. The tombs and monuments that have been discovered, however, in this vast necropolis, would not be exhausted by the sight-seer under several weeks, while, as for the students of Egyptology, a stay of several seasons, instead of weeks, might be made here with advantage.

The extraordinary wealth of antiquities in the Theban plain, and the great historic and antiquarian value of Karnak and Thebes, will require a longer chapter than usual, even for a superficial notice of the principal monuments.

For the practical purpose of getting some idea of the confusing topography of the site of ancient Thebes and its vast cemetery, as well as for the æsthetic enjoyment of an incomparable view, one of the peaks of the mountain barrier which keeps guard over the Tombs of the Kings should be climbed. Unique is the prospect of the smiling Theban plain, through which the Nile meanders like a silver thread, bounded by the Arabian Mountains. On the right are Hataus's Temple of Dar-El-Bahari and the Temple of Rameses III., and right before us is the Memnonium; on the left are the Temple and Palace of Rameses I. Some distance in advance of these stand, like videttes, the twin Colossi. Then, on the other side of the Nile, Luxor raises its gigantic columns from the river's edge, and gigantic propylons mark the Karnak temples.

"THE CITY OF A HUNDRED GATES." 283

The remarkable temple generally known as the Ramesseum, which "for symmetry of architecture and elegance of sculpture can vie with any other Egyptian monument," is really the cenotaph or mortuary temple (corresponding to the mastabas of Memphis) of Rameses II. In the entrance court a colossal figure of Rameses seated on a throne used to confront the worshipper. The ruins scattered round the pedestal show it to have been the most gigantic figure — to which the Abou Simbel colossi were but statuettes — ever carved in Egypt from a single block of granite. The fact that the granite of this statue would have made three of the great obelisks of Karnak will give some idea of its dimensions. It was probably destroyed by the Persians under Cambyses.

"By some extraordinary catastrophe this statue has been thrown down, and the Arabs have scooped their millstones out of his face; but you can see what he was, — the largest statue in the world. Far and wide his enormous head must have been seen, — eyes, nose, and ears. Far and wide you must have seen his hands resting on his elephantine knees. You sit on his breast and look at the Osiride statues which support the portico of the temple, and they seem pigmies before him. Nothing that now exists in the world can give any notion of what the effect must have been when he was erect. Nero, towering above the Colosseum, may have been something like it; but he was of brass, and Rameses of solid granite. Rameses, also, was resting in awful majesty after the conquest of the whole known world."[1]

This colossus forms the subject of one of Shelley's sonnets :

> "I met a traveller from an antique land,
> Who said : 'Two vast and trunkless legs of stone
> Stand in the desert. Near them, on the sand,
> Half sunk, a shattered visage lies, whose frown
> And wrinkled lips and sneer of cold command
> Tell that its sculptor well those passions read
> Which yet survive, stamped on these lifeless things

[1] A. P. Stanley, D.D.

The hand that mocked and the heart that fed.
And on the pedestal these words appear:
'My name is Ozymandias, king of kings;
Look on my works, ye mighty, and despair.'
Nothing beside remains. Round the decay
Of that colossal wreck, boundless and bare,
The lone and level sands stretch far away."

The proverbial poetic license must, of course, be accorded to Shelley's description of the "lone and level sands," which suggests the solemn associations of the more impressive Sphinx, sitting in lonely majesty in the actual desert. The Theban plain is a richly cultivated tract, and the colossus lies among plots of maise and lentils. But Shelley never visited Egypt. It is a little curious that Egypt, which offers such a rich field for poetic treatment, has never had justice done to it by modern poets of the first rank. Spain has had Southey for its laureate, and Germany, Coleridge and Longfellow; while as for Italy and Switzerland, a whole army of poets have sung their praises, from Shelley, Byron, and Landor down to the facile rhymester Rogers. Egypt, with all its wealth of material for an epic poem, has done little more than inspire a few fragmentary sonnets from Shelley, Leigh Hunt, and Moore.

The most popular, if the word is permissible in connection with these stupendous ruins of an extinct civilisation, of all the Theban monuments are the two Colossi, which for over three thousand years daily watched the dawn breaking over the Karnak temples. These two alone remain, though they probably formed but the vanguard of a procession of statues which guarded the approach to the palace of King Amen-Hetep III., which has now almost entirely disappeared. The most celebrated of these two statues is, of course, the one known as the Vocal Memnon, from a tradition that it emitted sounds when the sun's rays fell upon it. Many are the theories ventilated by scientists

"THE CITY OF A HUNDRED GATES." 285

to explain the origin of this legend; for, needless to say, the statue is mute now, and, indeed, has been silent, according to the chroniclers, since it was repaired in the reign of the Emperor Severus. Such inquiries are, however, futile enough, as there is little doubt that the credulous worshippers were deceived by a "pious fraud" of the priests, who were either possessed of ventriloquial skill, or contented themselves with hiding in the statue and secretly striking it. Certain kinds of granite have, it is well known, a musical ring. Humboldt has described similar sounding rocks in the Orinoco Valley, which yielded musical notes, supposed to be caused by wind passing through the chinks, and agitating the spangles of mica into audible vibration. The pedestal of this statue is covered with what may be considered testimonials of its musical merits, inscribed in Greek and Latin by visitors from the first century downwards. One of these inscriptions records the visit of the Emperor Hadrian.

The most important monument, from an archæological point of view, as well as the most interesting, is the famous Temple of Queen Hatasu (Hatshepsu), daughter of Thotmes I., and wife as well as half-sister of Thotmes II., who appears to have been the Cleopatra of the eighteenth dynasty. This temple is a fit memorial of the "spacious days" of a sovereign who has been felicitously termed the Queen Elizabeth of Egypt. Its principal features are admirably described by Miss A. B. Edwards, in the following passage:

"This superb structure is architecturally unlike any other temple in Egypt. It stands at the far end of a deep bay, or natural amphitheatre, formed by the steep limestone cliffs which divide the Valley of the Tombs of the Kings from the Valley of the Nile. Approached by a pair of obelisks, a pylon gateway, and a long avenue of two hundred sphinxes, the temple consisted of a succession of terraces and flights of steps, rising one above the other, and ending in a maze of colonnades and courtyards, uplifted high against the mountain-side.

The sanctuary, or holy of holies, to which all the rest was but as an avenue, is excavated in the face of the cliff, some five hundred feet above the level of the Nile. The novelty of the plan is so great that one cannot help wondering whether it was suggested to the architect by the nature of the ground, or whether it was in any degree a reminiscence of strange edifices seen in far distant lands. It bears, at all events, a certain resemblance to the terraced temples of Chaldæa."

The unearthing and restoration of the ruins of this great temple has been one of the most important works carried out within recent years by the Egyptian Exploration Society. The work had occupied them four successive winters, and was only completed last season (1896-7). The discoveries brought to light during this long and systematic excavation are of the greatest antiquarian and historical value. One of the most significant was the discovery of a large hall, in which was a huge stone altar, the only one discovered in Egypt. The altar is dedicated to Queen Hatasu's father, Harmachis. It is curious that Hatasu's cartouche is rarely found perfect. It is usually more or less erased, probably through the jealousy of her successor, Thotmes III. The cartouche, which is such an essential feature in all stone inscriptions, seems to have virtually served the purpose of a modern visiting-card.

Close to this temple is the deep pit in which were found the royal mummies in 1881. In all probability there was some kind of underground communication between this temple and the royal cemetery, known only to the priests.

The Temples of Rameses I. and Rameses III., lying respectively at the eastern and western extremities of the Theban necropolis, are of especial interest to the student of history on account of the paintings and inscriptions which cover the walls. The series of pictorial sculptures on the walls of the Medinet Abou (Rameses III.) Temple form a kind of panorama in stone, and are of the greatest value to the historian as a pictorial chronicle of

the conquests of Rameses III. No doubt they were intended to rival the famous illustrated epic of Pentaur, the poet laureate of Rameses the Great, in which the mighty achievements of that monarch were sung.

The temple has been recently completely cleared of rubbish. The second court, in the opinion of Mariette one of the most precious in any Egyptian temple, is the most interesting feature. The circular columns are very richly painted. The walls are covered with the inevitable battle-scenes. It was here that one of the most important discoveries of papyrus in Egypt was made. Among them was the famous Harris papyrus, now in the British Museum, which gives a very full précis of the reign of Rameses III.

In order to appreciate the importance of the excavations which have laid bare all these wonderful ruins in the Theban necropolis, thus adding to our knowledge of the political and social life of the ancient Egyptians, we must remember that the Theban temples were intended to serve many purposes. They are, of course, chiefly memorial chapels, like the Medici Chapel at Florence, or the Spanish Escurial; but they also served as a treasury, a kind of muniment room, a library, and even as a kind of national portrait gallery.

The Tombs of the Kings should be reserved for a whole day's excursion. They are hewn out of the living rock in the mountains, some three miles from the western bank of the Nile. The contrast between the fertile plain and these gloomy mountain gorges is very striking, and the name " Valley of Death,'' which has been given to these dreary and desolate defiles, is happily chosen. The kings of the nineteenth and twentieth dynasties were buried here, though, as we have seen, the royal mummies had been removed to Dar-El-Bahari, about 966 B. C., to secure them against pillage,— a precaution, we are reminded by the presence of the mummies at Ghizeh, quite ineffectual against the excavations of savants and antiquarians. Several of the best sarcophagi, too, are distributed among Continental museums; for instance, the sarcophagus of Rameses III. is in the Louvre, the lid in the FitzWilliam Museum at Cambridge, while the mummy itself is in the Cairo Museum. Though the chief interest of these tombs is therefore wanting, the tombs themselves are worthy of thorough examination. The principles of construction are similar to those of the Assouan tombs. They consist of long inclined tunnels, intersected by mortuary chambers which in some cases burrow into the heart of the rock for four or five hundred feet. "Belzoni's Tomb" is one of the "show" ones. Here was buried Seti I., the father of Rameses the Great. This magnificent sarcophagus is one of the chief treasures of the Soane Museum, London. It is nine feet in length, carved out of one block of translucent Oriental alabaster. It is covered both inside and out with hieroglyphic writing and figures from the mythology of Egypt, representing the judgment of the dead, and other subjects. This sarcophagus was discovered by Belzoni, in the year 1817, and purchased by Sir John Soane from Mr. Salt, in 1824, for the sum of £2,000.

According to Strabo, there are forty of these royal tombs, but the labours of the Government officials have not yet succeeded in bringing to light more than twenty-five of these sepulchres. Scarcely more than half of the tombs which have been opened are included, however, in the ordinary dragoman's programme. The walls of the corridors and of the mortuary chamber are covered with extracts from the "Book of the Dead," and with paintings, which show skilful and elaborate draughtsmanship.

"On one of the subterranean corridors leading to Belzoni's Tomb there is an allegory of the progress of the sun through the hours, painted with great detail: the God of Day sits in a boat (in compliment to the Nile, he lays aside his chariot here), and steers through

"THE CITY OF A HUNDRED GATES." 289

the hours of day and night, each of the latter being distinguished by a star. The whole circumstance of ancient Egyptian life, with all its vicissitudes, may be read in pictures out of these extraordinary tombs, from the birth, through all the joys and sorrows of life, to the death; the lamentation over the corpse, the embalmer's operations, and, finally, the judgment and the immortality of the soul."[1]

These royal vaults are known to the guides by numbers merely. One which is seldom visited possesses peculiar interest to Biblical students, and is numbered fifteen. According to Mr. J. A. Paine, an American Egyptologist, who has written a suggestive and well-argued article in the "Century," this tomb was prepared for Seti II., the firstborn son of the Pharaoh of the Oppression, who died in the last plague of the Egyptians. Though Seti II. is reckoned among the Egyptian sovereigns, records seem to prove that he sat on the throne with his father; so this need not upset Mr. Paine's theory that Seti died in his father's lifetime.

The above necessarily hasty and superficial glance at the more famous monuments will, perhaps, whet the appetite of the visitor for a more thorough exploration, and will at any rate help him to realise that a whole winter at Luxor would scarcely suffice to exhaust the tombs and temples of ancient Thebes. A consideration, then, of the claims of Luxor as a winter residence may appropriately close this chapter.

A whole winter here would be especially attractive to those who recognise the fact that Thebes is not a place to be "done," and who can appreciate the peculiar fascination of Luxor,—emphatically one of those places which, in common parlance, "grow upon you." Here, too, one is able to see more of the life of the people, and realise more of the native atmosphere than is possible at a popular cosmopolitan winter-city like Cairo. But apart from these æsthetic considerations, the material aspect of the case

[1] "The Crescent and the Cross."

is a factor which cannot be neglected. Living at Luxor is comparatively cheap.

The cost of wintering in Egypt is rather overrated, unless this implies residence at a fashionable Cairo hotel, where, if the visitor wishes to take part in the social life of the winter residents, he would no doubt find Egypt an unusually expensive residence, and it would be a difficult feat to keep the daily expenditure below two pounds a day. But the economical visitor, to say nothing of the invalid, must eschew the "flesh-pots of Egypt" so far as they are represented by the gaieties of this lively city; and if he makes Luxor his winter headquarters, he will find that his three months (including journey from England) will not cost him more than £80 or £85; that is, under a pound a day. Let us take the items:

First-class return by North German Lloyd steamers (the most moderate of the first-class steamship companies) from Southampton and Port Said . . .	£29.2.2
(From New York to Genoa, £32.8.0, first-class return.)	
Cairo to Luxor (second-class rail, first steamer) . .	6.9.0
Extras on voyage, rail from Port Said to Cairo, Cairo hotel, etc., say	5.0.0
Sixty days at Luxor hotel at 10s	30.0.0
Government tax for Egyptian temples . . .	1.0.6
Luncheon, wine, baksheesh, donkeys, and incidentals, at £1 per week	12.0.0
Total	£83.11.8

No doubt this amount would suffice almost for a whole winter at a cheap Riviera pension, but a sojourn of the same length at any extra-European winter-resort could scarcely be managed for less. The expense would be reduced from five pounds or six pounds by taking one of the cheaper steamship lines to Port Said or Ismailia, such as the *Anchor*, *Moss*, or *Papayanni;* but none of these services are altogether satisfactory, especially the two latter, and for an invalid they are impossible. In fact, a delicate person would be more comfortable travelling second-class in one of the Orient or P. and O. steamers. Then, another reason why Luxor is so economical a residence is that there are few opportunities for spending money in a place where there are no urban amusements, no society entertainments, no cabs, no cafés, and no shops (except for spurious antiques), and where vehicular means of locomotion are confined to donkeys, at a few piastres a day. The exploration of the temples and ruins is the one resource and recreation, and this entails no extra expenditure when once the Government tax of one hundred piastres (£1.0.6) is paid.

Baksheesh may, perhaps, be thought a formidable item in the incidental expenditure; but, as a matter of fact, the permanent visitors at Luxor are not usually regarded as a legitimate or valuable quarry by the natives, who confine their attentions, for the most part, to the short-time passengers by the tourist steamers. The amusing baksheesh stories, which form the stock of the *table d'hôte* humourist, are generally invented, or, at all events, considerably embellished. Few newcomers will be spared, for instance, the time-honoured yarn of the English medical man at Luxor, who used to doctor the natives,—of course, gratuitously,— and whose patients, after being cured, used to come down on him for baksheesh, on the plea that they had taken his medicines!

The hotel accommodation is good and comfortable; but the three hotels are hardly sufficient, and are apt to be overcrowded. The largest hotel, the Luxor, is expensive; but it is a particularly well-found and even luxurious establishment, and may rank as a first-class house, though, of course, it cannot compare with the palatial Cairo hotels. The cuisine reflects credit on the manager, considering the "commissariat base" is nearly five hundred miles distant, and that Luxor itself is but a large village. The terms here and at the Karnak are thirteen or fifteen shillings a day, according to the season; but visitors staying at least a month are taken at twelve shillings a day. The Thewfikieh Hotel (Gaze's) is a very comfortable house with particularly moderate tariff (twelve shillings a day all through the season), and by many is preferred to the more pretentious Hotel Luxor. For one thing, it is much quieter, and in this respect better adapted for those wintering in Egypt for health. Long-stay visitors are taken at ten shillings a day. Invalids find every comfort, including English doctor, English nurse and chambermaids, dairy, etc. Its one drawback is its noisiness. Four or five times a week passengers by the Nile tourist-steamers arrive and depart in throngs, and are apt to monopolise the hotel, to the dismay of permanent visitors.

It should be mentioned that, thanks mainly to the efforts of Mr. J. M. Cook, Luxor is now a chaplaincy of the Colonial and Continental Church Society. There is no chemist yet at Luxor, but necessary drugs can be obtained at the Dispensary of the Native Hospital. There is a post from Cairo three days a week. The post-office is attached to the Luxor Hotel, which is a remarkably self-contained establishment.

That Luxor has a great future before it both as a health-resort and a tourist centre is indisputable. The railway, now open almost as far as Keneh (three hundred and forty miles from Cairo, and only thirty miles from Luxor), is making good progress, and will probably reach Luxor in the course of next winter. This extension will do much towards making Luxor a favourite winter-resort for invalids. It will also popularise it as a goal of travel among ordinary tourists, who have only a few weeks for Egypt. Hitherto the Nile trip has made too great inroads on the time and purse of the short-time travellers. When the

railway is continued to the Theban plain, it will be possible to pay a hasty visit to the unrivalled monuments of ancient Thebes and be back in the Egyptian capital within three days, at an outlay of not much more than a five-pound note.

CHAPTER XXIII.

ASSOUAN AND PHILÆ.

BETWEEN Thebes and Assouan two interesting temples or groups of temples are passed, — Esneh and Edfu. Erment is no doubt included in the Nile itineraries, but this modern town is important merely as a flourishing manufacturing centre, — sugar being the chief industry, — and the antiquities are now non-existent. Every vestige has disappeared of the large temple, and the only survival of the smaller one are a few ruined columns.

Esneh is a populous market-town, and the capital of the province. Modern buildings occupy the site of the ancient city of Latopolis, but the ruins of the temple, which are not buried in the soil, are extremely beautiful. Like most other Ptolemaic monuments, — for all that remains is of Ptolemaic work, — this has been ignored by antiquarians and the Egypt Exploration Fund; and since Mehemet Ali cleared a part of the hypostyle hall of the temple, hardly anything has been done in the way of restoration. Yet from the elegant architecture of the columns now visible, systematic excavations and clearing away of rubbish would probably reveal a temple almost as beautiful as those of Denderah or Edfu.

Miss Edwards's graphic description, though written twenty years ago, applies in all essentials to the ruins as seen at the present day:

"This is what we see: a little yard surrounded by mud walls; at the farther end of the yard, a dilapidated doorway; beyond the doorway, a strange-looking stupendous mass of yellow limestone masonry. A few steps farther, and this proves to be the carved cornice of a mighty temple, — a temple neither ruined nor defaced, but buried to the chin in the accumulated rubbish of a score of centuries. This part is evidently the portico. We stand close under a row of huge capitals. The columns that support them are buried beneath our feet. The ponderous cornice juts out above our heads. From the level on which we stand to the top of that cornice may measure about twenty-five feet. Descending a flight of brick steps which lead down to a vast hall, we come to the original level of the temple. We tread the ancient pavement. We look up at the massive ceiling, recessed and sculptured, and painted like the ceiling at Denderah. We could almost believe, indeed, that we are standing in the portico of Denderah. The general effect and the main features of the plan are the same. In some respects, however, Esneh is even more striking. The columns, though less massive than those of Denderah, are more elegant, and look loftier. Their shafts are covered with figures of gods and emblems, and lines of hieroglyphed inscription, all cut out in low-relief. Their capitals, in place of the huge draped Hathor-head of Denderah, are studied from natural forms, — from the lotus lily, the papyrus blossom, the plumy date-palm. The wall-sculpture, however, is inferior to that of Denderah, and immeasurably inferior to the wall-sculpture at Karnak. The inscriptions, instead of being grouped wherever there happened to be space, and so producing the richest form of wall-decoration ever devised by man, are disposed in symmetrical columns, the effect of which, when compared with the florid style of Karnak, is as the methodical neatness of an engrossed deed to the splendid freedom of an illuminated manuscript."

The temple is dedicated to Khnum or Knept, who is represented as a ram with the asp between his horns, which is supposed to imply some idea of sovereignty over the gods, for in Roman times Khnum was considered to be identical with Jupiter. The magnificent temple of Edfu, a gem among Ptolemaic monuments, has already been noticed, with the other famous shrines of the Ptolemies, in the preceding chapter.

Assouan lies some one hundred and forty miles south of Luxor; but the scenic conditions are very dissimilar, and the immediate surroundings are more picturesque than those of ancient Thebes. Instead of a fertile plain stretching for miles on either side of the Nile, the river narrows, a mile or so above Assouan, to a gorge hemmed in by stupendous granite walls, which mark the approach to the First Cataract. The town stands well above the Nile, and has a decidedly imposing appearance from the river, the banks being lined with Government buildings, several handsome hotels, and large shops. The river-front is, indeed, rather too European-looking to please the æsthetic tourist; but the Oriental note is provided by an occasional minaret towering above the modern white buildings, and by the groves of palm-trees and acacias which surround the town.

Assouan, unlike Luxor, has few remains of the extinct civilisation of Egypt, most of the antiquities being late Roman or Saracenic, and regarded with little respect by Egyptologists, who are apt to be a little intolerant of all ruins of later date than the Ptolemies. The town, however, offers many points of interest to the traveller of wider sympathies than the dry-as-dust antiquary. The student of astronomy will no doubt remember that the Ptolemaic astronomers, erroneously supposing Assouan to be exactly on the Tropic of Cancer, carried out here their calculations for measuring the earth;[1] while to classical students it will be of interest as an important frontier city of the Romans, and Juvenal's place of exile, whence he wrote many of his Satires.

To come to our own days, Assouan will soon be a favourite goal of engineers and scientific men as the site of the greatest engineering enterprise, after the Suez Canal, ever carried out in Egypt. It is here that the great bar-

[1] Strabo, as is well known, says that in a certain well the sun at the summer solstice shone direct, without casting a shadow. The site of this well cannot be located, which causes some scientists to throw doubt on the accuracy of Strabo's story, especially as the actual tropic is a few miles farther south, between Philæ and Kalabsheh.

rage of Upper Egypt is to be built — a greater structure than the huge dam in the Delta, which for so many years proved a "white elephant" to the Egyptian Government — in spite of the agitation set on foot by Egyptologists, who naturally feared that the Philæ temples would be submerged by the artificial lake which would be created. However, every precaution against injury to these monuments will be taken by the Government. Besides, as embanking and damming the Nile at Assouan is estimated to increase the amount of crops in Egypt to *nine times their present yield*, it is probable that, in any case, purely sentimental and æsthetic reasons would not have been allowed to stand in the way of this enormous material benefit to the country. At the risk of being thought a " devil's advocate," I cannot help protesting against the conventional cuckoo-cry of vandalism so often raised by the superficial tourist to earn a cheap reputation for culture. In such a question the welfare of the Egyptian people should be the first consideration, and, as has been clearly demonstrated, the gain to a poverty-stricken and overtaxed population would be almost incalculable.

Assouan has some claim to be considered a potential health-resort. Its climate, except in the late spring months, is superior, perhaps, even to that of Luxor. In April and May, owing, no doubt, to its shut-in situation, it is, however, too hot to make a suitable or pleasant residence for invalids, — in fact, some observers have made its average temperature higher even than that of Wady Halfa, which is well within the tropics. Up to April, however, the climatic conditions are not surpassed by those of any place on the Nile.

Though the undeniable excellence of the climate of Assouan, for the greater part of the Egyptian season for foreigners, has been generally admitted by medical men, hitherto its comparative difficulty and costliness of access, and the great popularity of its rival, Luxor, have stood in the way of its development as an invalid station. Its situation is superior hygienically to that of Luxor. The latter is only a few feet above the Nile, and under water for a part of the year, while Assouan is beyond the reach of the annual inundation. This, of course, minimises the risk of malarial fever. Then, to a certain extent, Luxor suffers from those factitious drawbacks which make Cairo so ill-suited as a winter residence for the health-seeker, as distinct from the mere sun-worshipper. Luxor, indeed, like that cosmopolitan winter-city, is decidedly gay and fashionable during the height of the season, and altogether too noisy and crowded for delicate people. The Nile banks are lined with dahabiyehs, lavishly decorated with flowers and bunting, and at night glowing with hundreds of Chinese lanterns and fairy lamps. These brilliant illuminations, the crowds of fashionable visitors thronging the decks of these pleasure-craft, the twanging of the universal mandolin or banjo, may perhaps suggest to the correspondents of society journals an "Arabian Nights' Fairy-land," but to the ordinary visitor everything is unpleasantly reminiscent of Henley Regatta, with dahabiyehs for house-boats and tourist steamers for steam-launches. At all events, there is something bizarre and startling in the contrast afforded by the grim and solemn Theban temples which form the background to this scene of fashionable revelry.

Assouan, though the farthest outpost of invalid colonisation in Egypt, and situated some six hundred miles from the capital, is fairly well provided with what English residents in foreign watering-places regard as necessities of life, including a first-class, but expensive, hotel, a resident English doctor and chaplain, British vice-consul, post-office (three deliveries a week), telegraph-office, etc. In short, though at present but an incipient health-resort, and owing to the cost of the journey and the high hotel charges (there being only one first-class hotel, the proprietor can hardly be blamed for exercising the tyranny of a monopoly) practically confined to the richer class of invalid visitors, Assouan has a future. With the completion of the railway, which will enable the journey from Cairo to be performed in less than half the time and at less than half the cost of the present combined rail and mail-steamer service, an assured position as a climatic health-resort may be predicted for it, and a few years will probably see a large invalid colony established here.

It is not improbable that some time during the course of the season of 1897-8 the railway will reach Assouan, intended as the joint terminus of the Upper Nile and Soudan Railways. Considerable progress has already been made in the construction of the former railway, which has now reached as far as Keneh, some forty miles north of Luxor. Now that the Nile has been crossed at Nagh Hamadi, the continuation of the Assouan section offers little difficulty to the engineers. As for the Soudan Military Railway, the Wady Halfa and Berber section is now finished as far as Kirma, at the Third Cataract, only twenty miles north of Dongola.

Perhaps Mr. Cecil Rhodes's fond dream of a trans-continental railway from Cairo to Cape Town is not such a wild and visionary project after all. Who knows but that, in the dim and distant future, Nubia, with its incomparable climate, will replace the Riviera or Algeria as the world's great winter sanatorium?[1]

Nine out of ten visitors to Assouan are, however, quite indifferent as to the merits or demerits of the place as an invalid station, and therefore we will proceed to visit its

---

[1] These observations on the future of Assouan are taken from an article entitled "Assouan: a Potential Health-Resort," which I recently contributed to an English review.

lions. The chief objects of interest, next to the beautiful Island of Philæ, are the famous rock-tombs, the ancient quarries, and the Cataract.

The tombs, which, according to the absurd practice that prevails in Egypt of labelling remains after the name of the discoverer, are popularly known as Grenfell's Tombs, have only been partially explored. These rock-shrines were excavated in the cliffs of the western bank of the Nile by General Grenfell in 1887. In some respects they resemble the tombs of Beni Hassan, but it is only at Assouan that we see traces of the striking methods of transporting the bodies of the dead. It is a kind of slide cut out from the face of the almost perpendicular cliff, and on each side are remains of the steps for the bearers who drew up the mummy from the river.

The most striking tomb is that of Ra-Nub-Ko-Necht (Amen-Em-Hat II.), a sovereign of the twelfth dynasty; but it is generally — perhaps excusably, in view of the cumbrous designation of its tenant — known as Grenfell's Tomb. The entrance to this tomb is impressive, from the startling contrasts, and perhaps was intended to produce a dramatic effect on the spectator.

"The gloomy entrance, with its great, rough-hewn square columns and its mysterious side-aisles, unrelieved by a ray of light or a scrap of carving, leads to a square doorway some thirty feet from the entrance, which it directly faces. A narrow passage is then entered. At the very end, with the daylight streaming in full and clear upon it, is the shrine which bears the portraits of the sovereign and his family. The passage by which you reach it is unspeakably impressive. On either side are three deep niches in the dark walls. Before you yawns an apparently bottomless pit. Each of the niches is seen to contain an upright mummy, which gazes at you with sad eyes as you pass by. These six sepulchral figures are carved in stone and coloured, and form an appropriate line of sentinels to the entrance of the inner tomb."

Scarcely a mile from the town are the famous granite quarries of Syene, from which was hewn the stone for most of the famous obelisks and other monoliths of the early Egyptian kings. In fact, certain inscriptions show that even in the sixth dynasty stone was quarried here for Egyptian temples and sarcophagi. An obelisk entirely detached on three sides from the rock, nearly one hundred feet in length, may be seen *in situ*, as well as unfinished columns, sarcophagi, etc., which show that Syene in the time of the Pharaohs was not only a quarry, but what we should nowadays describe as a monumental mason's stoneyard. It is particularly interesting to see actual traces of the workmen's methods of cutting out an obelisk *en bloc* from the solid rock. A row of holes was bored along the whole length of the proposed obelisk, into which wooden wedges were driven. Water was afterwards poured on the wedges, when the swelling would crack the stone and separate it from the mass of rock. It was then roughly dressed at the quarries, hauled to the Nile upon a sledge run on rollers, and then floated down to its destination on a barge. The fact that even now engineers, although aided by all the resources of science, would not be likely to improve upon the methods (*teste* the removal of Cleopatra's Needle) of some four thousand or five thousand years ago, if they wished, for instance, to transport the one remaining obelisk, affords food for reflection.

The Island of Philæ is the chief feature of interest at Assouan. Though a mere rock, barely a quarter of a mile long, it is thickly covered with ruins of Ptolemaic temples and monuments, and is, perhaps, the " most beautiful, as well as the smallest, historic island in the world." The scenery about here is very striking and impressive. In fact, " The Approach to Philæ " has been rendered almost as familiar to the armchair traveller, by means of innumerable sketches, as the Pyramids or the Sphinx.

The most striking monument in the island is the beautiful Temple of Isis, one of the finest specimens of architecture the Ptolemies have bequeathed to Egypt. For picturesqueness of form and surroundings this magnificent temple cannot be equalled by any of the innumerable ruins of ancient Thebes. Its chief features are the Great Colonnade of thirty-two columns, and the massive towers of the Pylon, each one hundred and twenty feet wide and sixty feet high. The capitals of the noble façade of lofty columns are all of different patterns. Traces still remain of the vivid and varied colouring; for, according to the canons of art then prevailing, the shafts and capitals were painted. There are other courts and colonnades in the Temple, which, like the Great Temple of Karnak, seems rather a congeries of temples than one single building. The walls are covered with sculptures in low-relief. "Imagine walls," says the author of "The Crescent and the Cross," "whose height it wearies the eye to measure, all covered with gigantic hieroglyphics, where gods and warriors seem to move self-supported between earth and sky; then groves of columns, whose girth and height would rival those of the most corpulent old oak-trees, with capitals luxuriant as a cauliflower, and gleaming with bright enamel of every hue in heaven; every pillar and every wall so thickly covered with hieroglyphics, that they seem clothed with a petrified tapestry."

Another beautiful ruin is the Temple of Osiris, which, like the Palace of Charles V. in the Alhambra, never possessed a roof. It is rather absurdly known to tourists as Pharaoh's Bed, so called because of a fancied resemblance to a colossal four-post bedstead.

The island is thickly strewn with ruins of other temples, dedicated either to Isis, Osiris, or Horus, the tutelary triad

ASSOUAN AND PHILÆ. 303

of the island. In fact Philæ was the last refuge of this cult, a Greek inscription showing that these gods were worshipped here as late as 453 A.D., more than seventy years after the heathen religion was formally abolished in Egypt by Theodosius's famous decree. A portion of the Temple of Isis was converted into a Coptic church towards the end of the sixth century. To this period is due a strange mingling of the Egyptian and Christian faiths. For instance, Isis was represented as the tutelary deity of Saint John and Saint Paul. Even the shape of the bishop's mitre is considered by antiquarians to be directly borrowed from the characteristic horns of Osiris, as, according to tradition, Athanasius wished by this means to propitiate the Egyptians.

The First Cataract begins a little to the south of Assouan, and extends for several miles, Philæ marking the commencement. Cataract, as we understand the word, is, of course, a misnomer; it is actually a series of rapids. In fact, it is only at Low Nile, which is the off season of tourists, that the falls can be said to deserve the name of Cataract. Though the description of the awful character of this Cataract given by ancient writers is absurdly exaggerated, and may be relegated to the order of "travellers' tales," the feat of descending it is sufficiently exciting, though it is a somewhat costly amusement. The scenery, however, of the Nile at this point is grand and wild in the extreme, and no visitor should omit to get the full benefit of it by climbing one of the cliffs of the banks just above Philæ.

CHAPTER XXIV.

FROM THE FIRST TO THE SECOND CATARACT.

> Here Desolation keeps unbroken sabbath,
> 'Mid caves and temples, palaces and sepulchres;
> Ideal images in sculptured forms,
> Thoughts hewn in columns, or in caverned hill,
> In honour of their deities and of their dead.
>
> MONTGOMERY.

FEW tourists, compared with the crowds who throng the luxurious steamers to Luxor and Assouan, continue the voyage to Wady Halfa by the unpretentious little sternwheeler which runs weekly with the mails between the First and Second Cataracts. In fact, those who make this voyage may be considered to have graduated from the rank of tourist to that of traveller. The desolation of the banks and the absence of animal life, to say nothing of the inferior interest of the antiquities south of Assouan, make the voyage, short as it is, — for the whole expedition only takes a week, — rather monotonous to the ordinary tourist.

The geographical features of Nubia are very different from those of the country south of Assouan; in fact, Nubia might be in another continent. Instead of a richly cultivated plain extending for many miles on either side of the Nile, the bleak sandstone hills which abut on the desert come near the river, and the cultivated country, varying in breadth from a few hundred yards to a few miles, extends, a narrow palm-fringed strip, along either bank of the Nile. On the western bank there stretches beyond this sparsely cultivated littoral a savage and illimitable desert, while on the opposite side of the rapidly-flowing, coffee-coloured river an equally desolate wilderness is bounded only by the distant Red Sea. In the following description by Dr. Conan Doyle, the wild note of the scenery is very graphically presented:

"Between these two huge and barren expanses, Nubia writhes like a green sand-worm along the course of the river. Here and there it disappears altogether, and the Nile runs between black and sun-cracked hills, with the orange drift-sand lying like glaciers in their valleys. Everywhere one sees traces of vanished races and submerged civilisations. Grotesque graves dot the hills or stand up against the sky-line, — pyramidal graves, tumulus graves, rock graves, — everywhere graves. And, occasionally, as the boat rounds a rocky point, one sees a deserted city up above, — houses, walls, battlements, — with the sun shining through the empty window squares. Sometimes you learn that it has been Roman, sometimes Egyptian; sometimes all record of its name or origin has been absolutely lost. There they stand, these grim and silent cities, and up on the hills you can see the graves of their people, like the portholes of a man-of-war. It is through this weird, dead country that the tourists smoke and gossip and flirt as they pass up to the Egyptian frontier."

To the traveller accustomed to the never-ending procession of villages which stud the Nile banks between Cairo and Luxor, Nubia seems almost uninhabited. The vegetation is too sparse to support a large population, and the mainstay of life of the Nubians is the date-palm, instead of barley and rice. Every palm-tree, as is the olive-tree in Italy, is registered and heavily taxed.

In the two hundred miles' voyage between the First and Second Cataracts there is, however, one monument of superlative interest; namely, the famous rock-temple of Abu Simbel (called by an older generation of travellers, Ipsamboul), which in point of antiquarian interest is only second to the Pyramid field of Ghizeh and the Theban temples.

This unique ruin, in which some ancient race has hollowed out a vast shrine in the mountain as if it were a cheese, deserves a stay of several days, especially as the other ruins are nearly all of Ptolemaic or Roman origin. There is no doubt that the traveller, who has already explored Memphis and Thebes, and contemplated the very oldest buildings which the hands of man have fashioned, is naturally apt to regard with languid interest temples and tombs which are scarcely older than the Christian era. But the wonderful rock-hewn temple of Abu-Simbel will claim the attention of every traveller, however much he may be sated with the magnificent temples of Thebes and Karnak. Indeed, if it were the only goal of this extended Nile trip, the voyage would be well worth the time and expense.

The temple was built by Rameses the Great as a memorial of his victory over the Khita in Syria, — a race considered by some historians, but on doubtful authority, to be identical with the Hittites. The temple is hewn out of the solid rock, the eastern face, fronting the Nile, having been cut away, forming the most impressive and striking temple front in the world. In this stupendous façade four colossal statues, seated on thrones, stand out in bold relief. Each figure represents Rameses, and is some sixty-six feet high, without reckoning the pedestal, and "the faces, which are fortunately well preserved, evince a beauty of expression the more striking as it is unlooked for in statues of such dimensions.

An amusing incident in connection with these colossi is related by Miss Edwards in her " A Thousand Miles up the Nile," — a record of travel which now deservedly ranks as a classic. The face of one had been disfigured by plaster left when a cast was taken for the British Museum; so Miss Edwards set her boatmen to work to clean the stone by scraping off the lumps of plaster. The subsequent process—namely, tinting the white patches left, where the plaster was removed, with coffee — may be open to objection on the part of archæologists.

Some years ago, owing to overhanging masses of rock, these colossi were threatened with destruction. This was averted by some very skilful engineering on the part of Captain Johnston, R. E. The task was rendered especially difficult, as no explosives could be used because the vibration would probably have toppled over these titanic statues. One over-hanging rock weighed no less than two hundred and seventy tons. "Five stout iron cables were placed round the big block, and then it was broken up into small pieces, and thrown down into the sand. Rameses may now sit in peace, and watch the dawn break over the desert for another three thousand years. The two colossi which are out of balance are to be pinioned back to the rock behind by iron bands; the bands will be disguised as much as possible, but one regrets that a more dignified method of support for Pharaoh could not be devised." [1]

The entrance to the temple had been for thousands of years hermetically sealed by the drifting sands of the desert, till discovered by Belzoni, in 1817.

"A vast and gloomy hall, such as Eblis might have given Vathek audience in, receives you in passing from the flaming sunshine into that shadowy portal. It is some time before the eye can ascertain its dimensions through the imposing gloom; but gradually there reveals itself, around and above you, a vast aisle, with pillars formed of eight colossal giants upon whom the light of heaven has never shone. These images of Osiris are backed by enormous pillars, behind which run two great galleries, and in these torchlight alone enabled us to peruse a series of sculptures in relief, representing the triumphs of Rameses the Second, or Sesostris. The painting, which once enhanced the effect of these spirited representations, is not dimmed, but crumbled away; where it exists, the colours are as vivid as ever." [2]

[1] Cook's Handbook for Egypt.   [2] Eliot Warburton.

To the historian Abu-Simbel is mainly of importance as containing a long chronicle in stone of Rameses the Great, in which he describes at length the great work he has carried out in his temple at Thebes. Here is also inscribed the history in great detail of the king's famous campaign in Asia. This he evidently considered his greatest military achievement, for it is inscribed also at great length on the walls of the Theban Ramasseum, and at Abydos. These stone records, which are virtually a series of official despatches, form a kind of argument to a magnificent series of painted sculptures representing battle-scenes, and are written with all the terseness and precision of a modern official précis.

If possible, the temple should be explored at sunrise, when the sun's rays, shining directly through the entrance, light up the interior with a wonderful effect.

A smaller temple, also hewn out of the rock, is about fifty yards from the Great Temple. It is dedicated to Hathor, who is symbolised in the interior under the form of a cow. This temple is, however, of inferior interest, and might be regarded in relation to Rameses's great shrine as a "lady chapel," just as the third small temple, discovered in 1874, may be looked upon as a chapel of ease. Forty miles farther south lies the important fortified post of Wady Halfa, a kind of "breakwater of barbarism," which till 1896 formed the southern frontier of the Khedive's dominions.[1]

It has occasionally been found necessary, owing to the disturbed state of the country and the hostility of the dervishes, to furnish the post-steamers and steam dahabiyehs — sailing dahabiyehs were not allowed beyond the First Cataract — sailing beyond Assouan with a military escort. This escort, which gave a flavour of romantic adventure to

---

[1] At the time of writing (May, 1897), the frontier post is at Merawi, beyond Dongola.

the commonplace Nile voyage, was especially necessary for tourists exploring the Abu-Simbel Temple and the Pulpit Rock of Abusir; each party of tourists used to be accompanied by a corporal's guard of Soudanese soldiers, who carried out their duties with a conscientiousness which was rather embarrassing, and not a little irritating when the novelty had worn off. This escort was not, of course, intended as a defence against a raid of dervishes, for the proximity of the Wady Halfa garrison removed all danger of an open attack on travellers; but the authorities counted more on its moral effect in preventing independent excursions on the part of rash travellers who might be inclined to pooh-pooh any idea of danger from the disaffected dervishes. Besides, there was no doubt a certain risk of brigandage on the part of stray dervishes; for the movements of travellers were known days beforehand, and in the case of tourists under the charge of tourist agencies, freely advertised.

It may be mentioned that the famous novelist, Conan Doyle, has recently utilised the suggestion of exciting adventure afforded by these precautions of the military authorities in a thrilling story of modern adventure, in which he describes the experiences of a party of English tourists attacked by dervishes at Abusir.[1]

The one lion of Wady Halfa is the famous Pulpit Rock of Abusir, with the incomparable view of the Nile and the Libyan desert. This rock is a veritable "visitors' list" in stone, and the name of almost every traveller of note has been inscribed here. The dragoman firmly believes that Moses's name might once have been seen among the graven autographs! He is, however, careful to add, in order to take the wind out of the sails of the sceptical tourist, that it has long been worn away. At all events, the names of

---

[1] This decidedly up-to-date novel of adventure was running as a serial in the Strand Magazine during 1897.

Belzoni, Burckhardt, Warburton, and other famous travellers are to be seen there high up on the rock, and still higher, Gordon's.

Stern critics may, perhaps, be inclined to deprecate this habit of trying to impress one's own trivial personality on these immortal rocks, but it appears that for some reason it is considered almost praiseworthy at Abusir. Even the severe Murray gravely declares that "custom sanctions here, as innocent and not without a certain interest of its own, a practice which good taste and common sense alike condemn most strongly when indulged in to the injury of priceless monuments of antiquity and works of art." The distinction is a subtle one; and without arrogating to myself the office of the tourists' *censor morum*, I fail to see much difference between cutting one's name on the apex of the Great Pyramid, which every traveller of taste would strongly deprecate, and inscribing it on the *Livre des Voyageurs* of the cliff of Abusir.

There are few views which impress the spectator as does the grand prospect from the semicircular platform which forms the summit of the rock. Looking down on one side is the sunless and eddying Nile, studded with black shining rocks, dividing the river into endless channels, — these being the rapids known as the Second Cataract; the eastern bank is a wild jumble of black rocks and boulders, the débris brought down in high flood. The absence of any sign of habitation intensifies the sensation of wild desolation and awful grandeur. In the distance, too, misty blue mountains conceal Dongola, some one hundred and fifty miles south. Turning round and looking westward, the view is even more impressive. Again I borrow Dr. Conan Doyle's admirable bit of word-painting:

"It was a view which, when once seen, must always haunt the mind. Such an expanse of savage and unrelieved desert might be part of some cold and burned-out planet, rather than of this fertile and bountiful earth. Away and away it stretched, to die into a soft, violet haze in the extremist distance. In the foreground the sand was of a bright golden yellow, which was quite dazzling in the sunshine; but beyond this golden plain lay a low line of those black slag-heaps, with yellow sand-valleys winding between them. These in their turn were topped by higher and more fantastic hills, and these by others, peeping over each other's shoulders until they blended with that distant violet haze. None of these hills were of any height, — a few hundred feet at the most, — but their savage, saw-toothed crests, and their steep scarps of sun-baked stone, gave them a fierce character of their own."

A few miles south of Abu Sir, some excavations, cleverly executed by a detachment of English engineers under Major Lyons, have brought to light an interesting temple of respectable antiquity even for Egypt. It is at least as old as the eighteenth dynasty, for inscriptions prove that it was restored by Thotmes III. This monarch's name, it will be noticed, appeared in stelæ and other inscriptions more frequently than that of any other sovereign, not even excepting the name of Rameses the Great.

CHAPTER XXV.

RECENT EGYPTOLOGICAL DISCOVERIES.

THE most important fields of research of the Egypt Exploration Fund (the leading Egyptological Society of Great Britain and America), since 1890, have been Dar-El-Bahari (Thebes) and Beni-Hassan. Several seasons' continuous work was devoted to these temples and the Beni-Hassan Tombs.

The operations of this society are characterised by great thoroughness and scientific zeal, and are conducted with an elaborated conscientiousness which is not always appreciated at its full value by the ordinary tourist, who is naturally inclined to give greater credit to the more practical and less technical explorations of the Egyptological Department of the Egyptian Government. But the aims of these two bodies are different. The Egypt Exploration Fund is a purely scientific society. It is supported by archæologists and antiquarians, and their researches are undertaken for the benefit of Egyptologists rather than Egyptian travellers and students; and the exhaustive reports the society publishes annually are learned monographs, "caviare to the general," rather than popular descriptive handbooks.

Yet harmonious relations are preserved between the two bodies, of which the Egypt Exploration Fund may be reckoned the pioneer. The latter gives prominence to researches and excavations of sites likely to prove of scientific interest, while the Government Department chiefly devotes its attention to preserving and restoring the famous monuments and temples which attract the ordinary visitor.

During the last four winters the Exploration Fund have been carrying on extensive excavations at Thebes, with the view of thoroughly clearing out the wonderful Temple of Queen Hatasu. In the chapter on Ancient Thebes and its Monuments this temple is briefly referred to, but this account may be supplemented by the admirable and succinct description of M. Naville, who was responsible for the excavations:

"There is no other Egyptian temple known to us which is built on a rising succession of platforms; and we are therefore without comparisons for our guidance in seeking to ascertain how the architect was led to the adoption of this scheme. To some extent it may have been suggested to him by the nature of the site at his disposal, and by the huge steps in which the rock of the foundations descends to the plain. What was the distinctive use of each of the three platforms on which the temple was built? Our excavations have proved that the lowest platform was treated as the garden, or rather the orchards, of the temple, and that the trees planted in it were artificially watered. But the central and most extensive of the platforms — on the one side abutting against the cliffs, and on the other supported by a decorated retaining wall — seemed to have been a clear space, and may be considered as corresponding to the spacious colonnaded courts preceding the sanctuaries in temples of both Pharaohs and Ptolemies."

Neither have we any certainty as to the proposed use of the four unfinished chambers opening on to the colonnade on the northern side of the middle platform. Like the lateral chambers at Denderah and Edfu, they may have been intended as storerooms for the incense and sacred oils, and for the garments and numerous utensils necessary to performing the various rites of the complicated Egyptian ritual. Or, like the court of the altar of Harmakhis, they may have been sanctuaries, dedicated to the cult of divinities more especially worshipped in other parts of Egypt. But the more plausible supposition is, that they were meant to be funerary chapels for members of the queen's family.

Again, the similarity of Dar-El-Bahari to a Greek temple is striking, especially to the visitor coming from the Ramesseum, when first he catches sight of the long row of white columns at the base of the rock on the north side. This impression is borne out, not only by the often noticed resemblance between the fluted columns of Hatasu and those of the Doric order, but still more by a consideration of certain architectural proportions, and of the relations between column and architrave.

At Dar-El-Bahari nothing is on a gigantic scale, and it seems to me that when the Egyptians turned aside from the style which was here applied so successfully, in favour of the massive architecture of Karnak and Medinet Abou, they deviated from the path which would have led them to elegance, and preferred the majestic and the colossal.

Tourists will be glad to hear that the clearing of this beautiful structure is now completed, and that every part of the temple is visible. Many interesting discoveries of sculptures and paintings were made, among them some of the missing fragments of the famous series of sculptures portraying the Punt expedition of Queen Hatasu. These rather point to the probability that the goal of this expedition was not, as is usually supposed, a part of Asia, but that Punt was a portion of Africa.

It has always been a moot point with Egyptologists as to the manner in which the obelisks were transported from Assouan quarries to the ancient cities of the Delta. A remarkable discovery of a series of sculptures at Queen Hatasu's Temple by M. Naville clears up this disputed question. The obelisk was placed on a huge flat-bottomed

raft or barge, and this unwieldy craft, one hundred and twenty cubits long, was furnished with two pairs of rudders. In all probability the season of high Nile was chosen for the transport of an obelisk, when not only would the navigation be easier, but the monolith could be brought in the barge nearer to the temple where it was to be erected. The barge itself was merely a receptacle for the obelisk, and was towed by three parallel groups of ten boats, each group being connected with the barge by a thick cable. In the sculptures the rowers are represented on one side only; but if we suppose there were the same number on each side, there would be thirty-two oarsmen for each boat. If we add the reïses, the officers, and the helmsmen, we have a grand total for this flotilla, which conveyed an obelisk from Upper Egypt to the Delta, of over one thousand men!

But the most valuable work of the Egypt Exploration Fund within recent years has been the exhaustive archæological survey of the famous rock-tombs of Beni-Hassan. The results of this stupendous undertaking, in which thousands of wall sculptures and inscriptions were conscientiously transcribed and translated, supplemented and explained by an enormous number of plans, diagrams, and "squeezes," are to be found in the *magnum opus* of the society, which consists of four folio volumes. Naturally, such a work is only likely to be seriously read by students; but ordinary travellers, who are about to visit these remarkable tombs, will do well to consult these erudite and beautifully illustrated works.

Previous to 1883, when the Egypt Exploration Fund was founded, the historical value of many important discoveries had been considerably discounted, owing to the haphazard manner in which excavations and archæological researches had been undertaken; and this carelessness must be attributed to the insufficient supervision of the native diggers by the Cairo Museum authorities, who, in most sites, had the monopoly of research. For instance, the most valuable objects discovered near Abydos some thirty years ago were carted off wholesale to Cairo without any record being kept of the position or the circumstances in which they were found. It is to be feared that consular agents, who in the days of Ismail were little more than "protected" dealers, are as responsible for this waste of the precious relics of ancient Egyptian civilisation as are the regular dealers and unscrupulous curio-hunting travellers.

For instance, in the wonderful and almost sensational discoveries of Mariette, certainly the most zealous and indefatigable explorer and excavator of all workers in the field of Egyptological research, there was a frightful waste of scientific material. The results, no doubt, were magnificent, as the most casual inspection of the galleries in the Cairo Museum clearly shows; but there is no doubt that the excavations were conducted in a decidedly unscientific and unmethodical manner, the only aim being to get the "finds" transported as quickly as possible to the Cairo Museum, only the most hasty and superficial notes being made on the spot. Within recent years excavating has been carried on more intelligently, with a greater appreciation of the value of each record, and with accurate cataloguing, without which the most important discoveries from the dealer's point of view have little value in the eye of scholars and archæologists.

The discoveries at Naukratis, an ancient Greek settlement of the seventh century B. C., are of peculiar interest to art students. This ancient site is just beyond the native village of Neqrash (evidently a corruption of the ancient name), a few miles from Tel-El-Barud, a station on the Cairo and Alexandria Railway. Researches here have shown us the life of the early Greek settlers, who founded the city in the time of Psammetikos, about 660 B. C. The place was of great commercial importance till the rise of Alexandria eclipsed its fame. Professor Petrie brought away from the mounds of rubbish a large collection of Greek vases and statuettes, many of which can now be seen in the British Museum.

Another important work by Professor Petrie was the identification of the site of Pithom, the famous treasure-city which the Israelites built for Rameses the Great, in the mounds of Tel-El-Maskhuta in the Wady Tamilat.

One of the most startling discoveries in the whole field of Egyptian research was that of the Temple of Sneferu, the first king of the fourth dynasty, and the oldest sovereign of whom any remains are known. This was discovered buried some forty feet beneath the surface, by the accumulation of desert sand and rubbish of several thousand years, close to the famous "False Pyramid" of Medum, itself the very oldest *dated* monument in Egypt.

An extraordinary circumstance in the discovery of this almost prehistoric temple was that it was found absolutely perfect, and even the roof was entire and uninjured.

"The chances against the oldest dated temple in the world being quite uninjured," remarks Professor Petrie, "might seem beyond hope; yet, strangely, it still remains. Of course it needed to be very fully buried again to preserve it from destruction by the present natives; and it is much to be hoped that it will not be uncovered until better security is insured for Egyptian monuments. The priceless early tombs, near the Pyramids, have been battered to pieces where the boys can reach, and blocks taken away for building, thus destroying some of the finest sculptures known; and though these were all carefully buried to prevent injury a few years ago, some traveller has ruthlessly uncovered them again for destruction. Nothing can be left exposed in Egypt; it must be either deeply buried or else removed to a museum, if not constantly guarded. The Pyramid can be easily visited from Waita station, about five miles distant."

Tel-El-Amarna, some fifty miles north of Assiout, is the site of several interesting discoveries. The great temple of the "heretic king," Khu-En-Aten, was discovered by Lepsius, and systematically explored and described by Professor Petrie, during the winter of 1891-2. The fame of Tel-El-Amarna as a field of research dates from the finding of the famous cuneiform inscriptions, of which a short account has already been given in the chapter describing the principal antiquities from Cairo to the First Cataract.

"There, besides the well-known tombs, a large, painted pavement of the palace has been found in this ancient town; and it is now well preserved in a building, and accessible to visitors. The interest in it lies in the naturalistic style of the painting, and the link in taste and design which it shows to the Mykenæan Greek work. In the rubbish heaps of the palace waste were found fragments of many hundreds of prehistoric Greek vases, of the 'Ægean' style, apparently all of Rhodian and Cypriote sources, suggesting that they came by way of the Syrian coast; whereas, the Ægean vases of this same age, from Gurob, belong to the Peloponnesian forms, pointing to a trade along the African shores. The mass of remains, in a place which was only occupied for twenty or thirty years, gives the most certain dating of this style in Greece to the fourteenth century B. C., and thus fixes an epoch in the prehistory of Europe."

Side by side with the more scientific work of archæological research undertaken by the Egypt Exploration Fund is the equally important, but more mechanical, work of the Egyptian Government, which is mainly confined to the clearing of rubbish or unearthing the buried portions of the great monuments and temples of the Upper Nile, which may be considered as the great "show" places for travellers and tourists. The Karnak and Philæ temples have been for many years the site of extensive excavations, nearly all the money from the Tourist Fund being devoted to the work. The Philæ temples have now been completely cleared, and the able and thorough manner in which the work has been done under Captain Lyon's superintendence may be seen from the following extract from Lord Cromer's last report:

" The débris has been carefully removed from the whole of the area enclosed by the two colonnades, as well as from the open spaces to the south of the colonnades. The site of a temple of Augustus at the north of the island, and a small unfinished temple near the Kiosk, were also excavated. Subsequently the Coptic village, which covers three quarters of the island, was laid bare, the walls, stairways, and doors of the dwellings being left, while the streets and interiors of the houses were cleared from the rubbish of the fallen roofs and walls which encumbered them."

Then, in addition to these important works, the Great Temple of Isis has had its crypts cleared of the rubbish with which they were choked, and the columns of the eastern colonnade freed from the débris of a ruined Coptic village which had formerly buried that portion of the temple. All the operations have been most intelligently undertaken, and the aim has been to *restore* rather than to *repair*, a distinction which antiquarians will appreciate. The director of the excavations took the opportunity of carefully examining the foundation of the temple, when it was found that the foundation masonry, which in one portion had been carried down to a depth below the present high Nile level, was in excellent condition, and that there were no signs of any settlement of the soil. A great portion of the Temple of Isis is, indeed, founded upon the granite rock.

Indirectly, the Upper Nile Reservoir scheme alluded to in a former chapter, which was so bitterly opposed by archæologists, has been the means of promoting Egyptological research in Philæ; for the Government surveyors, when excavating in connection with this reservoir project, have cleared up several temples, including one of the Emperor Octavius on the north of the island.

At Karnak, also, important work has been done. All the money raised by the Government tax (levied on visitors to the ancient monuments of the Upper Nile) during last winter (1896-97) was devoted to the great work of clearing the Karnak temples. "Under the superintendence," to quote again the Government report, " of M. de Morgan, great progress has been made during the last year in the work of preserving these temples. A large amount of earth, which filled the great courtyard and the Hall of Columns, has been removed; the bases of the columns have been cleared from contact with the salted earth, and repaired with cement. The fallen stones have been numbered and collected, with a view possibly to their being replaced at some future time."

In the Ghizeh Pyramid Plateau we reach a site known, of course, to every tourist. Here it might naturally be supposed that systematic explorations had exhausted the potential wealth of antiquities. Unfortunately, however, this district — of the highest archæological interest — has never been properly worked, owing to the Government digging-monopoly; and though there is a vast amount to be done in the great district of the Pyramid and Memphis, yet, as Professor Petrie cynically remarks, "only the inadequate work of the Government Department and the plundering by natives is allowed, and all real scientific work is forbidden."

At the Pyramid of Dahshur, however, at the southern end of this extensive necropolis, some excellent work has been done by the new director of the museum, and his thorough and capable researches have resulted in a most valuable mine of tombs being brought to light. The magnificent sets of jewellery found here, now in the Cairo Museum, are familiar to every traveller in Egypt. "The exquisite delicacy, skill, and taste of this work surpasses all that is yet known. The pectorals are formed by soldering walls of gold on to a base plate, which is elaborately chased with details on the back. Between these walls or ribs of gold are inserted minutely cut stones, — cornelian, lazuli, and felspar, — to give the vari-coloured design. In this, and in the beads of gold, the astounding minuteness of the work and perfect delicacy of execution exceed the limits of mere naked-eye inspection."

To come to the latest discoveries, the winter of 1896-7 has been marked by some remarkable finds. The discovery of some extraordinary fifth-dynasty tombs at Deshasheh, by Professor Petrie, where a large number of skeletons was found which point to a method of burial anterior to the age of mummies, has already been referred to. In addition to these necrological finds were some objects of great artistic interest, including a remarkably well-executed portrait-statue of a certain royal priest called Neukheftka, the work of some fifth-dynasty sculptor, which shows that even at this early period the Egyptian artists had attained considerable technical skill. Some curious baskets of palm-fibre were also found, evidently used for carrying away the soil from the excavated graves. It is curious that baskets of a similar pattern are still used in India by women labourers for carrying away earth in railway cuttings and other public works.

In the same winter took place the sensational discovery, by Messrs. Grenfell and Hunt of the Egypt Exploration Fund, at Oxyrhncus, some one hundred and twenty miles south of Cairo on the edge of the Libyan desert, a few miles from the Nile, of a second-century papyrus containing some remarkable sayings attributed to our Lord (*Logia Jesou*). This document has aroused a considerable amount of interest among theological students, and has given rise to many problems. Some critics consider that this papyrus is a fragment of the well-known, but of course non-canonical, "Gospel according to the Egyptians."

A more satisfactory view, though not free from difficulties, is that this fragment is what it professes to be, — a collection of some of our Lord's sayings. These, judging from their archaic tone and framework, were put together not later than the end of the first or the beginning of the second century, and it is quite possible that they embody a tradition independent of those which have taken shape in our Canonical Gospels.

The above is, of course, the merest outline of the more noteworthy results undertaken within recent years in the field of Egyptian exploration. The able and suggestive summary of Professor Petrie, to whom I am much indebted for the information in this superficial sketch, will form a fitting conclusion to this chapter:

"The general result of all this activity of recent years is that Egypt has appeared in far closer relation to other ancient lands. Towards the East an entirely new view is opened by the cuneiform letters between Syria and Egypt; for no one had dreamed that an active correspondence in that writing had been going on in the fourteenth century B. C. in Syria. And the relations shown to exist between the Egyptian Power and the various princes of Syria far exceeded what has been supposed.

"But it is also to the West that equally unexpected relations have appeared. Instead of looking on Egypt as an isolated factor in the world's history, standing apart from all else, we now realise that there was much more civilisation outside of it than had been supposed, and that it was in pretty close relation with all the surrounding countries. The earliest light on the South European peoples comes from the Libyan invaders, who conquered Upper Egypt after the sixth dynasty. The connection of the prehistoric Cretan civilisation has lately been brought to light, each link of which points to the time of the twelfth dynasty as an age of intercourse. The considerable intercourse with prehistoric Greece in the eighteenth dynasty is now almost every year more fully cleared up. The early historic settlements of Naukratis and Daphnæ have opened a new chapter in Greek history, and given some of the actual links between Egyptian and early Greek art. And all these stages were absolutely unknown and unguessed as lately as eleven years ago, when nothing from the West was known in Egypt before Ptolemaic times. It is as new a world of history as the discoveries of Layard or Schliemann, and may well encourage us to hope for what the next ten years may yield to those who employ accurate research for opening up the buried story of the life of man."

INDEX.

A

Aah-hetep, Queen, 14.
Aahmes, founder of the eighteenth dynasty of Egypt, 13, 14; mummy of, 159.
Abbas, founder of the Abbasside dynasty, 151.
Abbas, successor to Mehemet Ali, 55, 245.
Abbasside dynasty, the, 150, 151.
Abu Simbel, famous rock-temple of, 305, 306, 308; four colossi of, 306, 307.
Abusir, pulpit-rock of, 309; excavations at, 311.
Abydos, traditional burial-place of Osiris, 9, 270, 271; tablet of, 271; most valuable discoveries here carried to Cairo, 316.
Actium, battle of, between Octavius and Antony, 40; its results, 41.
Africa, first complete circumnavigation of its continent, 20.
Ahmed, the tomb-robber, 162, 163.
Alexander the Great, founder of the Ptolemaic empire in Egypt, 8; subjugates the Persians, 20; his Egyptian campaign one of his most striking achievements, 22-24; his death, 24.
Alexandria, capital of Egypt founded by Alexander the Great, 24; besieged by Euergetes II., 38; Antony's celebration of a Roman triumph at, 39; bombarded by English fleet, 57; infection in, 81; and the Nile Delta, 90-104; aspects of, as approached from the sea, 90; few traces left of her ancient glory, 91; ignored by tourists and neglected by antiquarians, 92; peculiar shape of, 93; legend accounting for its site, 93; her fine harbour, 94; modern aspect of, created by Mehemet Ali, 95; best view of, 98, 99; can boast of few "lions," 100; its Serapeum and library, 101; its Mohammedan cemetery, 102; the cemeteries of Elmeks, 103; a city of sites rather than of sights, 103; its mosques, and convent of St. Mark, 103, 104; best route to Egypt *via*, 119-121; its museum, 167.
Alphabet, Phœnician origin of, cannot be substantiated, 6; probably originated in Egypt, 6.
Amen, worship of, 16.
Amen-Em-Het, 12, 266, 267; tomb of, at Assouan, 300.
Amen-hetep, II., III., IV., 15, 16.
Amru, conqueror of Egypt, and builder of Old Cairo, 42; mosque named for, at Cairo, 139, 182-184.
Antiochus, fights battle of Raphia with Ptolemy IV., 34-36.
Antony, Mark, his relations with Cleopatra, 39, 40.
Apepa II., the Pharaoh who raised Joseph to high rank, 14.
Apis, the sacred bull, cult of, 9; city of, 215-226; mausoleum of, 218, 219; common belief concerning, 219,

326 INDEX.

220; divine honours paid to, 220, 221, 229.
Arabi, Egyptian minister of war, rebellion of, 57.
"Arabian Nights," quoted, 53.
Art Journal, quoted, 146.
Arsinoe, wife of Ptolemy Philadelphus, 30, 31.
Assouan, health-resort in Egypt, 114, 115, 250; her quarries the source of many Egyptian obelisks, 280, 281, 301; situation of, 295, 296; great engineering work to be done at, 296, 297; its excellent climate, 297, 298; has a future inviting to the tourist and health-seeker, 299; tombs of, 300; ancient process of quarrying at, 301; island of Philæ at, 301–303; first cataract in the Nile here, 303; how obelisks were transported from, 314, 315.
Auletes (Ptolemy XIII.), his character described by Cicero, 39.
Ayyubides dynasty, the, founded by Saladin, 46, 150, 151.

B

Baalbec, 231.
Baedeker, quoted, 155, 264, 265.
Baker, Gen. Valentine, 77.
Balm of Gilead, the, Coptic tradition of, 234.
Barrage, the, great dam on the Nile, 71, 242, 244–246.
Bebars (Sultan), character and reign of, 50–53.
Bell, Moberly, quoted, 66, 164, 165, 180.
Belzoni, 288, 307.
Beni-Hassan, rock-tombs of, 262–267, 315.
Boulag, port of, 236, 237.
Brugsch Bey, an authority on Egyptian history, 9, 163, 228, 229.
Bubastis, 12.
Burckhardt (Sheik Ibrahim), 154.
Byzantine empire, 42.

C

Cæsar, his relations with Cleopatra, 39.
Cæsarion, reputed son of Cæsar and Cleopatra, 39.
Cairo (the "City of the Caliphs"): one of the dozen most interesting cities of the globe, 1; comparatively modern, and historically unimportant, 1; distinctively an Oriental city in its typical characteristics, 2; Europeanised by Mehemet Ali and Ismail, but still a magnificent field of study, 2; full of picturesque associations connected with the age of the Mameluke Sultans, 2; ignored by most of the books on Egypt, 2; offers richest material for the sketch-book, 2; its history goes no farther back than mediæval times, 5; is wholly a Mohammedan creation, 5; its two periods of history under Arab and Turkish rule, 5; improved and fortified by Saladin, 42–44; its original name, 43; its three creators, 45; what the Mameluke Sultans did for it, 48; scheme for thorough drainage in, 81, 82; at the time of the Suez Canal inauguration ceremonies, 113. As a resort for invalids, 114–121; malarial in November, December, and January, 115; climatic conditions of, 117, 118. In its social aspect, 122–131; its hotels, 123–126, 127, 128; an aristocratic winter residence, 128; three classes of visitors at, 129; bicycling in, 130; the official functions at, 130, 131. Bazaars and street-life of, 132–138; its two great thoroughfares, 132, 133; how to make purchases in, 135, 136; all races and nationalities to be seen in, 136, 137. Mosques of, 139–148; more than three hundred in, 140. Tombs of the Caliphs at, 149–156; never properly the seat of the Caliphs,

INDEX. 327

149, 150. Its National Museum, 157-168; origin, scope, and value summed up by Murray's Handbook, 158; a vast treasure-house of early Egyptian civilisation, 159; remarkable paintings, and Hall of Jewels, 160; the Museum of Arabian art, 167, 168. The Acropolis of, 169-180; built of stones from the Great Pyramid, 169; most striking landmark of the city, 176; view from, 179. Old Cairo and the Coptic churches, 181-190; the Egyptian Babylon, 181, 182; architectural interest and characteristics of churches described, 184, 185. Side-shows of, 191-201; most popular, 193; public festivals, 197; native weddings, 198-200; degraded position of women, 200, 201. Minor excursions from, 235-248; rich field for artists, 235, 236; its trading-port of Boulag, 236, 237; its royal residences, 247, 248; an expensive health-resort, 249; from, to Thebes on the Nile, 261-276.

Caliphs, the, rule of, in Egypt, 42-54; different capitals of the, 46, 149, 150; the title loosely used, 149; *de facto* and *de jure*, 150, 151.

Cambyses, king of Persia, invades and conquers Egypt, 20, 22; his brutal outrages of Egyptian gods, 23, 107, 181; slaughters the sacred bull, 221, 222.

Campbell's Tomb, 210.

Canopus, Decree of, 31, 32, 161.

Capitulations, the, privileges granted to foreigners in Egypt, 58, 63.

Cemetery of cats, the, 267.

Cheops, 10; pyramid of, 202; statistics concerning, 204, 205; ascent of, 206, 207; *raison d'être* of, 209.

Chephren, 10; statue of, 159, 160; pyramid of, 207; builder of the Temple of the Sphinx, 214.

Chess, origin of the game of, 223, 224.

Cicero, his estimate of Ptolemy XIII., 39.

City of the Caliphs (*see* Cairo).

Cleopatra, her relations with Cæsar and Antony, 39; her flight after the battle of Actium, and her death, 40, 41; attempts to escape by a canal between the Red Sea and Mediterranean, 108; her portrait in relief on the temple of Denderah, 273, 274.

Commission for the Preservation of Arabic Monuments, the, 141, 178.

Constantinople, a hybrid city in comparison with Cairo, 5; its chief temple dedicated to a Christian saint, 5; conquered by the Turks, 54; Conference of, 85; most cosmopolitan city in Europe, 136; titular city of the Caliphs, 150; menaced by the troops of Mehemet Ali, 173.

Continental, the (hotel), 114, 123, 125.

Cook, the Messrs., their tourist-steamers on the Nile, 252; the advantages they offer to the Nile traveller, 256-258; their Handbook quoted, 307.

Copts, the, and their churches in Cairo, 186-188.

Cornelia, mother of the Gracchi, refuses to be queen of Egypt, 37.

Cotton-plant, the, one of the most lucrative articles of commerce in Egypt, 234.

"Crescent and the Cross," the, quoted, 288, 289, 302.

Cromer, Lord, his report on Egyptian drainage, 71, 79, 247, 319.

D

Dahabiyeh, the, native sailing-boats on the Nile, pleasures and expense of, 250, 251, 255-257.

Damietta, 94, 105, 106.

Davey, Richard, quoted, 142.

Denderah, Nile city, Ptolemaic architecture here, 272-275.

Dervishes, Howling and Twirling, the, 193-196.
Deshasheh, important "finds" made here, 321.
Dion, his description of Cleopatra's death, 41.
Doyle, Conan, quoted, 305, 309, 310, 311.

E

Edfu, temple of, 276.
Education in ancient times B.C., from the Euphrates to the Nile, 269.
Edwards, Miss A. B., quoted, 15, 212, 230, 231, 261, 263, 271, 285, 286, 294, 295, 306.
Egypt: cradle of the oldest civilisation and culture, 1; of the highest importance to the tourist and sightseer, but of low rank among semi-civilised countries, 3; national importance of, 4; great highway between the Eastern and Western hemispheres, 4; under the Pharaohs, 5-21; all literature, ancient and modern, indirectly due to her ancient civilisation, 5, 6; the cradle of the alphabet, 6; her history fossilised in monuments, 6; the cardinal fact in her history one of foreign invasions and conquests, 6, 7; has preserved her racial continuity notwithstanding, 7; little known of her prehistoric history, 7; her first earthly kings, 7; scholars disagree as to the origin of her people, 7, 8; the five principal divisions of her history, 8, 9; dates in her chronology only approximate, 9, 10; her political centre shifted under different kings, 11, 12; her twelfth dynasty an important period, 12; dark period of, 12; invaded by nomad tribes of Syria, 13; expansion of her national spirit, 14; most popular period of her history, 16, 17; enters on the stage of disruption, 19; a satrapy of the Persian empire, 20, 21; under the first Ptolemy (Soter), 21, 24; easily conquered, but perpetually revolting, 22; power of her priesthood, 23; her people welcome Alexander as their deliverer from Persian tyranny, 23; her history during the three hundred years of Ptolemaic rule difficult to unravel, 32; under Roman rule, 38; under Antony and Cleopatra, 39, 40; under Arab rule (the Caliphs), 42-54; picturesque period of her history, 42; her one hundred and forty-four Saracenic rulers, 45; her history uninteresting from the Ottoman conquest till the French occupation, 54; the making of, 55-89; her leaning towards Western civilisation under Mehemet Ali, Said, and Ismail, 55, 56; her financial embarrassment, 56; rebellion of Arabi, 57; England in, 57, 60-67; hampered by the Great Powers, 58-60, 66; most important reforms of England in, 63 et seq.; delicate diplomatic relations between the two governments, 64; her army disbanded, 65; kind and wise action of English officers, 66; her finances reorganised by England, 67; her material productiveness only a question of irrigation, 68, 69; Herodotus's epigram concerning, 69; two systems of agriculture in, and why, 69, 70; drainage, 71, 246, 247; proposed reservoir for the upper Nile valley, 72, 319; confidence of the people in the English engineers, 73, 74; unsatisfactory condition of the courts of law, 75 et seq.; police system, 76, 77; department of the Interior, 77, 78; sanitation and sanitary reform, 78-82; education and legislation, 82-84; attitude of England in her policy of intervention, 84 et seq.; French her official language, 85;

INDEX.

England's withdrawal from, considered, 87 *et seq.;* three Egypts to interest the traveller, 94; climatology of, 116, 117, 119; best way of reaching, 119–121; her ecclesiastical property, how vested, 142; fanaticism of sects, 145; methods of burial in, 165, 166; under Mehemet Ali, 170–175; the cry of "Egypt for the Egyptians" impossible of realisation, 175; Christianity established as the state religion of, by Theodosius, 186; degraded position of woman, 200, 201; pyramids of, 202–214; animal worship of, 219–221; her most ancient object of worship, the sun, 229; modified monotheism ascribed to her, 230; destined to be the granary of Europe, 242, 243; her climatic conditions unfavourable to textile manufactures, 243; produces three crops annually, 247; as a health-resort, 250, 251; state of education in, in times B.C., 269; architecture, Ptolemaic and Pharaonic, 272–276; her fifty-five historic obelisks, 280, 281; neglected by the poets, 284; cost of wintering in, 290; recent discoveries in, 312–323.

Egypt Exploration Fund Society, its important work, 312 *et seq.;* should be distinguished from the Egyptological department of the Egyptian Government, 312; its work at Beni-Hassan, 315.

Eiffel Tower, height of, 204.

Elamites, the, 12.

El-Azhar University, 82.

El-Makrizy, Arab historian, 53.

El-Muizz, first of the Fatimite dynasty, 43.

El-Muizz-Ebek, founder of the Mameluke dynasty, 49.

Emin Bey, legend of his escape from the slaughter of the Mamelukes, 176, 177.

England in Egypt, 57, 60–67; most important reforms of, 63 *et seq.;* delicate diplomatic relations between the two governments, 64; reorganises the Egyptian army, 65, 66; moral and educational service of her officers to the Egyptians, 66; reëstablishes Egyptian finances, 67; important work of drainage, 71; proposed great reservoir in the upper Nile valley, 72; perfection of Irrigation department, 73; department of Justice and Police, 74 *et seq.;* mistakes in the police system, 76, 77; department of the Interior, 78; Public Health department, 78–82; educational system, and government schools, 82, 83; legislative reforms, 83, 84; her policy of intervention considered, 84 *et seq.;* her relations with France, 85–87; her hostility to the Suez Canal project, 86, 111-113; her withdrawal must be gradual, 87 *et seq.;* her Public Works department in, her one great apology for being there, 243.

Epiphanes (Ptolemy V.), deplorable state of affairs under his rule, 38.

Esarhaddon, King of Assyria, invades Egypt, 19.

Esneh, temple of, 294, 295.

Euergetes I., 31.

Euergetes II., the ninth Ptolemy, reigns jointly with Philometer, 37; puts to death the infant King Neos, 38; his death, and what ensued, 38–39.

F

Fatima, daughter of Mohammed, 46.

Fatimite dynasty, the, origin of, 46; 150.

Fellaheen, the, make good soldiers when intelligently led, 65; overburdened by taxation under Ismail, 67; their confidence in the English engineers, 73, 74; filthy condition of their huts, 80; twenty-

five thousand of, work on the Suez Canal, 112; sliding scale of their taxation, 189; naturally unfitted for manufactures, 243, 244.
Fergusson, writer on architecture, quoted, 152, 263.
Fostat (old Cairo), founded by Amru, 42, 181.
Fraas, Professor, quoted, 241.
France, partner of England in Egypt, 61, 62, 85–87; encourages Mehemet Ali, 173.
Friday, the Mohammedan Sabbath, 145.

G

Gebel Abu Faydah, the Nile Palisades, 269.
Ghawazee dance, the, 191, 192.
Ghezireh Palace, the (hotel), 114, 123, 125, 126.
Ghizeh, pyramids of, 202–214; plateau of, neglected by archæologists, 320.
Gohar, general under El-Muizz, 43.
Gorst, J. L., 78.
Granville, Lord, memorable despatch of, 61, 62.
Great Powers, the, their relation to the Egyptian question, 87, 88; intervene between the Porte and Mehemet Ali, 172–175.

H

Harris papyrus, the, 287.
Hatasu, Queen, 14, 15; her famous expedition to the Land of Punt, 17, 314; obelisk erected by, at Thebes, 279, 280; temple of, at Thebes, 285, 286, 313, 314, 315.
Hathor, temple of, 308.
Heliopolis, the "city of the sun," 227–234; its one curiosity, 227; age of its famous obelisk, 228; chief seat of learning during the Middle Empire, 230; mother city of Baalbec, 231.

Helouan-les-Bains, oldest health-resort in the world, 115, 237, 238, 250.
Herodotus, his aphorism concerning Egypt, 69; his account of the building of the pyramids, 205; his story of Rhodope, 210.
Hogarth, David, quoted, 6, 32, 33, 92.
Homer, his description of Thebes, 277, 278.
Hotel d'Angleterre, the, at Cairo, 127.
Hotel du Nil, the, at Cairo, 128.
Hotel Royal, the, at Cairo, 127.
Hyksos, the (*see* Shepherd Kings).
Hypatia, scene of her triumphs and tragedy at Alexandria, 92.

I

Isis, Temple of, 29, 302, 319.
Ismail (Khedive), his hausmannising of Cairo, 2, 113; fall of, 9; his passion for European institutions and exalted aims, 56; wrings heavy taxes from the fellaheen, 67; refuses to supply labourers to dig the Suez Canal, 112; mania for building palaces, 125; walls up the "Needle's Eye," 184; gives the Virgin's tree as a present to his guest, the Empress Eugénie, 233.
Issus, one of the most decisive battles of the world fought at, 20.

J

Johnston, Captain, his engineering feat in saving the colossi of the Abu Simbel temple, 307.
Joseph (Jewish patriarch), 14; his well, 178, 179.
Josephus, quoted, 234.

K

Ka-mes, 14.
Karnak, the Great Temple of, 15, 264; tablet of, 271, 278–280; important archæological work done at, 320.
Kerouan (the "Holy City"), 43.

INDEX.

Khalig Canal, the, fête of, 189, 190.
Khu-en-Aten (*alias* Ame 1-hetep), 16, 268; record office of, 268, 269; temple of, 318.
Kinglake, quoted, 213.

L

Lesseps, M. de, 108-113.
Lloyd, Clifford, 77.
Luxor, 15, 114, 115, 250; occupies part of the site of ancient Thebes, 277; temple of, 280; cost of living at, 290-292; has a great future before it as a health-resort, 292, 293; compared with Assouan and Cairo, 298.
Lyons, Colonel, 32, 311, 319.

M

Macgregor, John, quoted, 107.
Mahaffy, Professor, quoted, 36, 40, 100, 273, 274.
Mamelukes, the, 47-52; meaning of the name, 47; the true founder of their dynasty, 49; length of their reign, 51, 151; great mosque-builders, 146; tombs of, 154; rivals of Mehemet Ali, 170-172.
Manetho, historian of Egypt, 29, 230, 231, 238.
Marco Polo, 50, 52.
Mariette Bey, 107, 218, 219, 222, 223, 226 (*Note*), 316.
Mark, Saint, his bones not in Alexandria, but in Venice, 103, 104.
Maspero, Professor, discoverer of the pyramid-tomb of Unas, 10; 163.
Mastabas, the, meaning of the word, 224; described, 225, 226.
Matarieh, village of, 232-234.
Mehemet Ali, rebuilds and Europeanises Cairo, 2; invents system of perennial irrigation for Egypt, 70; looks to France for aid in his attempt to civilise Egypt, 85; creator of modern Alexandria, 95; his romantic career, and resemblance to Napoleon, 96, 169-175; great blot of his reign, 97, 172, 176, 177; equestrian statue of, at Alexandria, 97; his rivalship with the Mamelukes, 170-172; conflict with the Porte, 172-175; dares not withstand "the lucky queen," 174; greatest ruler of Egypt since the Ptolemies, 175; mosque of, 177; failed to appreciate the agricultural importance of the Nile, 243; began the Barrage, 244, 246; disgraceful vandalism in time of, 274.
Melik-es-Salih, 49.
Memphis, capital of Egypt under Menes, and chief centre of the worship of the god Ptah, 9; first historical capital of Egypt, 11; importance of, as capital of the Ancient Empire, 215; compared with Thebes, 216; its statues of Rameses II., 216, 217; necropolis at, 217.
Mena House, the (hotel), 115, 116, 126, 127, 250.
Menes, first really historical king of Egypt, 9.
Menzaleh, Lake, 109, 112.
Mer-en-Ptah (Seti III.), the Pharaoh under whose reign the Exodus of the Israelites took place, 18, 162.
Milnes, Sir Alfred, 73.
Moeris, an artificial lake, 12, 30, 71.
Mokattam Hills, the, 169, 241.
Moncrieff, Sir Colin Scott, 72, 244, 245, 246.
Montbard, quoted, 236, 237.
Morgan, M. de, quoted, 320.
Moses, at Heliopolis, 230; his well, 241.
Mosques, unsanitary condition of, 80; of Cairo described, 139-148, 152-154.
Murray's Handbook, quoted, 143, 158, 162, 189, 190, 209, 216, 239, 265, 266, 275, 310.
Mycerinos, 10, 210.

332 INDEX.

N

Napier, Admiral, his interview with Mehemet Ali, 173, 174.

Napoleon, compared with Mehemet Ali, 96; his scheme for a maritime canal through the Isthmus of Suez, 108; curious coincidence concerning, 170.

Naukratis, an ancient Greek settlement in Egypt, discoveries at, 316, 317.

Naville, M., quoted, 313, 314, 315.

Necho, one of the Pharaonic kings of Egypt, 20.

New Hotel, the, at Cairo, 126.

Nile, the, its antiquities of surpassing interest, 3; the one and only highway of Egypt, 3; Herodotus's epigram concerning, 69; the beneficent providence of Egypt, 189; its annual increment to the soil of the Delta, 227, 228; worshipped as the creative principle of Egypt, 243; as a health-resort, 249-260; its dahabiyehs, 250, 251, 255-257; animal life and scenery of, 252, 253; its wonderful sunset afterglow, 254, 255; rare sightseeing on, 257; hints to sportsmen on, 259, 260; from Cairo to Thebes on, 261-276; first cataract of, 303; from the first to the second cataract of, 304-311; second cataract of, 310.

Nilometer, the, 12, 188, 189.

Nitokris, Queen, 10.

Nubia, geographical features of, 304, 305.

O

Octavius, his chief *casus belli* with Antony, 39; temple of, discovered, 320.

Omar, Caliph, 42; his advice to his viceroy, 68; destroys the Serapeum collection, 101, 102.

Osiris, his reputed burial-place at Abydos, 9; legendary phœnix sacred to, 231; temple of, 302.

Ostrich Farm, the, 242.

Othman, first leader of the Ottoman Turks, 54.

Oxyrhncus, *Logia Jesou* found here, 321, 322.

P

Paine, J. A., quoted, 289.

Palmerston, Lord, opposes the Suez Canal project, 111.

Pelusium (Sin of the O. T.), 107.

Pentaur, poet laureate of the Theban court, 18, 271, 272.

Persians, the, subjugated by Alexander the Great, 20; their sway in Egypt cruel and bloody, 22.

Petrie, Flinders, quoted, 9, 165, 166, 203, 204, 205, 263, 269, 317, 318, 320, 322, 323.

Petrie papyrus, the, 31.

Petrified Forest, the, 240-242.

Pharaohs, Egypt under the, 5-21; their twenty-six dynasties, 8; the name Pharaoh convertible with that of Rameses, 16; their reign covered four thousand years of Egyptian history, 21; mummies of, 162-165.

Pharos, the, at Alexandria, 29.

Philadelphus (second Ptolemy), his coronation ceremony described, 26-28; orders the Septuagint translation of the O. T., 28; builds the famous Pharos, 29; establishes the port of Berenice, 28, 29.

Philæ, island of, 301-303.

Philometer (Ptolemy VII.), sketch of his life by Polybius, 37, 38.

Phœnix, the, 231, 232.

Photographers, etc., in Egypt, warned, 97, 98.

Pithom, famous treasure-city built by the Israelites for Rameses the Great, 317.

Plato, a student at Heliopolis, 230.

Pliny, quoted, 31.

Plutarch, quoted, 37.

Pollard, Mr., quoted, 155, 156.

INDEX. 333

Polybius, his description of the battle of Raphia, 34–36; sketches life of Philometer, 37, 38.
Pompey, 107.
Pompey's Pillar, at Alexandria, 100, 101.
Poole, Stanley-Lane, quoted, 2, 43–50, 141, 144, 151, 168, 186, 187, 197, 198, 201, 228.
Port Said, 94, 105, 106, 107, 120.
Posidippus, epigram of, 29.
Prissé papyrus, the, oldest book in the world, 6, 166, 167.
Psammetichus, founds the twenty-sixth Pharaonic dynasty, 19, 20.
Ptah, creator of gods and men, 9.
Ptolemaic empire, the, fall of, 42.
Ptolemies, the, empire of, founded by Alexander the Great, 8, 21, 22–41; their comparatively peaceful rule in Egypt, 23, 24; their rule of Egypt during three hundred years characterised, 32 *et seq.*; end of their dynasty, 42; some kind of water communication in time of, between the Red Sea and Mediterranean, 108; where the architecture of their age may be studied, 272; ruins of their temples and monuments at Philæ, 301, 302.
Ptolemy IV. (Philopater), early events of his reign summarised, 33–36; a patron of literature, and builds a temple in honour of Homer, 36.
Ptolemy VI., what followed his death, 38.
Ptolemy Soter, founder of the dynasty of the Ptolemies, 21, 24; his museum and library at Alexandria, 24–26.
Pulpit Rock of Abusir, 309, 310.
Pyramid-builders, the great, 10.
Pyramid of Dahshur, sets of ancient jewelry found here, 320, 321.
Pyramid of Medum, built by Seneferu, 9.
Pyramid of Unas, 222, 223.

Pyramids, the, theories concerning, 202–204; Dean Stanley on, 208.
Pythagoras, a student at Heliopolis, 203.

R

Rae, Fraser, quoted, 164.
Ram, Colonel, 211.
Rameses I., least important sovereign of the Pharaohs, 17; cut the first canal between the Red Sea and the Nile, 17.
Rameses III., founder of the twelfth Pharaonic dynasty, 18; last of the warrior-kings of Egypt, 19; temple of, at Thebes, 286, 287.
Rameses the Great (II.), 11; the dominant personality in the history of Egypt, 17; his greatest achievement in arms, 18; built the oldest road in the world, 107; colossal statues of, at Memphis, 216, 217; temple of, at Abydos, 270, 271; colossal statue of, at Thebes, 283; built the temple of Abu Simbel, 306, 308.
Ramesseum, the, 281, 283, 308.
Ramleh, 115.
Raphia, battle of, described by Polybius, 34–36.
Rogers Pacha, proposed sanitary reforms of, 79–81.
Rosetta, 94, 105.
Rosetta Stone, 161, 231.

S

Said Pacha, beneficial results of his reign, 55; grants right of way to the Suez Canal, 110, 111.
St. Peter's, Rome, height of dome, 204.
Sais, 12.
Sakkarah, tablet and cemetery of, 217–219.
Saladin, improves and fortifies Cairo, 42, 43; his character and deeds, 46, 47, 150, 151, 176, 179.
Salisbury, Lord, his despatch to the

334 INDEX.

English envoy to the Porte, 62, 63.
Sandwith, Dr. F. M., quoted, 117.
Saracenic era, the, of Egypt, 8, 42; art fostered by, 48, 49, 51.
Scott, Sir John, 75, 76.
Sequenen Ra, 13, 164, 165.
Serapeum, the, 218, 219, 222.
Seti I., temple of, at Abydos, 271, 272; his tomb, 288.
Seti III. (*see* Mer-en-Ptah).
Shashank (Shishak of the O. T.), founder of the twenty-second Pharaonic dynasty, 19.
Shelley, quoted, 283, 284.
Shepheards, the (hotel), 114, 123, 124.
Shepherd Kings, the, 11, 13, 161.
Sinai, inscriptions on the cliffs at, 9.
Sneferu, temple of, 317.
Solar Disk, temple of the, 16.
Solon, a student at Heliopolis, 230.
Sphinx, the, 211-213; temple of, 214.
Stanley, Dean, quoted, 208, 212, 283.
Step Pyramid, the, 222.
Strabo, quoted, 31, 271, 288, 296 (*Note*).
Suez Canal, story of, 105-113; emphatically the work of one man, 108; not preëminently a monument of engineering skill, 109; its *genius loci*, 109; main difficulties in the way of its construction political, 110; opposition to, of the British government, 111; change from manual to mechanical labour in digging, 112; splendour and cost of the inauguration ceremonies of, 112, 113.
Syria, nomad tribes of, invade Egypt, 13.

T

Tanis (Zoan of the O. T.), at one time capital of Egypt, 11; ruins of, 107.
Taylor, Isaac, quoted, 279.

Tel-El-Amarna, city of Lower Egypt, 11, 16; rock-tombs of, 268; fame of, as a field for research, 318.
Tewfik, placed on the throne of Egypt by the Porte, 57; more nearly a constitutional ruler than any other Egyptian sovereign, 155; ceremonies attending his funeral described, 155, 156; Helouan his favourite residence, and where he died, 237.
Thebes, capital of Egypt under the Middle Empire, 11, 15; admirable site of, 277; for more than two thousand years the capital and ecclesiastical seat of Egypt, 278, 279; ruins and antiquities of, 278-289; view of, from one of the surrounding mountain peaks, 282.
This, earliest historic city of Egypt, supposed birthplace of Menes, 9, 270; cradle of the first Egyptian kings, 11.
Thotmes I., II., III., 14, 15.
Tombs of the Kings, the, 287-289.
Traill, H. D., quoted, 99, 137, 138, 162, 177, 196, 254, 255.
Trojan War, the, its date in connection with Egyptian history, 19.
Tunis, seat of the Fatimite dynasty, 46.
Turin papyrus, the, 167, 217, 227.
Turkey, her protectorship of Egypt considered, 88.
Turks, Ottoman, the, 42; beginning of their empire, 53; distinguished from the Saracens and Arabs, 54; date of their invasion of Egypt, 150.
Turra, quarries of, 238-240.

U

Unas, his pyramid-tomb, 10.
Usertsen I. and II., reigns of, 12.

V

Vandalism, European and American, of Egyptian and other antiquities, 274, 281, 316.

Verdi, composes the opera "Aida" for the Khedive Ismail at the inauguration ceremonies of the Suez Canal, 113.
Vincent, Sir Edgar, financial adviser to the Khedive, 68.
Virgin's Tree, the, legend of, 232, 233.
Virgin's Well, the, legend of, 233, 234.
Vocal Memnon, the, 284, 285.

W

Wady Halfa, fortified post of, 308; pulpit rock at, 309, 310.
Wakfs Administration, the, has charge of all Egyptian mosques, 141, 142.
Wallis-Budge, E. A., quoted, 14, 15, (*Note*); 160, 161, 167, 262, 271.
Warburton, Eliot, quoted, 170, 171, 307.
Washington Monument, the, height of, 204.
Wolseley, Lord, subdues the rebellion of Arabi in Egypt, 57.
Wood, Sir Evelyn, reorganises the Egyptian army, 65.

Z

Zoan (*see* Tanis).

APPENDIX

CONSISTING OF LETTERS FROM
ASSOUAN
DESCRIBING THE NEW BARRAGE
BY DANA ESTES, M. A.
AN AMERICAN TOURIST
OF
1901

ASSOUAN BARRAGE, LOWER LEVEL SLUICES WITH NILE RUNNING THROUGH.

APPENDIX.

THE GREAT NILE VALLEY IMPROVEMENT.

LETTERS FROM ASSOUAN BY AN AMERICAN TOURIST.

BEYOND question this place is destined to play an important part in the evolution of the new Egypt, as indeed it did in the Egypt of ancient times. Situated at the foot of the first cataract, and thus being at the head of steamboat navigation, and of pretty much all navigation for heavy merchandise, and at one of the nearest points to the Red Sea on the great caravan routes, across the Libyan and Arabian deserts; it is a focal point between Egypt proper and Nubia, or ancient Ethiopia; or, as it is now called, "The Soudan." But a short time since it was an outpost of civilisation, a stronghold held almost in fear and trembling against the Mahdists, who were drunk with the success against, and the bloodshed of, the great Egyptian armies under Hicks Pacha and others, which they had annihilated. Every hilltop commanding the post was fortified, and the remnants of these are now fast falling to pieces, being abandoned and neglected as of no further use. The desert route toward Khartoum was picketed for many miles to prevent a surprise.

Since the destruction of the hosts of the Kalifa, all is peace and plenty in Assouan. New buildings are springing up; fine schools and churches are being established. The garrison is reduced to a single regiment: a troop of cavalry, and one field battery, — all composed of fine stalwart Nubians, who are pronounced by good judges, who have seen them under fire, to be as fine soldiers as any in the world. A happier looking set of soldiers I have never seen, and my observations in this direction have been somewhat extended. They are fortunate in one respect. They have no fatigue duties, or dirty work of any kind. All this is done for them by convicts from all parts of Egypt. These are in squads under sergeants and corporals, who overlook them with loaded rifles, and the worst class — murderers, and those who may not be trusted at all — are in chain gangs; but the most of them are simply designated by a yellow uniform and work quite freely without fetters, and appear cheerful and contented. The soldiers' quarters are wonderfully neat and clean, and on parade they present a fine appearance; a good proportion of them being nearly six feet in height, and as straight as arrows. Their wives dwell near them in separate quarters, and wear a white costume of uniform character. I had the good fortune to see about a thousand of them coming out of their quarters, and moving slowly like an animated snow-storm to the parade-ground to witness some native races. The only bit of colour in the whole mass was the charcoal faces — all the rest clean white; and at a distance the scene was a wonderfully impressive one.

These races are called in Egypt "a gymkana," and consist of horse, donkey, camel, and foot races of every imaginable variety. They are organised and patronised by the hotel guests, and afford great amusement to the natives as well. The most interesting event was a race between eight camels ridden by almost nude Bisharin Arab boys. The skill of these boys and the speed attained by these awkward beasts was simply marvellous. A splendid Arabian race-horse, ridden by a skilled rider, was distanced by the winning camel. These Bisharin Bedouins are from the desert between Assouan and the Red Sea, and the young men and women are the finest physical specimens of dark-skinned folk that I have ever seen. They also have the finest teeth I have ever seen in any human beings.

The future of Assouan and indeed of all Egypt is bound up in the Great Barrage, now about half built. I cannot in this letter speak appropriately of this immense work, but only of one feature especially important to Assouan. It is intended to utilise the vast water-power of the cataract, now running entirely to waste, in a great electrical plant to supply light, heat, and power to this section, and it is expected to revolutionise the country, and it seems reasonable to suppose that it will. Already building sites and islands in the Nile are being sought for. Lord Kitchener has acquired a large island opposite Assouan, between the famous Elephantine Island and the Libyan Desert. Juvenal was banished to Assouan as the farthest outpost in the Roman Empire for punishment for his satires on the imperial court. Such a punishment now would mean living in one of three first-class hotels, at unfortunately excessively high prices, but in the finest climate in the world. A person banished might, however, not have the luck to get in at all, even at Waldorf-Astoria prices, as the rush this season has been so great that hundreds have been turned back to Luxor and Cairo, and some have been compelled to sleep in bath-rooms and offices. The season is, however, short, beginning December 1st, and at its height in January and February, and waning and finally ending in March. The chief occupations of the guests are camel and donkey rides, visits to the antiquities of Assouan and beautiful Philæ, the ancient quarries, the Barrage, and the Soudanese bazaar; but the air is so fine that one only needs to be and not to do.

At the last full moon I invited a party of twenty, chartered a special train, and visited the temples of Philæ under the white light of a tropical night. It was a scene never to be forgotten, tinged with the regret that it can probably never be repeated, for beautiful Philæ is doubtless doomed to destruction in the interest of more corn, wine, and oil for the long oppressed fellaheen, who at last, thanks to our English cousins, is having a fair chance in the world. Your correspondent is one of the fortunate who in coming early secured an Arabian horse for the season. Camel and donkey riding is very interesting as a novelty, but give me a desert horse if I may have my choice. Mine is a small beast, with the smallest ears I have ever seen on a horse, and a great aversion to donkeys. While in town he is as quiet a hack as one would find anywhere. But get him on his native heath, the open desert, and he becomes another kind of proposition. His nostrils dilate, up go his small ears and long tail, and not infrequently both his heels, and for a brief space it becomes a question as to which shall maintain the mastery. Nothing but a firm seat and will, and a vigorous application of the koorbash, a cruel rawhide whip made from the skin of the hippopotamus, will bring a rider safely out of such an encounter.

I intended to speak of Assouan from an archæological and historical point of view, but fear my letter is already too long.

Since the conquest of the Soudan and its occupation in the name of the Khedive, and the Queen of England, to the distinct inferential elimination of the Sultan of Turkey from the problem, it appears to be assumed on all hands that it is no longer a question as to whether the Briton will leave Egypt, but simply, "What will he do with it?" The Sultan of Turkey, it is true, censors Lord Cromer's speeches, and, as far as possible, hides his head in the sand by keeping the facts from becoming known to his subjects;

but the young Khedive, who, a few years ago, kicked over the traces by dismissing his enlightened Prime Minister, Nubar Pacha, and appointing his reactionary favourite, Riaz Pacha, and who also insulted General Kitchener and his English officers to such an extent that they resigned, and who was compelled by Lord Cromer to eat humble pie in each case, has now evidently seen a new light, and is most friendly, not only with the English powers that be, but with his own subjects who have all along favoured the English occupation.

The facts that the English have given freedom and practically equal rights to a people accustomed to oppression and the lash from a habit of at least ten thousand years; that they have reduced the immense debt, both principal and interest, incurred by "Ismail the Plunger," also called "The Regenerator" by his French parasites, by about twenty-five per cent., and have at one fell stroke abolished forced labour, the wicked system of the corvee, and the tax on the commerce of the Nile at the Cairo Barrage, would alone seem to settle all doubts in the minds of the people as to the necessity of the permanent occupation and administration of the country. The commercial elements of all nationalities are unquestionably a unit in its favour, even including the sore-headed French, who are compelled to see the country which was exploited for a generation by their speculators becoming Anglicised at an extraordinary rate.

A simple fact illustrating this has just come under my observation. Five years ago the scholars in the Assouan government school elected French as their language, to the extent of eighty per cent., and English twenty per cent. This year they elected English to the extent of ninety per cent. of the whole school, and practically the same rule holds good in the mission schools for girls, supported by English contributors, who are doing a noble work in giving the downtrodden sex a distinctly secular and ethical education, quite removed from any attempts to proselyte or convert to any change in religious belief.

All this, however, is somewhat apart from my visit to the Assouan Barrage. I have been led into political and economical questions, by the fact that the question of all questions is one of water. Under the blighting rule of "the unspeakable Turk" a large proportion of the most fruitful land on earth, the Delta, became a howling wilderness; in part a malarial marsh, and in part, including the famous world granary, the Land of Zoan, once occupied by the Israelites, simply a sandy desert. Ismail the "Regenerator" began at a frightful cost, owing to the influences by which he was ruled, to build canals, and the Cairo Barrage, an immense dam or weir to impound the waters of the Nile, and deliver them as needed to the thirsty lands of the Delta. The conception was grand; the execution by the flighty French defective; and the Barrage was useless until English engineers rebuilt the foundations.

Its immediate success raised the question of other dams, and there are two in course of construction, both by an English firm of contractors, John Aird & Son, who not only do the work, but receive no pay until after the completion and successful operation of the Barrages. Mr. Aird, whom I had the pleasure of seeing during his recent stay at the Cataract Hotel, was recently knighted by Queen Victoria for his great enterprise here.

THE ASSOUAN BARRAGE, ONE OF THE DAMS OF THE RIVER NILE.

The Assouan Barrage is in the first cataract, about halfway between the town and the island of Philæ, the beautiful temples of which it is feared are destined to destruction by the improvement, notwithstanding the fact that the

ASSOUAN BARRAGE, BATTER WORK ON DOWN-RIVER SIDE OF BARRAGE.

THE GREAT NILE VALLEY IMPROVEMENT. 345

Barrage was lowered fourteen feet from the original plan in the hope of preserving them, and so on the boundary line between upper Egypt and Nubia or ancient Ethiopia, now generally called the Soudan. A visit to "the works" and the Barrage is one of the occupations of the great crowd of sightseers and semi-invalids who dwell in this favoured spot, which has beyond doubt the finest climate in the world. By the courtesy of the eminent government engineers, Messrs. Maurice Fitzmaurice and Louis Neville, who were also associated in building the great Forth bridge, I was taken in hand by the latter and shown this stupendous work. It was begun in February, 1898, and was contracted to be completed in about six years at a cost of ten million dollars, payable, including interest, in thirty half-yearly payments of about four hundred thousand dollars each. Its foundations rest on the solid granite ledges, for which this spot is famous, and the materials of construction are from the quarries which have for six thousand years supplied Egypt with its most durable stone for temples, tombs, statues, and pyramids. Its dimensions, roughly stated, are as follows: Total length, a little more than one and one-half miles; extreme height and depth, including foundations, about 120 feet; extreme width at base, about eighty feet; width at top, which forms a roadway across the Nile, protected by heavy parapet walls, twenty-five feet. Its contents are about 1,250,000 tons of masonry, and the sluices, 180 in number, with their frames, will take about ten thousand tons of steel and iron. All of the masonry in sight is of rough hammered granite, quarried in massive blocks. The interior is of granite splinters of good size, solidly cemented together. The sluices through which the whole of the volume of the Nile, even during the inundation, must run, are at various heights, that the water may be loosed or held at pleasure. During the inundation, when the water is charged with its fertilising mud, all the water which can be possibly passed through the lowest sluices must go that way, that the life-blood of Egypt may not be stopped in its way, and the fellaheen robbed of his manure, and the lake at the back of the Barrage become filled with the silt. No water will ever pass over the dam.

It is, of course, a fine engineering problem to provide sufficient sluiceway for all the water which heaven may send down from the lakes of equatorial Africa and the mountains of Abyssinia. Were upper Egypt and the Soudan subject to rainy seasons, it would doubtless be an impossibility, but rains here are so infrequent as to be practically left out of the account, not only in engineering works, but in the dwelling-places of the people. When one comes, it leaves them stunned and almost helpless. For instance, a washout on the railway last month left this section cut off from the lower world for ten days, except for the infrequent steamers bringing and taking tourists. We were in our hotel, calmly informed that the world had not supplied us with butter or eggs, and we frequently ran out of ice. When the great electric plant in connection with the Barrage is completed the latter can be manufactured at a minimum cost, and it is expected to revolutionise this section. The increase in the price of land has many times paid the cost of the Cairo Barrage, and it is estimated that the Assouan and Assiout Barrages will add to the annual income of the country almost immediately upwards of thirty million dollars, and ultimately many times this vast amount. Should the result prove anything like the figures estimated, it will be easy to extend the system to the other cataracts, and doubtless Egypt will soon become one of the richest, as it is now one of the most fertile, spots on the face of the globe.

It is estimated that the water impounded by the Assouan Barrage, after all lower Egypt is fertilised by the inunda-

THE GREAT NILE VALLEY IMPROVEMENT. 347

tion, will amount to many billion gallons, and will raise the level of the river for about 120 miles.

The contractors have been favoured by two seasons of low Nile since they began their work, and in consequence they are about one year ahead of time on their estimates. This will prove an important factor in their profits and in the ultimate advantage to the country from its early completion. It is now expected that the foundations will be completed before the next flood, which comes in August. All of the river is now running through the sluices, and coffer-dams are built for the remainder of the foundations, and are nearly all pumped out.

An important, and, indeed, absolutely necessary adjunct to the Barrage, is the canal, which is built outside of the bed of the river in the solid ledge on the west or Sahara side of the river. The desert comes down to the river on both sides at this point. This canal is one and a half miles long, just about the same length as the dam, and is of sufficient width and depth to accommodate the steamers and dahabiyehs plying on the Nile. It is fitted with a series of four locks about four hundred feet long and thirty-five feet wide, and it will spoil the occupation of the hundreds of wild-eyed Nubians who used to levy blackmail on the tourists who wished to pass up or down the cataract in boats or dahabiyehs. It will save great delays, and the transshipment of vast quantities of merchandise, and tend to equalise prices and stimulate enterprise throughout the whole land, and thus prove a blessing to the nation.

A trifling fraction of the sums spent by our Cousin John in killing a handful of patriotic, if mistaken, Boers, would make the Nile valley the garden spot of the world. And John can afford it, too, for he has made a cool, clean profit of about one hundred million dollars on his Suez Canal shares, which the bankrupt Egypt had to part with at a forced sale. It must be admitted, however, that this is the chief thing he has to show on a profit and loss account. He lets us all trade and travel as freely here as he does himself, and, with an immense amount of care and responsibility and no direct gain, is giving the world a splendid object-lesson of the immediate benefits derived from Anglo-Saxon freedom and civilisation. When one contrasts the conditions in Egypt with those in the Barbary States on the west, even with those administered by republican France, and with the Ottoman Empire on the east, he cannot but admit the benign influence of our Cousin John, and I trust I may not lay myself open to the charge of becoming an Anglomaniac, if I express the view that a more enlightened or even altruistic experiment in international interference was never undertaken in the history of civilisation.

DANA ESTES.

Assouan, February 25, 1901.

www.ingramcontent.com/pod-product-compliance
Lightning Source LLC
Chambersburg PA
CBHW041436300426
44114CB00025B/2904